T0329776

A PRECARIOUS GAME

A PRECARIOUS GAME

The Illusion of Dream Jobs in the
Video Game Industry

Ergin Bulut

ILR PRESS

AN IMPRINT OF CORNELL UNIVERSITY PRESS   ITHACA AND LONDON

First published 2020 by Cornell University Press

Library of Congress Cataloging-in-Publication Data

Names: Bulut, Ergin, author.
Title: A precarious game : the illusion of dream jobs in the video game industry / Ergin Bulut.
Description: Ithaca : ILR Press, an imprint of Cornell University Press, 2020. | Includes bibliographical references and index.
Identifiers: LCCN 2019020927 (print) | LCCN 2019980590 (ebook) | ISBN 9781501746529 (cloth) | ISBN 9781501746536 (paperback) | ISBN 9781501746543 (pdf) | ISBN 9781501746550 (epub)
Subjects: LCSH: Video games industry—Employees—Job satisfaction—Middle West. | Video game designers—Job satisfaction—Middle West. | Video games industry—Social aspects—Middle West. | Ethnology—Middle West.
Classification: LCC HD9993.E452 B86 2020 (print) | LCC HD9993.E452 (ebook) | DDC 331.7/6179480977—dc23
LC record available at https://lccn.loc.gov/2019020927
LC ebook record available at https://lccn.loc.gov/2019980590

To Gülüzar and Metin Bulut

Contents

Preface   ix

Acknowledgments   xi

Introduction: For Whom the Love Works in
Video Game Production?   1

1. The Unequal Ludopolitical Regime of Game Production:
Who Can Play, Who Has to Work?   30

2. The End of the Garage Studio as a Technomasculine Space:
Financial Security, Streamlined Creativity,
and Signs of Friction   54

3. Gaming the City: How a Game Studio Revitalized
a Downtown Space in the Silicon Prairie   73

4. The Production of Communicative Developers in
the Affective Game Studio   89

5. Reproducing Technomasculinity: Spouses' Classed
Femininities and Domestic Labor   105

6. Game Testers as Precarious Second-Class Citizens:
Degradation of Fun, Instrumentalization of Play   122

7. Production Error: Layoffs Hit the Core Creatives   141

Conclusion: Reimagining Labor and Love in and
beyond Game Production   159

Notes   175

References   181

Index   197

Preface

At the beginning of each academic semester, I ask undergraduates majoring in media studies what their postgraduation plans are. Regardless of the industry they would like to get into, they want to do something fun or something they love. They desire creative jobs. Not interested in joining the white-collar workforce, my students are keen on being employed in workplaces where informality rules.

The video game industry is an ideal venue where job descriptions come very close to the aspirations of my students. Producing video games is definitely fun and glamorous. In fact, video game industry jobs are described as among the best jobs that U.S. workplaces offer. With its transnational connections and a truly networked labor force, the industry does offer lively workspaces. It is also positioned as an industry that thrives despite the adverse effects of the economic downturn.

This book suggests that things are a bit more complicated. By delving into the everyday experiences of video game developers in a studio that I call Desire, I reveal how the glamorous working lives of game developers are equally precarious and unpredictable, depending on many other factors that they cannot always control. In fact, the whole industry is structured around various forms of inequalities and surrounded with illusions about what it means to do what one loves. Even when Desire's developers work really hard, love what they do, and produce profitable games, their economic and social well-being do not always thrive equally well, rendering them anxious about their futures.

Not all of Desire's workers are employed on equal terms, either. There are the more privileged core creatives, such as programmers, artists, and designers, and there are the marginalized video game testers, whose labor is undervalued compared to the rest of the workforce. Game workers' partners' reproductive labor is also rendered invisible, even though they are vital to the success of a whole industry. There are cultural inequalities where a predominantly white-male industry's definitions of "fun" give us questionable game content with respect to gender and race. That is, work itself is extremely racialized and gendered. So, then, it seems that inequality is not a bug but a major feature of this industry. Doing what you love as a game worker can be a mixed blessing, because failure and production errors are endemic to this highly innovative industry, even though it is represented and imagined as a meritocratic utopia.

The fusion of work and play, desire and work, and performing a labor of love have become a hegemonic narrative across the globe. The video game industry stands out like a natural center of this fusion in the form of a dream job. This book interrogates the politics of this dream through the lens of inequality. It poses one main question: Who can play and who has to work in this industry? Grasping the personal, social, and emotional cost of racialized and gendered labor practices through the lives of Desire's creative workers, the present work critiques liberal conceptions of creativity and discourses around quality of life in this unpredictable industry. It politicizes love at work and invites readers to consider universal basic income, unionization, and a radical postwork imagination. By pointing to the illusions of game development as a dream job, it emphasizes the immediate necessity to make radical demands about how we can possibly disautomatize ourselves, deconstruct our naturalized commitment to work, and liberate play from its one-dimensionality.

I hope this book is a thoughtful and provocative call for becoming killjoys against a supposedly ludic future, which in fact is very much limited to instrumentalized and unequal relations of social domination.

Acknowledgments

Intellectual life has never been easy in Turkey, but I wouldn't have imagined the level of the uncertainty it has reached since I returned home in 2014. To that end, I would like to thank friends, colleagues, and institutions that supported me as I wrote this book.

First I want to thank numerous game developers and their partners who shared their stories with me amid their hectic lives. I hope this book contributes to the formation of a more equal video game industry. I also want to thank anonymous reviewers for their feedback, which has significantly helped me to reframe the book. Let me also thank Fran Benson and the editorial team for believing in and helping with this project.

Şükran Özkan, Leman Çınar, Meltem Çullu, Susan Robertson, Ayşe Buğra, and Özden Cankaya have been lifelong mentors and sources of inspiration. I am grateful.

Fırat Kaplan, Evren Dinçer, Emre Ergüven, Seçil Yılmaz, Yasin Kara, Aslı Filiz, Nurçin İleri, and Bora Erdağı deserve special thanks for being wonderful friends and intellectual interlocutors since the 2000s. My friends for life, you all rock! Mustafa's and Duygu's existence in my life has been nothing other than immense joy. They rock! Our WhatsApp group How I Met Your Mother has been my daily feed of political news, Brazilian music, and laughter. I am grateful to Garett and May for being my family in the United States. I thank Serdar, Ayşegül, Giray, Aslı, Gökhan, Emre, Eren, Deniz, and Ozan for immensely enriching my life back in the United States.

I fondly remember my memories at the University of Illinois and want to thank my friends and colleagues for listening to the stories in this book so many times. Thank you, Bryce Henson, Karla Palma, Nina Li, Darren Stevenson, Safiya Umoja Noble, Sarah Roberts, Matt Crain, Mandy Tröger, Nick Rudd, Alicia Kozma, Martina Baldwin, and Arnau Multu. Robert Mejia has been a wonderful colleague to work with and learn from.

Let me also thank Srirupa Roy, Thomas Allmer, Ben Birkinbine, Nina Huntemann, Aphra Kerr, Zsuzsa Gille, Kylie Jarett, Dal Yong Jin, Dan Schiller, Lisa Nakamura, John Nerone, Fazal Rizvi, Michael Peters, Aswin Punathambekar, Zeynep Devrim Gürsel, Suncem Koçer, Casey O'Donnell, Michelle Rodino-Colocino, Jack Bratich, Mutlu Binark, James Hay, Bilge Yeşil, Nick Dyer-Witheford, Victor Pickard, Anita Say Chan, Jack Qiu, Winifred Poster, Luke

Stark, Rolien Hoyng, Murat Es, Alison Hearn, and Enda Brophy for their support, friendship, and conversations in various academic venues. Many thanks to Jayson Harsin for his support and solidarity. Nicole Cohen and especially Greig de Peuter deserve special thanks for providing comments and feedback at various occasions on the earlier forms of the manuscript. Vicki Mayer's work has been a formative influence in this project. I am especially thankful for her encouragement in the earlier phases of my career. With her immense intellectual inspiration and political energy, Paula Chakravartty has been a formidable mentor and I am grateful.

Since I became a faculty member at Koç University, Bilge Ulutürk's invisible support at the Suna Kıraç Library has been priceless. I want to thank my colleagues at Koç University, especially Dikmen Bezmez, Çağla Turgul, Didem Pekün, İpek Çelik Rappas, Çetin Çelik, Gizem Erdem, and Lemi Baruh. Dean Aylin Küntay's leadership and support is much appreciated. My conversations with Can Nacar and Burak Gürel have helped me shape various parts of the manuscript. Erdem Yörük's motivation has pushed me along the way. Alexis Rappas deserves special thanks for numerous conversations in our hallway. Thanks to Megan MacDonald, who kindly read and gave feedback on portions of the manuscript.

Students at Koç University have been delightful to work with. I want to thank Ege, Suzy, Sidar, Zeynel, Aybike, Önder, Mert, and Aslı for both insightful conversations and research support.

I have given various talks as I was writing this book. I want to thank Galatasaray University, Leeds University, Pennsylvania State University, Rutgers University, Simon Fraser University, Kadir Has University, and the University of Pennsylvania's Annenberg School for Communication for inviting me to share my research with them. I want to especially thank Christian Fuchs and Westminster Institute for Advanced Studies for providing the precious intellectual time to rethink some of the theoretical issues in this book through the International Research Fellowship.

Meeting Niko Besnier and learning from him in 2018 was one of the top moments of my professional and intellectual development. I can only hope to have satisfied Niko's high standards of writing. In addition to Niko, I have been fortunate to have worked with such terrific and caring mentors including Angharad Valdivia and Clifford Christians. Cameron McCarthy's intellectual guidance and affective friendship has been something I could only have wished for before my graduate studies. Thank you, Cameron! A big "thank you!" to the Buluts and my new extended family.

Başak, thank you for listening to my disorganized and impatient thoughts every day. Thank you for reminding me of the value of love, patience, and kindness. I am honored to be your partner.

A PRECARIOUS GAME

FOR WHOM THE LOVE WORKS IN VIDEO GAME PRODUCTION?

One of the competing titles I considered early on for this book was "The Deluxe Suite on the *Titanic*: Precarious Playbor in the Digital Game Industry." Clunky, without a doubt, but James Cameron's historical drama has a lot in common with labor practices in the video game industry. The idea of using the *Titanic* as a metaphor for precarious labor in the video game industry goes back to a team meeting at Studio Desire, the ethnographic setting for this book.

Almost all Desire employees attended this meeting, which was held just a couple of months after the studio's major franchise had broken a sales record. Gathering in a historical building within walking distance of the studio, Desire's developers were jubilant. They were thrilled by what they had accomplished. Still, the developers were not quite able to enjoy the moment since their parent company was not financially thriving. The meeting was organized to discuss this issue with representatives from Desire's parent company, the publicly traded Digital Creatives, which was going through a "rebuilding process."[1] The representatives were on a tour to communicate their restructuring plans to the studios they owned; their first stop was Desire, the flagship studio of Digital Creatives.

The meeting started with PowerPoint presentations about Desire's record-breaking franchise and its international success. The audience was delighted. They loudly cheered. Years of labor had paid off, financially and emotionally. Desire had finally established itself as a voice in the competitive triple-A game market.[2] The joy in the room, however, was displaced by a relatively low-spirited atmosphere when the discussion moved from Desire's promising numbers to the not-so-bright financial condition of Digital Creatives. The representatives complained about how online rumors related to the company spread very quickly. The parent company, the representatives highlighted, was not going broke. They had funds "for two years, with the most conservative guesses and numbers." They hoped this would assure Desire's developers that things were not as gloomy as social media speculations claimed. According to the representatives, the remedy was to "keep our heads down and produce quality games. We're going to rebuild the company." In the minds of Digital Creatives' representatives, dedication and creativity were key to future success.

Following these hopeful remarks, Desire's workers put questions to the representatives of Digital Creatives. Their tone revealed that there was a funk at Desire. The developers criticized the lack of communication from Digital Creatives, suggesting that their parent company was "dragging down Desire." The representatives did hear the criticism but not necessarily in the way that Desire's developers expected. They responded with a meritocratic discourse, highlighting the significance of dedication: "Only the actions and your work will do it." In other words, if you work hard enough, there shouldn't be any reason to worry. But, in addition to failing to get the financial, organizational, or emotional support they asked for, Desire's developers were left on their own in dealing with the adverse economic condition caused by Digital Creatives.

The feeling of "being dragged down" resurfaced during another meeting, this time conducted internally at the studio. Held at the same location and attended by most of the developers and Desire's own management, this meeting's goal was to reflect on the previous one, throughout which the representatives' core message was clear. There was no reason to be worried. Showing the trailers of highly anticipated games produced by their other studios, the representatives had tried to preserve an upbeat mode and assure Desire's developers that they should not be alarmed, especially because Desire was Digital Creatives' most successful studio.

But the developers were far from being convinced. During the Q and A, one of them, Harold, said that the representatives' consolations just didn't work. Harold was a highly approachable white man in his thirties. He almost always wore a baseball cap. Originally from Georgia, he had a cynical sense of humor when discussing Digital Creatives. For Harold, the parent company's financial situation wasn't promising. In contrast to the bright future projections expressed by the parent company's representatives, which one of the developers after the meeting described as "shenanigans," Harold likened Digital Creatives to the *Titanic*. Desire was the "deluxe suite on [the] *Titanic*." Being in the "deluxe suite" was not enjoyable for Harold. He didn't want to be on the *Titanic* in the first place.

In response, one of the managers said: "It is not about who owns you. It is about what you do. We happen to have most of the lifeboats. You guys are the keys, the assets. You are not going to miss a paycheck." Again, meritocracy was the key to success. Yet such assurances regarding the safety of Desire weren't helpful. The ship was clearly sinking, and the captains' guarantee about the likelihood of survival based on individual responsibility was not convincing.

In addition to depicting the "sink or swim" business dynamics of game development, the metaphor of the *Titanic* is useful for pointing at the transnational and networked nature of this creative industry.[3] Even though imagined to be unsinkable, the *Titanic* sank as it was making its transatlantic voyage, and so too did Digital Creatives go bankrupt partly due to its transnational investments. Digital Creatives boasted about these investments to appeal to its shareholders. Yet, for Desire's workers, Digital Creatives' global growth strategy, tied to the mandates of the financial markets, was ultimately "reckless," as an assistant producer at Desire told me. In a way, just like the *Titanic* ignored warnings from other ships on its voyage, Digital Creatives shut their ears to Desire's workers' criticisms. Despite not being the largest game publisher of its time, Digital Creatives was big enough to be heard when it filed for bankruptcy in the 2010s. Unlike the *Titanic*'s sinking, the bankruptcy of Digital Creatives did not lead to any regulations to prevent "reckless" growth strategies among game publishers. Finally, just like *Titanic*, Desire's passengers—that is, their labor force—presented a stratified picture. Depending on their disciplines and skills, some of the developers were in a more precarious position than others in the industry, which itself was imagined to be "unsinkable."

This crisis moment was very different from the atmosphere when I entered the lives of Desire's developers in 2010. My first encounter with Desire was in a large room full of vibrant developers, who were all applauding their colleagues for receiving such annual awards as Rookie of the Year, Design Excellence, Artistic Excellence, Production Excellence, and the President's Award. Every time the name of an awardee was announced, her or his digitally manipulated photograph resembling a celebrity was projected on a wall, making developers burst into laughter. Back in 2010, Desire's workers felt that their jobs were secure because their franchise was expanding its fan base. Market sales were growing and, in fact, reaching record levels, which put Desire's workers under the impression that the 2008 crash would be tangential to their studio. Nevertheless, in a couple of years, the impact of the 2008 crisis had become tangible, ultimately leading to the bankruptcy of Digital Creatives.

A Start-Up Dream Becomes a Precarious Nightmare

The story that this book recounts starts with a youthful start-up dream, which then turns into a nightmare intrinsically related to finance capitalism. The following pages demonstrate that failure is endemic to the push for newness and novelty in the highly innovative game industry, which unleashes not only creative outbursts and financial success but also missteps and failures. Although the industry thrives on creative destruction with respect to game technologies, there are also major moments when what results is "destructive destruction, something that becomes visible, even if it does not become totally clear (far from it), with the crisis of 2008" (Stiegler 2016, 81–82).

Examining an industry that supposedly works on meritocratic ideals, this book provides a sobering account of the inequalities that structure the lives of game developers in the aftermath of the 2008 crash. It recounts Desire's transition from its early days as an independent studio to a financialized structure after its acquisition by Digital Creatives in the 2000s.[4] Investigating the creative, spatial, and domestic impact of this expansion on a stratified labor force, the book explores how the bankruptcy of Digital Creatives affected Desire's game developers. While labor analyses often take precarity among low-wage service jobs as a given, the present study extends that assessment to include the ranks of middle-class game producers. I conclude the book with a discussion of the unequal and toxic implications of "DWYL: do what you love" (Tokumitsu 2015), a mantra within and beyond the video game industry, and propose alternative ways to imagine work and love in the digital age.

Rather than assuming a rhizomatic labor force in the game industry, I take materiality seriously. Responding to Toby Miller's (2006, 10) call to "follow the money, follow the labor," I unpack Desire's story as it unfolds through four interlinked processes: rationalization upon acquisition, spatialization, financialization, and precarization. Among these, precarization anchors the whole story.

Rationalization upon acquisition refers to Desire's commercial and bureaucratic transition from an independent studio to being Digital Creatives' most successful internal studio. I am not suggesting that Desire's production prior to acquisition by Digital Creatives was irrational or completely chaotic. Rather, with rationalization upon acquisition, I evoke Bill Ryan's (1992) "formatting" to emphasize cultural industries' financial logic that seeks to streamline creativity to mitigate market risk. Specifically, I refer to the major cultural shifts involved in Digital Creatives' organizational plans to rationalize Desire's creative production in line with commercial mandates (chapter 2).

Spatialization follows as a logical next step from rationalization upon acquisition. When Digital Creatives bought out Desire, they had to relocate since the new ownership structure required Desire to produce competitive triple-A titles. That meant hiring new developers, necessitating a spatial fix. While spatialization fundamentally refers to the deployment of communication technologies to overcome the crisis of capital (Harvey 1990; Mosco 2009), it also reveals the vitality of constructing a functional and affective workplace to maintain the well-being of the game developers (chapter 3).

Rationalization upon acquisition and spatialization are both embedded in the broader political economy of *financialization*, which I consider the networked and intensified dimension of rationalization upon acquisition. Being acquired by Digital Creatives brought financial relief to Desire, which would no longer have to seek out funding for each new project. But being part of a publicly traded company put the developers at the mercy of financial networks, marketing schemes, and investment plans over which they had no control. Thus integrated into the financial markets, Desire's developers found themselves perpetually working to satisfy the investors and shareholders of their parent company.

Financialization, then, had become a control mechanism in Desire. The financial performance of Digital Creatives' stock prices were now used as the measure of workers' performance and well-being. Given its market position back then, Digital Creatives had no other choice but to do more with less in the triple-A market. Therefore, the financial resources that Digital Creatives brought to the table were a double-edged sword. As Maurizio Lazzarato (2015, 174) has argued, "capital is driven by a dual movement" in that the moment it comes as a liberatory force, it creates new forms of subordination. Being offered stock options by Digital Creatives was appealing at first. Many of Desire's workers had indeed bought stocks, but once a developer invested in the stock options, this produced a form of social bond, leading in turn to the financialization of work and self-surveillance of productivity. The financialization of work and formation of this particular bondage created an especially intricate situation for Desire as it was the flagship studio of Digital Creatives. In spite of its privileged position as a successful studio, financialization—coupled with the perpetual production dynamics and competitive upgrade culture of the industry—produced a feeling of endless work entrenched in precarity, which constitutes the heart of Desire's story.

Precarization is the dynamic process characterizing the existential conditions at Desire. My use of the term *precarity* doesn't refer to an absolute or static structure. Rather, I am suggesting that we approach precarity as an emergent form, as "compositional and decompositional" (Stewart 2012, 524). This means that precarity rises or decreases in its scope and intensity. For instance, in the case of Desire, precarity fluctuated temporally. Although most of Desire's workers were not feeling the force of precarity at the beginning of my fieldwork, they were sending out their résumés as I was concluding my research. The feeling of precarity is also relative in that a temporary entry-level game tester is more precarious than an experienced programmer since proof of having successfully shipped games matters. But still, even the creatives, especially those without sufficient experience, can be precarious. As the designer Silvio, who had taken loans to study game design in his forties, said to me during our interview in a Japanese restaurant: "It's harder for me to get into another job. These all make it tough. Once you ship a game, though, you are sort of part of the club because the industry asks for everyone in shipping titles."

Given the persistence of precarity across the creative industries and emerging forms of resistance (Brophy, Cohen, and de Peuter 2015), precarity is neither a novel condition nor an inevitable trap. At a very basic level, I understand precarity as the hegemonic form defining employment relationships within the neoliberal context. However, the fact that subjectivity and life have become key sources of value in the information economy differentiates the precarity of our times from that of Fordism. Precarity under Fordism was different as there was a more visible distinction between labor and leisure time (Fumagelli and Morini n.d.). In the neoliberal information economy, this distinction has become blurred as life itself has become work, leading to the individualization of the safety net on which workers depend. The struggle for more free time has become trickier.

Therefore, post-Fordism's precarity is to be seen beyond the limiting economistic framework of the short-term contract and rather as part of an "affective atmosphere" (Berlant 2011), entering "directly into the perceptions of individuals" (Fumagelli and Morini n.d., 4). Precarization, then, has to be understood in its relationship with governmentality and as an ambivalent condition, which involves not just subjugation but also self-empowerment (Lorey 2014, 13). In other words, precarization is not simply the top-down imposition of insecurity. Rather, the government of subjects—in our case, video game developers—actively depends on workers' participation from below, which is enabled by their creative autonomy, passion for work, the ethos of hard work, and game development's cool status; these aspects not only empower the workers in their everyday practices but also deepen precarization. Simply put, precarity is productive of subjectivities especially because it is entrenched in love. It doesn't exist just because there are fewer jobs. On the contrary, precarity is strong especially due to the game developers' ideological tendency toward abstract promises of play and the materiality of glamorous employment. As Silvio's earlier remarks regarding the conditions of acceptance into the "club" suggest, precarization depends strictly on hard work, willingness to take risks and get into debt, and hope of entering the club, which promises that once you're in, you are in for good.

At the same time, the precarity specific to Desire is one that is experienced by a predominantly white, heterosexual, middle- or upper-middle-class group of developers. It is a privileged precarity, different from what one finds in outsourced film production in Europe (Curtin and Sanson 2016) or soap opera production in Turkey, where workers experience heart attacks, cerebral bleeding, or at times lose their lives (Bulut 2016). This necessitates addressing the racialized and gendered dimensions of the highly bodily hardware and recycling work in the Global South (chapter 1) and practices of inferential racism (Hall 1995) that justify problematic game content through various discursive strategies at Desire (chapter 1).[5]

Ultimately, if even game developers who love their well-paid and symbolically valuable jobs are not immune from precarization (chapter 7), this book is an invitation to reflect on what the precarization of glamorous middle-class jobs means with respect to labor broadly considered, especially in the current context of debates regarding the future of work. In addition, game workers in North America and across the globe are currently organizing to improve their work conditions, a strong indication that workplace perks and passion for work are inadequate for happiness. Game workers' organizing attempts suggest that contemporary capital's strategy to enlist subjectivity for work is likely to face resistance. In that regard, perhaps we should start imagining work and democracy in new ways, without limiting ourselves to a liberalism that demands alienating trade-offs at work and in civic life. Simply put, it is time to politicize love at work.

After the 2008 Crash: The Future of Work and Labor in the Game Industry

This book is situated vis-à-vis the mythic aura surrounding video games. On the one hand, we are told that video games can improve education and health and ultimately fix our dysfunctional society (McGonigal 2011). On the other hand, urban and federal policy makers imagine the video game industry as a remedy to unemployment, providing tax incentives to attract investment (de Peuter 2012; Kerr 2013; Kocieniewski 2011).

The fetishization of a particular kind of labor or technology is not new. Years before Richard Florida acknowledged his indifference to inequalities in his work on the creative city (Wainwright 2017), it was the prophets of postindustrialism who promised to liberate society from labor conflicts. And of course, who can forget the dot-com fever and following bubble in the late 1990s? With the internet emerging as a new frontier for commercial success, start-ups were smashing workplace hierarchies (Ross 2003). People were willing to invest in start-ups, where "the amount of money available to venture capital funds ballooned from $12 billion in 1996 to $106 billion in 2000, leading many doomed ideas to be propped up by speculative backing" (Taylor 2014, 30). This had devastating consequences for some of those willing to take risks back then (Henwood 2003; Neff

2012; Solnit 2001). Less than a decade later, the whole world witnessed the collapse of the financial markets in 2008, bringing to the fore broken social promises, increasing personal and public debt, the intensification of racial inequalities (Chakravartty and da Silva 2012), record levels of unemployment (even in a country like Sweden), and deteriorating work conditions, where recovery meant the replacement of unemployment with underemployment (Piketty 2013; Rushkoff 2016; Streeck 2016, 18).

A decade after the 2008 crash and two decades after the dot-com bubble, the future of work dominates the public agenda.[6] On the one hand, robots and automation are collectively imagined as uncontrollable aliens that take not only service jobs but also white-collar ones. But serious historical perspectives alert us to how the science-fiction-like talk around automation disguises the class project behind it. It is not robots but capitalist decisions and actions mediated through robots that threaten jobs (Taylor 2018). On the other hand, apps and the so-called gig economy promise new income avenues through driving idle cars and sharing idle bedrooms.

Not coincidentally, automation, the gig economy, and their leading promoters emerged right around the 2008 crash. The current reality is so dark that Wolfgang Streeck (2016, 28) defines our political condition as "oligarchic inequality" or "neo-feudalism." Therefore, the excitement around the future of work has to be situated "in the history of 40 years of wage stagnation, the decline of benefited employment," (Schor and Attwood-Charles 2017) and the broader tendencies regarding labor precarization (Kalleberg 2011). This history is important because in the United States, 160,000 people rely on Uber for income and only 4,000 are regular employees (Streeck 2016, 26), hinting that the gig economy gained legitimacy partly by buffering the damage of the crisis on the middle and working classes (Sperling 2015).

Whether one calls it gig economy, sharing economy, or platform economy, its prognosticators have a flawless narrative. In addition to its income-generating dimensions, this brand-new world of work puts pressure on legacy services (e.g., hotels, taxi) and empowers consumers. This is all possible thanks to the algorithmic management of labor (Rosenblat and Stark 2016). The convenience of touching a screen, however, doesn't terminate inequality, discrimination, and labor exploitation (van Doorn 2017). Workers' decisions are ignored in the opaquely automated decision-making mechanisms embedded in the labor process (Gandini 2019). Externalizing investment costs, companies also abuse enormous amounts of consumer data through "digital market manipulation" (Calo and Rosenblat 2017) and subject human sociality to market mandates.

Aside from these economic inequalities, there is the ideological work that words like *gig* or *sharing* perform in our consciousness. Naming things matters. What is commonly called the gig or sharing economy is digitally intermediated, platform-based capitalism (Huws 2016; Srnicek 2016). Uber's refusal to pay workers benefits rests on the claim that algorithms have transformed the employment relationship (Kennedy 2017). In refusing to call workers "workers" and renaming them "independent contractors," companies like Uber are redefining labor as "humans as service" (Prassl 2018). This discursive move is possible thanks to what Jeremias Prassl (2018) calls the "platform paradox," enabling companies to present themselves as a marketplace for matchmaking. Yet these companies are still employers who track and regulate workers without calling the process as such. This political logic informs what Elizabeth Pollman and Jordan M. Barry (2017) call "regulatory entrepreneurship" through which companies in the gig economy emerge as political actors to either exploit legal gray areas or make laws like the state by mobilizing its users through campaigns against regulation.

But such corporate actions create antagonisms where workers, refusing to be reduced to code and data (Irani 2015), reclaim their rights, demand regulation and national minimum wage, and form co-ops (Hayns 2016; Scholz and Schneider 2016; Slee 2015; Taylor 2014; Zamponi 2018). At the end of the day, gig workers are increasingly aware that even if they seemingly have reclaimed the means of production, property relations are intact mainly because the algorithms beneath the sharing economy are completely black boxed (Pasquale 2015).

Even though jobs in the game industry are more glamorous than those in the gig economy, the industry is haunted by the same technophilic discourse, which itself is a "technology of distraction" (Frase 2016), making us forget capitalism's various crises and the game industry's own collapse in 1983 due to market greed. The amnesia is such that the game industry has steadily been characterized as immune from crisis, but that is far from the reality. In the early 1980s, Atari had released two consoles, Atari 2600 and 5200, but this double release had been planned too hastily and without a thoughtful strategy. When Atari 5200 was launched, the company was also flooding the market with games designed for Atari 2600. Coupled with a poorly performing *E.T.* game and the news of an insider-trading story related to the company's CEO, the stock of Warner Communications, the owner of Atari, stumbled, leading the parent company to sell Atari in three pieces in 1984 and 1985 (Trautman 2014).

In fact, Mirko Ernkvist (2006) demonstrates that although the 1983 crash is a primary event in the video game industry's history of failures, there have been other crashes, which have consistently followed periods of growth. Similarly, the impact of the 2008 crisis on the industry is systematically ignored. Although they didn't declare bankruptcy, leading companies like Take-Two and Square Enix went through financial difficulties during the crisis (Kerr 2017, 49). The profit margins of Electronic Arts (EA) shrank from 27 percent in 2004 to 8 percent in

2008, leading EA to downsize 6 percent of its workforce in the fall of 2008, whereas this figure rose to 11 percent (1,110 employees) toward the end of the year. Due to the crash, EA shut down twelve studios (Dyer-Witheford and de Peuter 2009, 68). Consider the gaming website Kotaku's long list of the studios that closed between 2006 and 2012. There are one hundred studios in this list and seventy-six of them were closed between 2009 and 2012. Although the relationships between the closures and the workers' experiences need to be uncovered, it is evident that the game industry is far from crisis-prone.

In addition, the sustainability of the game industry's console segment has been called into question given intense competition, increasing costs, decreasing profit margins, and the advent of the free-to-play model. In fact, only one in twenty-five games will be profitable, and it's the top twenty games that bring in 80 percent of industry revenues (Whitson 2013, 123). In sum, multiple disorders shape the game industry, hinting at structural problems in the play factory.

But myths regarding the emancipatory potential of game labor persist. There are concrete reasons behind the erasure of narratives with respect to market failure and the proliferation of myths around video game production. Our historical moment is defined by what I call the "ludic contract." In the context of late capitalism, governments across the globe desire predominantly playful kinds of capital, playful kinds of cities, and playful subjects that are willing to engage with precarious work. Video game production shines with playful practices and mythical discourses that promote this ludic contract.[7]

The field of video game studies has critically addressed these myths. Some have pointed to the emergence of a new form of labor—"playbor"—as the distinction between work and play gets blurred in the information economy (Kücklich 2009; Wark 2007). Others have examined the game industry and algorithmic materiality of games through Michael Hardt and Antonio Negri's theory of empire and cognitive capitalism (Dyer-Witheford and de Peuter 2009; Galloway 2006). Scholars have also investigated how fans' pleasurable activities are valorized to sustain the industry through cocreative activities in virtual worlds (Banks and Potts 2010; Postigo 2010); how the economies of online games affect culture, politics, and commerce (Castranova 2005); the massive use of video games beyond purposes of play (Bogost 2011); the transnational racialization of in-game labor and racism in game design (Leonard 2009; Nakamura 2009); and digital contestation and aesthetic resistance (Coleman and Dyer-Witheford 2007; Raley 2009). Researchers have written excellent ethnographies of virtual worlds (Boellstorff 2009) and the techno-liberal politics endorsed by the creators of *Second Life* (Malaby 2009). From the perspective of science and technology studies, Casey O'Donnell's (2014) *The Developer's Dilemma* provides an in-depth description of game development as a creative and collaborative practice and differentiates between game development and other kinds of software production. O'Donnell's work has been invaluable in terms of his description of the legal terrain within which the industry is embedded.

This book draws decidedly on critical political economy, feminist theory, and autonomist Marxism. Specifically, this book builds on critical game studies (Dyer-Witheford and de Peuter 2009; Kerr 2017; Mejia 2012; Nakamura 2009; Nieborg 2014; Woodcock 2019), the political-economic insights derived from Nicole Cohen's (2016) work on journalism, feminist theories of labor (Federici 2012; Jarrett 2016; Pateman 1988), digital labor studies (Andrejevic 2013; Burston, Dyer-Witheford, and Hearn 2010; Fuchs 2014; Noble 2018; Roberts 2019; Scholz 2013), critical studies of media and creative work (Banks 2007; Duffy 2017; Hesmondhalgh and Baker 2011; Gregg 2011; Mayer 2011; Ross 2003; Stahl 2012), and philosophical explorations on work, universal basic income, and the post-work society (Chamberlain 2018; Lordon 2014; Read 2003; Weeks 2011).

Integrating these interdisciplinary insights, I critically deploy the term *immaterial labor*[8] to define game production. As a crystallized form of immaterial labor, game development serves as an entry point to deconstructing the hype regarding the pleasures and promises of video game production in the neoliberal context. In revealing this hype, I offer the notion of ludopolitics to describe how Desire's organizational capacities involve not only resourcefulness, cooperation, and communication but also various inequalities.[9] Through ludopolitics, I question the unequal politics of who can play and who has to work in the game industry at the local and global level. Specifically, ludopolitics allows for understanding inequality at various levels. While the strict intellectual property regime and the obsession with work alienate Desire's privileged workers at the workplace level, one should also note that their pleasure depends on the exploitation of others, both in their own houses and in the Global South. In other words, the pleasures of a predominantly white-male labor force depend on the pain of others in different nodes of global game production.

To that end, I examine how unequal power relations around game production unfold not only within the boundaries of the workplace but also at home and at the urban level. I ground and materialize game labor, embed it within the workplace, and connect the workplace to financial markets, the urban, and the domestic space. Without taking into consideration the networks that link the workplace to other nodes of production in the context of the "social factory" (Negri 1989), we cannot understand the uneven political economy of fun and pleasure that fuels the game industry at large. But researching how game developers perform immaterial labor in the networks of this "social factory" is not an easy task.

Researching Game Developers

I was curious about how game industry professionals, as creative workers, were doing in a postcrash context. With the help of a wonderful friend, I reached out to Studio Desire. After two months without a response, I decided to find an alternative site, but right around that time, Desire invited me to discuss my research. I met them, shared the broad framework of my research, and gained access. Yet the joy of having access soon turned into anxiety as I was no longer the avid gamer I had been in high school. I bought a game console to play Desire's games so that I could talk with them about their work. Now I was playing games for ethnographic work.

It was at a companywide meeting in 2010 that I first met Desire's developers, who discussed financial issues, retention, crunch,[10] and future plans. Right at the beginning of this meeting, the president of Desire projected my photograph on a large screen and shared my name. The game developers welcomed me warmly. Fast-forward three years from 2010, and Desire was in a completely different context. Digital Creatives had filed for bankruptcy, selling Desire to a private company.

I was invited to a meeting where Desire's new owners were about to meet the development team. The developers were nervous but relieved since they had a new owner. During this meeting, I wasn't on the same floor with Desire's new owners. They were on the third floor whereas I and half of Desire's workers were on the second floor. We were seeing the new bosses only virtually on a large screen thanks to a camera located on the upper floor. If the developers next to me had questions about their future or other issues, they asked a designated employee to send a text message to the IT staff on the third floor, who would then relay the question in person to the new owners.

All of this is to say that Desire constituted a highly mediated, networked, and swiftly changing work environment, posing peculiar difficulties for ethnographic research. While people did have face-to-face meetings, a lot of work was done via email, forums, spreadsheets, conference calls, Skype, and VPN (virtual private network). The computer had become the canvas of the game developers. I had naively expected a lot of interaction with the developers. But impromptu conversations proved harder than I thought since wearing headphones while working, for instance, indicated that the developers had completely focused on work and did not want any interruption.

Regardless, I was able to attend team meetings, studiowide meetings, and a game launch party. I spent time with game testers and participated in two different in-house training programs. I attended school visits where game developers talked to aspiring developers. For about three years, I collected ethnographic data, conducting fifty-six semistructured interviews with managers, programmers, artists, designers, producers, testers, spouses of developers, a city official, and a real estate developer. The studio kindly gave me a computer station to work with. This allowed me access to online forums, informal culture, and flows of work and communication. I conducted a small survey to understand developers' perceptions about job security with respect to Desire, Digital Creatives, and the broader industry.

Since I did not have the occupational skills to work as a game developer, my primary access to information was through participant observation and interviews. This created some uneasiness on my part. I desired to grasp the totality of social relations within which the developers worked, lived, and played. I wanted to be in their minds and hearts to understand how their days went, how they worked with their colleagues, and what they felt throughout. I also wanted to be in the hallways of Digital Creatives to explore how the parent company's management perceived the financial market, the future of products, and the studios they owned. There were times that I wished I could be in China to talk to people who produced art content for Desire. As love, passion, and working with machines are central to game development, excavating the emotions at work was also vital to this project. In sum, I wanted to study game production in its totality.

Yet, is that ever possible? Does the social present itself as it is in networked environments shaped in real time by different kinds of social, economic, and legal forces (Howard 2002; O'Donnell 2008)? Posing similar questions, Michael Burawoy (2000, 1) underlines his frustrations about the impossibility of "appreciat[ing] the fate of Manchester textiles without knowing about America's slave South or the progress of colonization in India." Similar difficulties in grasping the spatial and temporal interconnectedness of capitalist life and work were relevant for my case, as well. It was impossible to understand the fate of the financialized and precarized nature of work at Desire without comprehending the stock prices of Digital Creatives, whose own fate depended on a set of other factors, such as the sales of their other games, performance of certain products made by Digital Creatives and its other studios, or the market sales of their competitors. A potentially negative event for Digital Creatives and Desire would adversely affect the city where Desire was located, given that the downtown area hosted up to two hundred game developers, who fueled the economy of the city.

The question of method thus became, how does one immerse oneself in the production of a video game—an ephemeral puzzle in continuous production—by approximately two hundred people to whom a researcher cannot have instant and simultaneous access? If subjectivity is put to work in these work spaces, how could it be explored? How does one grasp the aesthetic value that employees attach to their labor and the game they produce every day? Studying emotions, immateriality, and aesthetics in the creative labor process is a challenging task because passion, aesthetics, and visuality are scholarly blind spots (Fineman 1993; Strangleman 2004). Thus, in addition to ethnographic research, I implemented photography to illuminate the emotional and invisible aspects of material culture and labor in the game industry. I asked volunteering video game developers to "show me how it feels to work" (Warren 2002). For reasons of privacy, I do not use these photographs but describe them in detail in the book. But the elicitation of photos led to productive conversations that my regular observations or interview questions were not delving into, primarily because ordinary objects can be invisible to the researcher. In fact, the idea of exploring the tensions between commerce and creativity emerged when a technical artist went out of his way to Desire's storage to capture an old desk, which led to a new line of inquiry about the cultural shifts following Desire's acquisition by Digital Creatives (chapter 2).

I also conducted what one might call "playful interviews." I asked designers to take me to a certain section of the game and depict the joys and frustrations of working in that particular project. I was able to assemble the fragments of the labor process diffused in email lists, chat boxes, and computer screens. These interviews provided clues about the disagreements, negotiations, and agreements pertaining to production.

A final methodological issue to address is my own reflexivity as a male researcher. As I illuminate in chapter 4, developers describe their work using such words as "parenting," "love," and "fighting battles." Initially, I wasn't critical of such gendered language. I am not a militarist person, and I was certainly not buying into the neoliberal dream of passionate work, but perhaps I had a romantic vision of love, ignoring its gendered and exploitative dimensions at work. "Parenting," "love," and "fighting battles" imply a gendered subject position occupied by male game developers. These words and the pleasure they suggest are embedded in unequal social relations. As I began to think about gender, love, and work through interdisciplinary conversations in media production studies,[11] I was better able to consider the racialized and gendered inequalities involved in discourses and practices of love and work in game production and its industrial dynamics.

The Game Industry and Studio Desire

The emergence of video games as a medium goes back to a moment of "refusal of work" (Dyer-Witheford and de Peuter 2009) when Pentagon scientists, tasked with beating the USSR during the Cold War, ended up creating ludic experiences on their work computers during times of boredom. Atari (and later Nintendo, Sega, Sony, and Microsoft, along with hundreds of studios and independent game producers) turned these experiences into commodities and laid the foundations of the present-day global games industry.

Today, contemporary video game production is a serious, lucrative business. In 2017, the global worth of the industry was more than $100 billion, excluding hardware and gambling-related revenues (Kerr 2017, 32). The production of games played on consoles, computers, and smartphones is a truly global phenomenon. Companies scattered around the United States, Japan, Europe, and Canada dominate software production, the most lucrative arm of the industry. Asia is the primary site for manufacturing hardware, though South Korea, China, and Singapore also engage in some software business and are struggling to create original intellectual property (Fung 2016).

Desire's main target is the console market. It generally takes eighteen to forty-eight months to make a console game. The number of employees required varies depending on the scope of a project, but, to give one example, more than one thousand people worked to produce Rockstar's *GTA V*. Corporate players in the console market must acquire the technological and legal infrastructure, investment, and authorization of Sony, Nintendo, or Microsoft, as producing console games requires the development kits produced by these giants of the field. Sony, Nintendo, and Microsoft thus dominate the market as gatekeepers because it is technically and legally impossible for a studio to produce console games without these kits and accreditation.

In addition to game studios and such console manufacturers as Sony, Nintendo, and Microsoft, there are also publishers in the industry. They finance, market, and distribute the games. Publishers are the financial protagonists in the story since it's not typical for an average game developer to have the capital investment required for console game production. That is, publishers have immense power as they own considerable capital to hire the labor force, invest in technology, and organize worldwide physical and digital marketing. Electronic Arts, for instance, is the behemoth publisher, employing almost ten thousand employees for whom it has built campuses so that they enjoy work.

Geopolitics heavily shape power relations and structure the value chain in game publishing. When I started my research in 2010, the top ten companies in the publishing market were from Japan, France, and the United States, and Digital Creatives was on this list. The number of companies is not evenly distributed, though. The United States was the base for six of these companies (Kerr 2017, 50) and still dominates the industry. According to the Electronic Software Association (ESA), the United States video game industry earned $36 billion in 2017. It directly or indirectly employs 220,000 people in all fifty states. California, New York, Washington, Texas, and Massachusetts are the top five states in terms of the number of video game companies. For comparison, Desire's home state has roughly

10 percent of the total number of game studios based in California. In this midwestern state, there are fewer than one hundred game companies, and there are only three other game companies in the city where Desire is located. None of these companies operate at close to the organizational capacity of Desire.

I conducted my research in a medium-sized city in the U.S. Midwest, with a population of about ninety thousand. The racial composition is as follows: almost 70 percent white, 15 percent African American, 10 percent Asian, and 6 percent Hispanic. The city is a college town and a primary node in the Midwest's technology networks. The city houses diverse industries, including agriculture, health care and medical research, and retail and distribution, and it does aspire to attract visitors to boost the consumption-based economy. One key branding strategy that the city has used to market itself is that of a "micro-urban community," where people enjoy a somewhat healthy work-life balance, although the poverty rate in the city is more than 20 percent (see chapter 3).

In 2010, Desire had 239 employees, including artists, programmers, designers, audio designers, producers, project managers, studio directors, vice presidents, game testers (quality assurance, or QA), human resources, finance, information technology, office administration, and marketing. By the time I left the field in the summer of 2013, the studio had 186 full-time employees and 26 temporary testers. Desire had its first layoff in April 2011 and was acquired by their new parent company in early 2013. Between these two events, 52 people left the studio. Based on my conversations with the management and game developers, the financial condition of Digital Creatives was not the sole reason but definitely a significant factor behind this flight. The flight has continued to this date. At the time of writing, there were about 160 employees at Desire, and of the 56 people I interviewed, fewer than 20 were still there. Some had quit and moved to California, Canada, or Seattle to continue game development, whereas others were laid off.

During my fieldwork, I witnessed the release of two games and the bankruptcy of Digital Creatives. My workstation was relocated a couple of times since employees were shuffled based on the status of their project. In that sense, Desire was reminiscent of Richard Sennett's analogy concerning the modern corporate environment and the MP3 player, where "linear development is replaced by a mind-set willing to jump around" (Sennett 2006, 48). However, Desire is also different from Sennett's flexible organization primarily because it resembles a playground.

From the very entrance of the plaza where Desire is based to its interior offices, the studio tells its workers and visitors that people are working in an open, creative environment and simultaneously having fun. This "playbor" space, to evoke the wonderful term coined by Julian Kücklich (2009), boasts about how its move away from the cubicle enables free communication and the exchange of creative ideas. As you pass through the entrance, you are greeted by a trophy case, a display of the studio's history of successful games. If you need to wait for somebody, like I did numerous times, you can relax and read *Wired*, *PC World*, or *Business Information Week*. Since a considerable amount of work is accomplished in meetings, meeting rooms are fully equipped with technology to allow networked work. Kitchens are especially important in Desire's broader culture. Developers enjoy snacks and free soda, talk about work, and sometimes complain about the amount of work they have to do or how they have to redo something. Nerf guns are an important aspect of the culture, turning the workplace into what one technical artist's wife called a "fraternity house." As a playground, Desire provides every opportunity to blur work and play and ultimately harness creativity.

This is the primary goal of the book, film, and game libraries at the studio: to help developers escape for a moment or look for inspiration. The books on the shelves cover a diverse set of topics, including lean manufacturing, consumers, programming language C, architecture in the Islamic world, weapons and swords, Photoshop, gothic art, and brand culture. The game library covers many video games produced by both Digital Creatives and its rivals. It is not uncommon to see developers playing video games or board games in a designated area next to the libraries. If you fancy playing arcades, Desire has them. Outside the regular work hours, interested developers organize what they call a "terrible movie" night and watch a terrible movie at the studio. The studio also at times takes the developers to the movies to sustain team spirit. In sum, Desire is a workplace you want to live in, but this playful workplace is enabled by intense practices of communicative labor.

Communicative Labor Process at Desire

Developing games with a team of more than two hundred people is like being part of a crowded and somewhat tipsy band. It is hard to attain a coherent sound. Writers, programmers, artists, designers, and testers come together with their aesthetic and technological skills to produce long hours of game play. Giving life to digital games is a very complicated process, "a creative collaborative practice," through which developers work together under cultures of secrecy dictated by strict intellectual property regimes (O'Donnell 2014).

Collaboration, communication, and negotiation are key to game development, an intensely emotional labor process. As Trip Hawkins, the founder of Electronic Arts, puts it, making games is a complicated business where "creative people need to get out of the ivory tower and pay attention to the tests in the Petri dish. And the scientists need to understand that it takes creativity to make something fun" (Ramsay 2012, 15). Articulating a whole social process where creativity is valorized through collaboration and responsible communication, a Desire designer once vividly explained, "People's work depends on you. You can't just sit. Everyone is so connected. People will notice. You need to be on top of things."

To collaborate, team members communicate pervasively in meetings, informal gatherings, studio hallways, emails, forums, instant messaging, and Facebook. Communication is crucial for the maintenance of team spirit and the production of a cohesive game. It is not a coincidence that the studio has posters on the walls constantly reminding the developers of the broader vision, the direction of their project, and their focus as a studio. Vision is tough to establish as the direction of a game can swiftly shift or may not even be clear from the beginning. Therefore, communication in general has itself become a form of labor (Brophy 2008) within which different actors work not only on the game but also on their subjectivities to become good team players. Who, then, are the parties involved in these pervasive communicative practices, and what exactly do these communicative laborers at Desire do?

Desire's Creative Workers

Programmers typically write the code for a game, read code written by others, and are involved in developing support infrastructures for the studio. They mainly deal with logic and the manipulation of numbers, which constitute the technical basis of the experience that the designers and artists have in mind. The programmers' position can at times be a frustrating one, most often because of time and budget issues, but it is also not uncommon that other colleagues' demands lead to creative conflicts.

I was once talking to Matthew, a person of color and an experienced programmer. He worked at Desire for many years and was a self-confident employee. He was never afraid of criticism and always willing to help others at work. Although he was also vocal about industry practices, he had endorsed the post-Fordist work ethic. He had read Daniel Pink's (2009) *Drive* and understood work in terms of an internal energy. When communication with designers and artists was not smooth, Matthew got frustrated: "You are working with a machine that only understands zeroes and ones. Black and white. Therefore, you need to think about every possible scenario. Nonprogrammers never think about these things. I always ask them not to be too ambitious and a bit more conservative."

Working with machines on the one hand and human beings on the other can be particularly hard. Matthew said: "We run into situations like having to deal with difficult demands. We translate the demands of design into numbers. For example, they want the character to look angry . . . We ask them: What does angry mean? We need to deal with numbers and hard rules. We know what a doorway is, but a computer doesn't know. We have to give it rules." In sum, programmers' primary role is to create a game that not only runs smoothly on the machine but also satisfies the demands of design, a role that requires communication, translation, and interaction between machines and humans.

Artists are responsible for the game's aesthetics. They produce the environment in the game, its characters, and the interfaces. They also work closely with sophisticated technological tools. Unless involved in the concept design with designers, they typically begin to work after projects enter the production phase. At Desire, artists have a peculiar position in that some of the environment art is produced in China. This practice of outsourcing initially created anxiety about job security. But my discussion with artists about Desire's cost-reduction policy revealed that their anxiety was not simply about job security. They were also concerned about their creativity. As important as job security was, artists complained about how working with fellow artists in China had turned them into managers. Rather than producing art, they were now lost in corporate spreadsheets so as to manage artwork done by Chinese artists.

Designers are the stars of the industry. Playing a lot of games to learn from other industry practices, designers' primary concern is to make a game fun, compelling, and competitive. Design involves communicating certain emotions to the players. One essential question they keep asking, as I witnessed in a design meeting, was "What are the emotional goals for the player experience?" One designer's response to this question was "to get overwhelmed. You shouldn't feel that you can stay there very long, you gotta keep moving." Designers' primary role is to guide players through visual tricks in the game so that they get a sense of what future moves to make. At Desire, designers and those who work closely with design meet regularly, exchange ideas, and share industry publications to create Desire's own design culture. The appeal of the profession is such that recent years have witnessed the emergence of game design schools and degrees in the United States and across the globe. They go to conferences and are interviewed in game magazines, which gives them a certain amount of celebrity value, as I heard from designers a few times.

Testers (quality assurance, QA) are the most vulnerable workers in Desire. Testers' vulnerability is derived from their temporary employment status. Describing a major event in Desire's history will prove helpful in underscoring testers' distinct precarity. In 2009, there were 102 employees at the QA facility when the majority of the workforce (84%) was laid off, reducing the chance for getting a full-time position to almost nil. Only a few have permanent positions; the majority are hired on a temporary basis. Specifically, while there are usually 11 full-time testers in the studio, there are 10 to 15 temporary testers at any given time, and this number fluctuates depending on the status of the project. Toward the end of my research when a major title was launched, there were 50 temporary testers (28 onsite, 14 outsourced, and 8 for localization).

Testers are responsible for helping the core development group (designers, programmers, and artists) release a relatively bug-free game, though they don't have much agency in the broader creative process. This is not meant to undervalue the important work that testers do. On the contrary, testers are crucial since it is their attention-based labor that helps Desire ship games with as few bugs as possible. The value of testers and the repetitive tasks they perform under precarious conditions can be even more appreciated given the gigantic scope of console games, which involve the interaction of complicated hardware and software, which itself is comprised of lines of code, art assets, artificial intelligence, and different logics of design. Nevertheless, despite their important skills as competent video game players, testers do not have as much creative impact on a game's vision, which leads to feelings of "second-class citizenship."

Desire also employs producers and project managers who are in charge of whole teams. Leads (programmers, artists, and designers) are the bridge between their teams of fellow artists/designers/programmers and the producers or the project managers. They communicate the concerns or work schedules of their fellow workers to the upper management and vice versa. Project managers ensure that resources are allocated to team members and the team is on schedule. They remind team members what needs to be done within a given time frame, which might position them as a source of discontent for the creative team. Producers are responsible for the production of a cohesive and profitable game. They communicate between the studio and the parent company. When creative disagreements occur, it is the producer who ultimately drives the game and makes the final call.

Desire's team consists of a workforce (predominantly white and male in terms of demographics) with different levels of cultural capital, skills, personalities, personal histories, and work experiences that need to be harnessed. The team's faith in the game is crucial. Team morale is equally important as it affects the well-being and performance of the labor force. For instance, when experienced staff left the studio due to the unfavorable financial conditions of Digital Creatives, this not only demoralized the team but also meant difficulties in terms of recruitment and replacing lost talent.

In sum, game production is not purely about fun or love. As a few game developers underlined during our conversations, game production at its core means that developers have to "fight battles" with other disciplines and sometimes hate what they do. Frustrations occur when upper management does not provide sufficient information. Alienation is inevitable when testers are hired more than once but not promoted to full-time positions despite the quality work they perform. But such problems are universal and exist in other creative industries, as well. So then what is distinct about the video game industry and games?

Video Game Production: A Distinct Amalgam of Technology and Creativity

In fashion blogging, new media, music, freelance journalism, or television and film, workers are granted significant autonomy (Cohen 2016; Duffy 2017; Mayer 2011; Ross 2003; Stahl 2012). In that regard, the video game industry has commonalities with other creative industries. For instance, the requirement to waive intellectual property through nondisclosure agreements in the game industry is similar to the exclusive contracts signed by recording artists in the music industry (Stahl 2012). Even if not quite publicly visible like a recording artist, game industry professionals also enjoy the symbolic capital granted by society. Likewise, both the film and game industries share the blockbuster mentality. Or if we were to make a comparison between the aspirational labor behind fashion blogging and video game production, aspects of the "future return system" (Duffy 2017, 7) defining the former are also evident in the latter, especially in the do-it-yourself (DIY) and independent game production scene (Keogh 2015).

Video game production has distinct features too, though. First, the political economy of the video game industry presents a peculiar case. Surely, the dynamics of conglomeration are similar to other media industries (Kerr 2017). Yet the video game industry works in a hybrid way in that it combines the revenue model of television with new media economics (Dyer-Witheford and de Peuter 2009). Having recognized how design is central to video games, Microsoft, Nintendo, and Sony—as publishers and console producers—sell consoles at or below cost. As the analogy suggested by Nick Dyer-Witheford and Greig de Peuter (2009) reveals, the implication is that the money is in the software (blades) that are played on the hardware (consoles, i.e., razors), which are also produced by the three aforementioned companies. In this model, these game industry giants lose money on the consoles but make money on the software thanks to their dominance in the market and the proprietary nature of game platforms they produce. That is, the political economy of video games is platform dependent, which differentiates a game from a song, an e-book, or a movie. As David B. Nieborg (2011, 19) has argued, "a console game is anything but an interoperable software format and is ultimately shaped by a computational platform defining the technical and economic properties of the triple-A commodity form."

What defines this commodity form then? Not completely unrelated to this economic model, games are unfinished commodities, and they have an afterlife (Nieborg 2011). Games' afterlives derive from the production of paid downloadable content, free downloadable content to reward loyal customers, and franchising based on the blockbuster model. The production of game expansion packs is primarily intended to satisfy financial investors, another aspect of Desire's distinct political economy.

Aside from the distinct political economy and the peculiar commodity form, the industry works on the premise of constant technological change. Since games are future-oriented commodities, they sell dreams to consumers. Selling dreams based on faster game play, deeper immersion, and greater connectivity necessitates a "permanent upgrade culture" (Dovey and Kennedy 2006). In line with this techno-logic, game consoles are regenerated every five to seven years. Therefore, technology and the level of high capital investments essential to the game industry distinguish it from other creative industries.

This has implications for both creative labor and consumption practices. On the one hand, workers have to learn the specificities of each new console generation since new consoles come with new affordances and enhanced capacities. On the other hand, consumers share the ideology of innovation and progress, and their expectations keep rising. Similar expectations regarding technology and upgrade culture do not exist, at least in the same intensity, in book or magazine publishing. Magazines and books are finished commodities with a relatively fixed life, whereas games have a modular design structure not independent from the ideology of upgrade and progress and perpetual innovation dynamics (Nieborg 2011). Although this potentially empowers and reskills workers as they learn how to work with new technologies, they can also become alienated because cycles of permanent upgrades deliver nothing but more work.

In addition to their political economy, commodity form, and techno-economic logic, the materiality of digital games matters. Video games are machinic experiences. One needs a console, a TV, and internet connection. Due to the materiality of their interactive and code-based structures, digital games transform users into active authors. Through machinic play, they lift both producers and players of digital games out of the banality of their ordinary lives. Games are also embodied experiences. When we play a game, we don't just follow the narrative but also play its code. We play against a system (Galloway 2006, 90–91), which, in return, does something *to us* (Ash 2015). By engaging the player through the materiality of code, this system quite efficiently inculcates both the love for the practice of play and the desire to become a game developer. Understanding how this love operates has major implications with respect to labor and citizenship.

Games and Democracy: Time to Be a Killjoy?

Since the 2008 crash, there has been considerable debate about work and employment. Automation, algorithms, artificial intelligence, machine learning, robots, gig economy, and sharing are only some of the keywords used in these debates, revealing hopes, anxieties, and criticisms about how the future of work and employment should look. The 2008 crash has also caused major political and cultural upheavals around the globe. Right-wing populism and its toxic political culture are on the rise globally, the U.S. symptoms of which include Gamer-Gate,[12] the 2016 presidential elections, and the Kavanaugh hearings in the U.S. Senate. Although I do not imply a causal relationship between these events and right-wing populism, the cultural infrastructure of the game industry and high-tech production substantially inform politics. Given the problematic representations, misogynistic trolling, and techno-masculine geek cultures (Taylor and Voorhees 2018) of video games, this book has relevance beyond Desire in terms of imagining democracy, free speech, and citizenship. Thus, as a techno-masculine (Johnson 2018) workplace informed by white masculinity, Desire and the precarization of middle-class lives therein have lessons for us.

First, jobs and employment constitute a major portion of our daily conversations. The memorable meme of Steve Jobs is a wonderful case about how we imagine the economy and employment vis-à-vis the high-tech sector. Reflecting the cynical mood toward the dysfunctional economy, this meme showed Steve Jobs, Georgios Papandreou (the former prime minister of Greece), and Silvio Berlusconi (the former prime minister of Italy), each paired with different phrases containing the word *Jobs*: "Steve Jobs" under Apple's cofounder; "No Jobs" under Papandreou, who had to resign due to Greece's debt crisis; and "Blow Jobs" under Berlusconi, who was infamous for his lifestyle as a politician and a media mogul. Amid the dire circumstances of the crisis, politicians told their constituents that the nation as a whole needed to stick together, act responsibly, and work harder to compete in a global economy. Citizens, especially those employed in the creative industries, responded positively. They worked at home, at the coffee shop, and even during vacations.

This mandate to work has continued and is not simply about unemployment anxiety. Work has now been redefined in positive terms. That is, a dominant discourse of love and enjoyment informs how we imagine work. In that regard, the command to be passionate about work when there are not enough jobs needs to be considered in relation to the broader ideological framework that redefines work along the lines of enjoyment. In what Todd McGowan (2003) describes as the "society of enjoyment," lack of enjoyment counts as failure; work is no longer supposed to involve toil. Labor has been gamified in many respects (Cherry 2012), and it should be about love. Steve Jobs's remarks at Stanford University's commencement in 2005, now considered one of the ten commandments regarding work, prescribed that we should do what we love because our work will be a big part of our lives. Jobs had advice for those who haven't found love at work: "keep looking."

Jobs was right. Today's world of work does fill a large part of our lives, and many aspire to follow his advice. As a Desire developer's T-shirt said: "I work to support my videogame habit." There is possibly nothing wrong about associating work with love. What is not terrific about getting paid for doing something that one is passionate about and the rest of society admires?

Yet love comes with inequalities. On the one hand, becoming obsessed with their jobs and having to comply with the requirements of a strict intellectual property regime was not always pleasant for Desire's workers. That is, alienation emerges in both psychological and legal ways (chapter 1). On the other hand, Desire's workers' love for work takes a bigger toll on certain demographics, such as their partners. Through an old, gendered logic, this same mechanism also classifies partners' love at home and domestic labor as trivial, marginalizing domestic labor and attaching more value to paid work at Desire (chapter 5). I was once talking with Gina in a local coffee shop. She was in the IT sector and knew firsthand the difficulties of being on call 24/7. Unlike her husband, she was pro-union. Married to a technical artist at Desire, Gina told me how her children's friends and sometimes strangers (once, a fireman) would ask her if her husband could help them get a job in the industry. This might be flattering for industry professionals, but the glamor around certain professions fetishizes only certain kinds of work as more worthy of social respect and monetary reward (Tokumitsu 2015).

The association of labor with love also renders invisible the unequal gatekeeping mechanisms that shape the field of game production. How egalitarian is an economic structure when we use the phrase *break into* to describe access? Or what if game development does not respond back to your love despite your good credentials? And in these creative communities, what are the mechanisms of inclusion and exclusion with respect to race, gender, sexual orientation, and class background? Who can play and who has to work? Who are the proper subjects of our ludic democracy?

According to an International Game Developers Association (IGDA) survey in 2015, 75 percent of developers are male and 76 percent are white. This report described the "prototypical game industry workers/developers as a 32 year old white male with a university degree who lives in North America and has no children" (Paul 2018, 4). Dominant discourses of love and creative meritocracy fail at serving marginalized communities as these discourses thrive on racialized and gendered inequalities. This is important because in an industry that defines itself through meritocracy, talent or love become self-explanatory for success whereas social inequalities based on race, gender, and the legacy of colonialism become irrelevant to understanding games' success. As pointed out, the genres and aesthetics of lucrative games are closely linked with dominant social norms and market imperatives (Alexander 2013; Anthropy 2012; Bulut 2018; Mukherjee and Hammar 2018).

In addition to how discourses of love marginalize broader inequalities in a supposedly meritocratic system, this book reconsiders play and its productive dimensions. Popular discussions regarding video games have overwhelmingly constructed them as wasteful objects of violence, sidelining their productive features. I do not mean to promote gamification as a remedy to fix our "broken reality" (McGonigal 2011). Rather, based on their productive capacities, developing a critical approach toward games' design structure is important because games are influential sites for the cultivation of skills, habits, and subjectivities (Yee 2006, 70). Games teach us how to race, war, network, raise a family, and collaborate (Dyer-Witheford and de Peuter 2009). As Lazzarato argues (2015, 188), our contemporary economy is defined by a "tremendous acceleration of investments in machines and this involves much more than 'production' alone." Following this point regarding machines and production, it seems appropriate to state that the labor force in the game industry is trained not only within educational institutions but also on consoles and computers, which shape the subjectivities of prospective workers of the industry from early ages. Therefore, although this book is a media ethnography and takes the reader into Desire, it underlines how the production of video games is never restricted to the workplace, the formal work hours, or limited only to the formal skills defined by the market. That is, the productive and pedagogical dimensions of play and its fusion with work make it crucial for us to consider game production as embedded within broader processes of social reproduction involving the domestic space, educational institutions, and game technologies.

Finally, game development stands as an odd profession at a historical period when we both fetishize work as an economic activity and have less respect for work. The cultural legitimacy of work seems to be at a crossroads, perhaps in crisis (Fleming 2014). Work, at one level, is about money, but jobs are scarce. If we are lucky to be employed, we work more to prove our worth but we gain less. We have even less time to enjoy the financial rewards, if there are any. This is not simply the case for dead-end jobs. It applies to game labor and Desire, as well. The very professionals that enjoyed what they did and invested long hours could not always receive the desired economic gains or pleasure. At times, work seemed to have no visible end. As Matthew, the programmer, emphasized with respect to his colleagues, considering passion to be endless "is a double edge sword. They really love video games. But then they get burnt out quickly. You can't do this forever; you can't work 100 hours a week forever."

More than a decade has passed since the 2008 crash, but problems associated with the economy and employment have not disappeared. Digital technologies and new forms of labor had promised to deliver peace, prosperity, and democracy, but we ended up with right-wing authoritarianism, environmental crises, and political conundrums. Ordinary workers earn less and unions are weaker. Gigs do not seem to be fun. At the same time, workers in the game industry and beyond are organizing. In that regard, the current crisis can be an opportunity to question what the future of work could be like, how we relate to time, what kind of working lives we want, and what kind of citizens we want to be.

This moment of critical reflection should start by coming to terms with the fact that the social contract is no longer social. It has been unmoored from its social dimensions and currently defined by individualized precarity and play. Our ties with the state and the rest of society rely on vulnerable bonds, but then, we are still invited to enjoy these fragile relations. If you don't want to play the game, then one becomes a killjoy, the undesirable and disposable citizen. What's to be done then? Perhaps it is time to *become* a killjoy. To that end, this book questions the political implications of the fact that market mechanisms have permeated the most intimate aspects of humanity: desire and love. The normalization and celebration of this process is alarming because capital is more than happy to provide the ludic infrastructures for digital labor only to consolidate property relations.

Feminists have long challenged the instrumentalization of love in the heterosexual family unit and argued for a radical notion of love. Following this call, we need to rescue love from its essentialist, privatized, and compulsory mode. We may perhaps demand our right to like work "just fine" and "reimagine love as a revolutionary force, the energies of which could be enlisted in transformative political projects" (Weeks 2017, 55). If we reinstate our ability "to call work what is work," we can, following Silvia Federici's (1975) contributions to the International Wages for Housework Campaign, "rediscover what is love." This is possible and desirable, but we have to be careful not to reproduce the dominant ludic discourses and practices but construct them from the margins in a diverse fashion. Only then can we claim to be whole persons, both at work and in love (Pateman 1988; Stahl 2012). This might be a vital step to reclaim love, labor, and citizenship in a nonprivatized and truly democratic fashion.

Overview of the Book

The narratives in this book suggest that working in the video game industry is fun but also precarious. In fact, failure and precarity are endemic to this industry, but even the precarity of game developers itself rises on various inequalities.

To that end, chapter 1 introduces the notion of ludopolitics to center economic and cultural inequalities in the game industry. We need to move beyond grasping game production as simply an economic process based on trade-offs between two supposedly equal parties. Game production is a problem of social reproduction rooted in politics. A two-part question thus follows: Who can play, and who has to work in the game industry? This question illuminates how Desire's workers are alienated at work but sheds further light on how this very alienation depends on the exploitation of others in different locations and settings. I also introduce ludic religiosity as a heuristic device to examine how the definition of fun and escapism in the game industry relies on a dominant white masculinity, as well as the commodification of the Other. That is, one's creative pleasure and escapism are enabled by somebody else's pain. This new broad emphasis on inequality and social reproduction allows for shifting our focus from labor to life and life's materiality.

Chapter 2 illuminates how Desire's workers were managed after acquisition by Digital Creatives. I interrogate the tensions between the game developers' desire for autonomy and management's push for a more rigid structure geared toward the requirements of competing in the triple-A market. By examining how game developers deploy passion in their descriptions of work, the chapter provides a distinct focus by gendering labor practices and reframing the "garage" as a gendered space. The chapter demystifies the language of "trade-off" and brings politics back in, as far as acquisition of media companies is concerned.

Chapter 3 deepens the story by introducing a spatial dimension to Desire's acquisition by Digital Creatives. I examine how Desire's relocation contingently brought about the revitalization of a midsized downtown area. This revitalization was possible as discourses, imaginaries, and alliances at the local level converged around neoliberal public-private partnerships that fetishized creativity, privileged middle-class values, and promoted art as the engine of economic growth. The chapter unravels how geography, materiality, and space in the digital economy are far from being dead and are, in fact, indispensable to the reproduction of life.

The workplace is never free from frictions even when developers move to a corporate plaza. To that end, chapter 4 documents the difficulties experienced by studio management in measuring the productivity of Desire's workers. I examine the logic behind turning the workplace into a playground and the attempt to cultivate communicative laborers (Illouz 2007). The broader argument is that capital cannot afford to forego investing in the well-being of video game developers for whom strictly defined work schedules and work spaces are no longer feasible.

Capital does care about the well-being of game developers, but its reproduction is a completely different question. Chapter 5 moves out of Desire to foreground the domestic dimensions of the unequal ludopolitical regime. Keeping the discussion on social reproduction alive, it asks: What kind of classed femininities are at work in the domestic space, as far as the reproduction of techno-masculinity at Desire is concerned? Drawing on interviews with developers' partners, the chapter reveals the dialectical relationship between Desire's techno-masculine work culture and the domestic labor behind it. The taxing emotional toxicity at work is rendered tolerable thanks to the mobilization of women's emotional capacities at home. The chapter's distinct focus lies in its framing of women not simply as providers of domestic work but also as active agents who politically critique industry practices. Overall, this chapter provides a sobering response to techno-utopian claims about how digital technologies would terminate social inequalities within the domestic space, pointing to continuities in terms of love's exploitative dimensions.

Work for game testers is fun, but playing as one works can be a mixed blessing. In chapter 6, another group of marginalized actors are under consideration: game testers. As a means of getting one's foot in the industry, video game testing constitutes an arena of "cruel optimism" (Berlant 2011). Video game testing is a decidedly temporary position appealing mostly to young people with fewer occupational skills than the core creatives. Testers endure extreme precarity in hopes of garnering the symbolic capital they gain in the industry, a permanent position, or new job in one of development's other disciplines, such as design, art, or programming. Following Harry Braverman ([1974] 1998), I coin the term "degradation of fun" to illuminate the process through which the joy derived from testing is diminished due to precarity, instrumentalized play, and surveillance in the workplace.

Video game testers are the most vulnerable working subjects at Desire, but they are not the only vulnerable ones. Chapter 7 reveals how even upper-rank workers are not exempt from layoffs, financial insecurity, and the anxiety of working in a hit-driven industry. While being bought out by Digital Creatives initially provided financial security for Desire's developers, Digital Creatives' hasty, adverse investment decisions destabilized their flagship studio. When Digital Creatives eventually declared bankruptcy, Desire's developers found themselves working in a perpetual-growth machine without much morale. The chapter concludes by addressing workers' indifference toward unions.

As a critique of liberal attempts at achieving "quality of life" in the industry, the conclusion considers universal basic income, game industry unionization, and the radical imagining of a postwork society. It emphasizes the immediate need for making demands based on utopian hopes. Through hope and praxis, game developers and workers can provide partial answers as to how we can disautomatize ourselves, denaturalize our commitment to work, liberate play from its instrumentalized forms, and reconstruct work as collaborative and creative activity outside relations of domination. The book concludes by making a call for being killjoys against a future that is primarily shaped by the unequal regime of ludopolitics because game workers—and we, as players and citizens—deserve better.

As a glamorous profession, game development transnationally has immense cash value as a "labor of love." In *The Dialectic of Sex: The Case for Feminist Revolution*, Shulamith Firestone (1970, 128) describes love as "a situation of total emotional vulnerability" and adds that "anything short of a mutual exchange will hurt one or the other party." The book you hold poses two questions: If love is about mutual vulnerability, what is the politics of this romantic relationship in video game production? And if video game production is a dream job, whose dream is it?

THE UNEQUAL LUDOPOLITICAL
REGIME OF GAME PRODUCTION

Who Can Play, Who Has to Work?

I am in a college library. Desire's employees are about to meet with students aspiring to become game developers. The room is packed, full of ludic energy. It is
decorated with posters of blockbuster games, including those Desire makes. Some
of the developers are proudly wearing the T-shirts of their franchise. The meeting starts, and the vibrancy in the room transforms into laughter and serious conversations about having a future in the industry.

Attending some of these recruitment meetings alerted me to two issues about
the conception of video game production as a glamorous profession. First, college students had no idea about the cost of producing a triple-A game, which they
called a "dream job." Their guesses were astoundingly off: $300,000, $1 million,
and $1.5 million. The answer back then was around $50 million, whereas a game
with the scope of *Grand Theft Auto V* costs more than $200 million. This gap be-
tween students' imagination and reality struck me. While the attractiveness of
video game development had considerably infused educational settings, the fetish for the interactive commodity had apparently concealed the scope and value
of labor that went into producing the game. The complexity of video game production had not registered in the minds of the aspiring students, who seemed to
fancy that their portfolio in and of itself would help them join the industry.

The second issue that came up during these promotional meetings was an inquiry into the employment prospects and the work ethic in the industry. One
student asked: "What matters in this business?" A developer responded: "Education definitely matters. But what really matters is teamwork. Managing other
people is important. Learning to work with others and learning to take critique

and move on and not be hurt. It is not necessarily the classes you take." But then, another student asked: "How does one get a good portfolio?" The response: "It's about passion. Be willing to put something beyond school. Not simply projects that you had to do for school." Another developer intervened: "If there are people with equal . . . skills, the person who is hungry and ambitious will be hired." In addition to being "hungry," one needed to be willing to work in one's free time. As associate producer, Margaret, who initially joined the industry as an intern in the audio department, recommended, "Download movie trailers and make your own audio and sound effects." Working on independent projects or practicing interactive music projects was not enough, though. Entering this competitive industry required aspiring students to undertake a lot more work, but not always in paid form. As an audio designer in his early thirties, wearing a reverse baseball cap, somewhat timidly said: "If there is an independent studio with no money, it is terrible to say this, but work for free." Developers across the board—artists, programmers, QA, designers—advised students to primarily be passionate, driven, and self-directed team players and to do what they loved. If one wanted a job in the video game industry, taking the pills written down on the neoliberal work prescription was mandatory.

Let us now go inside Desire. I am observing a usability test in the usability test lounge equipped with furniture and new tools. Usability tests are vital since the studio pays avid game players to get valuable feedback for improving their games. As Harold, a game developer involved with usability tests, emphasized, "as soon as you have something playable, put it in front of the players. If you have cut scenes, test it." The data gained from these tests is later analyzed and shared with the designers and producers and may result in redesigning certain features of the game. Through usability tests, Desire monetizes gamers' passion and extensive play skills.

Desire prefers to hire experienced players for these tests. One player I talked to had spent almost 250 hours playing one of Desire's games. Nevertheless, it was not just the money that motivated him to participate in the usability test. It was more about love and feelings of belonging to a community:

> I love it when game developers are open to their fan base about the development process. One of the reasons I don't like Apple is that they are so clandestine with their product development. They are afraid that people will copy them. In the games industry, people copy other people all the time. That is how we developed genres. . . . As someone who aspires to develop games myself, I love being involved in the bugtesting of products. It is why I have been running the Developer Preview of Windows 8 since day one. When you involve the community in the

creation of a game, the community feels like they own the game. They are more willing to accept it because they realize that they took part in its creation.

The usability tests themselves were constructed like a game. There were two rooms separated with dark glass. While the developer in charge of the test and I were able to observe the gamer next door, he couldn't see us. As the gamer played the game and provided feedback, his motions were recorded with four different cameras focusing on his hands, the entire body, his face, and the game itself. The gamer's desire was being monetized as his complete body was at work. "We got some new toys" was how Harold expressed his excitement about the newly equipped lounge. Then, he initiated the test through which the following conversation took place:

> GAMER: I like the user interface.
> HAROLD: What's your objective here? What is that object there?

During these playful interviews, Harold carefully took note of what was coming out of the gamers' mouth. He was performing live data mining and valorizing the information given by the player. By asking questions about the weapons or other nonplayable characters in the game, Harold was trying to dig into the emotions and experience of the player in order to write a report for the designers.

What do we make of these two different scenes? On the one hand, as opposed to toil and financial reward, nonmonetary motivations like passion and love characterize work ethic in the game industry. The narratives from the school visit point to the consolidation of what Kathi Weeks (2011) calls the "post-Fordist work ethic," which requires contemporary subjects to be on the lookout for new opportunities, stay alert for competition, and therefore prove the worth of one's labor. On the other hand, when I asked the usability play tester if he would be interested in joining the industry, his response exemplified the opportunity-seeking character of an aspiring game developer: "I don't know if you have any connection in the industry, but if you do, I am looking for an internship. Email me if you know someone!" While this same player did think that he "got paid less" for what he did, he underlined that by not wasting Desire's time, they would "be more likely to consider calling me up again to test another game." Looking for an internship went hand in hand with paying attention to not wasting Desire's time as a potential employer.

These encounters reveal the making of workers for one of the most glamorous professions of our time. Desire's school visits point to the disassociation of work from toil as a common thread across the creative industries, whereas the usability test involves the valorization of information and the cultural taste of the players. The affective force behind each of these settings is love[1] toward game play and hope toward game production, where work is imagined to be fun.

Following Lazzarato (1996, 132), I call this particular form of labor immaterial labor, which is "the labor that produces the informational and cultural content of the commodity."[2] Desire's designers, artists, and programmers perform immaterial labor, the product of which is communication and affect reflected on our screens. They are the model workers of our time, enjoying creative autonomy in their workplace, just like those employed at Google, Facebook, or Electronic Arts. While they are typically paid well, they claim not to be simply driven by money. They love being creative and love collaborating with cool people. As I use Lazzarato's term, through ethnography, I materialize immaterial labor by not only focusing on how game developers work but also how their working capacities are reproduced on unequal terms. Kylie Jarett's (2016, 56) point about "the mutually constitutive relationship between production and reproduction—between economic and social organization" is vital to materialize immaterial production outside the formal boundaries of the labor process. That is, to understand how immaterial labor works through various forms of inequalities, we need to center social reproduction as a critical perspective.

Introducing Ludopolitics, Centering Social Reproduction, Materializing Love

We should dialectically understand game workers' labor of love through what I call the regime of ludopolitics, which emphasizes the local and global inequalities in the performance of this labor. Capitalism has always produced inequalities, but the field of video game production presents a distinct form of inequality, since the affect of love and social glamor make it a highly desirable job where work *looks* and *feels* more like play. The love and glamor of game production is so strong that developers—both aspiring and actual—can barely see and acknowledge the inequalities involved in making games. Inequalities are made invisible because play, as a central activity to humanity, implies freedom. And unless informed by the historical and theoretical insights of feminism (Firestone 1970; Gunnarsson 2014; Jackson 2001; Jarrett 2016; Nash 2011), one does not typically appreciate how play and love can involve exploitation and inequality.

What exactly does love render invisible then? First, the alienation experienced by Desire's workers is partly alleviated or ignored due to the material reality of pleasure at work. Desire's workers love what they do. Who wouldn't? They play games in the middle of the day. They drink beer as they stream Netflix at work. But love has its frictions. It is at times frustrated as it does not always function smoothly. The moment work becomes fun and flexible, work's temporality becomes infinite, pushing these workers into "the social factory" (Negri 1989) where workers work all the time, even when taking a shower. Moreover, even though these workers enjoy spaces of creative autonomy, their relationship with Digital Creatives is political: the moment they sign an employment contract, they waive any rights over their creative output due to intellectual property clauses.[3]

Second, even though it is not recognized as such, the love fueling Desire's labor force and the broader industry is deeply racialized and gendered. The love of Desire's predominantly white-male labor force, its creative self-realization at work and social reproduction beyond the studio depend on unequal forms of economic production at the local and global level. On the one hand, when Desire's male workers passionately work, their partners perform extra labor to maintain a smoothly functioning domestic life. At the end of the day, it was the infamous EA Spouse that exposed the deeply gendered roots of the game industry's labor conflicts (Dyer-Witheford and de Peuter 2006). On the other hand, the exploitation of other bodies has a global dimension. Without the exploitation of racialized and gendered bodies and nature in the Global South due to manufacturing and recycling, there would be no creative labor of love or game play at Desire.

Making inequalities visible in game production and materializing immaterial labor therefore requires a fundamental intellectual step to acknowledge how the workers themselves are reproduced on a daily basis, because, as Astra Taylor (2018) so astutely suggests, "every bridge, every factory, every Silicon Valley app is merely the visible tip of a hidden iceberg of reproductive labor." If Desire's workers love what they do, what enables their love? Responding to this question is possible only if we center social reproduction as a framework. Social reproduction acknowledges the complex social processes behind any economic production. Tithi Bhattacharya (2017, 2) suggests that the theory of social reproduction, complicating the broader context in which commodity production takes place, is "an approach that is not content to accept what seems like a visible, finished entity—in this case, our worker at the gates of her workplace—but interrogates the complex network of social processes and human relations that produces the conditions of existence for that entity."

This emphasis on social reproduction will shift the focus from the abstract discourse of love to a *materialist investigation of love and labor*. This is crucial because love is far from an abstract, individual matter. It is social in that it is already cultivated, communicated, and practiced in educational institutions well before it enters production. It is produced within game consoles before one becomes a game developer, but love then flows beyond the workplace as an essential actor in the reproduction of labor power (chapter 5). It is a communicative contagion that not only defines the moment of employment and the workplace but also acts as a material force in the reproduction of labor power. When understood as a matter of social reproduction, love enables us to challenge the conceptualization of game production as yet another form of economic arrangement and situate it as a problem rooted in politics and the society at large. Centering social reproduction is especially important given the debates around automation and claims around how a jobless future is ahead of us. Without the social reproduction of life, there is no production of economic value. After all, that is what the EA Spouse in 2004 taught us. It was only when women recognized their labor in reproducing a whole video games industry that the industry started to have discussions about quality of life and had to consider improving working conditions.

Then, as far as the ludopolitical regime in game production is concerned, the reproductive interdependence between North America, Asia, and Africa involves a political-economic relationship. Similarly, the reproductive interdependence between Desire's workers and their partners is mainly an economic one, although the ideology of a heterosexual family is clearly at work. And yet, there is also a cultural form of exploitation derived from white masculinity, the dominant subjectivity at Desire. At the end of the day, Desire's workers are racialized and gendered subjects. That they can deploy a language of sacrifice—"work for free if necessary"—is not independent from their white masculinity because this language of sacrifice, as a form of addressing others, is never independent from power relations involving race and gender.

As privileged subjects, Desire's workers produce powerful narratives, artwork, and characters, mostly dependent on what Stuart Hall (1997) calls "the spectacle of the Other." Assuming the position of the universal subject, they are unable to see the cultural logic behind their game design. That is, the dominant design logic in the industry—games are for fun and escapism—renders invisible how profitable game content thrives on inequalities embedded within the domain of cultural consumption. As I demonstrate later in this chapter, as a highly racialized and gendered domain, game development offers a particular demographics a "free space" to engage in problematic cultural production practices justified by logics like "this is what the consumer wants" or "it's just a game." While seemingly neutral and innocent, such strategies unfortunately obstruct critical conversations about games, especially when it is gender and racial inequalities that inform producers' conception of "fun" in the first place.

The goal of this chapter, then, is to theorize the economic and cultural inequalities surrounding the labor of love in game production through the notion of ludopolitics. At the studio level, ludopolitics materializes the conditions of alienation of a privileged labor force that prefers to imagine itself as a creative class rather than workers. It materially foregrounds the alienation of Desire's workers, whose relations with their company sit on uneven grounds. However, ludopolitics has a broader dimension that considers the social reproduction of Desire at the global and local level. Globally, the regime of ludopolitics allows privileged populations like those at Desire to play but only because the same regime classifies populations in the Global South in racial and gendered terms, marking them as less worthy than others. Locally, despite being overworked and alienated, Desire's workers are able to celebrate success only because others have taken care of their families while they are at work. That is, Desire's ascent from being a small start-up to Digital Creatives' flagship studio relied not simply on an ideal regime of meritocracy enabled by Desire's work ethic but heavily on the social reproductive work of Desire's workers' partners.

My suggestion of using ludopolitics[4] to uncover the inequalities in game production is inspired by Achille Mbembe's (2003) "Necropolitics," where he argues that politics is a form of war, and sovereignty resides in the power and capacity to decide who can live and who must die. I take a similar path and embed Desire's labor force within a regime of ludopolitics, which I define as the complex assemblage of multidimensional, uneven power relations at the local and global level, ultimately setting the political terms of who can play and enjoy work as opposed to those who have to work. Ludopolitics allows for grasping how various control strategies are deployed to maximize profits and create either play worlds or work worlds. While the former are constructed for the desirable subjects of the global economy, human beings in the latter are subjected to such conditions of life that they become what Mbembe calls the "living dead." As labor is increasingly gamified and mediated through algorithms in the new economy, ludopolitics offers new possibilities to understand emerging forms of gamified, algorithmic labor across the globe.

Specifically, Desire's workers are governed through a flexible labor regime, which harnesses their productive and living capacities. Desire's core developers had the freedom to go jogging during lunch, come back, take a shower, and keep working. Testers, however, were subject to a playful shop floor disciplinary regime, steeped in camaraderie, where productivity was measured by a combination of digital and analog techniques. That is, from paternalistic to biopolitical, a multiplicity of techniques coexists to control Desire's privileged workforce. But then again, as opposed to these playful techniques targeting the well-being of Desire's workers, there are also manufacturing and recycling workers in the global game industry whose labor conditions are a lot more physical and exploitative.

Finally, the success of Desire and its labor force are intricately linked with a dominant production logic, a belief system that I call ludic religiosity. As a powerful belief system, ludic religiosity enacts and justifies the cultural inequalities within the regime of ludopolitics. As the cultural pillar of the regime of ludopolitics, ludic religiosity works through the "spectacle of the Other" (Hall 1997) and rationalizes every game mechanic based on whether it serves a ludic function. Beyond being simply a technological phenomenon, ludic religiosity is culturally powerful among developers as it is strictly tied to Desire's white masculinity. In this racial and gendered echo-chamber-like environment, whiteness becomes the sociocultural infrastructure behind discourses of fun, success, or escapism. That is, whiteness breeds financial and social relationships both in the world of production and consumption, enabling networks of fraternity that ultimately set the monetary and cultural parameters of fun. Without a conscious, critical effort, recognizing that one operates in an echo chamber is not easy, especially when one assumes that his identity is the universal one. Justifications of problematic game content through statements such as "this is just fun" not only forecloses critical thinking about games but also marginalizes cultural inequalities based on race and gender, even though it is these same inequalities that set the parameters of "fun" in the broader industry. Finally, without critically considering the racialized and gendered economic and cultural materiality of game production, we are unfortunately bound to think of structural inequalities as individual problems of diversity.

Ludopolitics at the Local Level: Material Roots of Alienation; or, What Liberal Approaches to Creativity Miss

Desire's creatives wear flip-flops at work. The studio provides them with free soda, snacks, and beer during meetings. They can enjoy the pool table, the Ping-Pong table, and the margarita machine at any time. They customize their workplaces as they wish and benefit from the flexible work environment policy. They get into Nerf gunfights at work. Desire's management does not deny life but affirms it through enhancing labor's autonomy. At the end of the day, when game developers describe their jobs as a "labor of love," what relevance, if any, does the concept of alienation have? Constituting a direct contrast to the explicitly exploitative practices at Foxconn, the industrial end of our ludopolitical regime, can we really talk about alienation as a form of friction at Desire?

Perhaps understanding capitalism as a regime of desire (Lordon 2014) might be helpful to rethink alienation beyond the dualistic perspective exemplified in Marx's depiction of industrial work, juxtaposing workers' misery with the wealth of the bourgeoisie. According to Frédéric Lordon (2014), post-Fordism produces a joyful alienation. We have become automobiles and affective robots that move based on their desires. Desire for play and creative production move

Desire's developers. We may be tempted to think that such desires are internal, but Lordon (2014, 74) warns us that these desires are "induced from outside but turned into authentic internal desires."

In Desire, it makes less sense to think about alienation as the loss of autonomy, since developers enjoy work based on positive affect (fun, play, autonomy, freedom) rather than negative affect (debt, hunger). Following Lordon, we may rethink alienation as *fixation* in Desire. Fixation manifests itself through the ubiquitous discourse and flow of love in and outside the studio. Alienation becomes a "stubborn affect" (Lordon 2014, 145) where the mind is completely occupied. It becomes such that developers think about work all the time. The joyful working subjects in the new economy are similar to cocaine addicts, and we should therefore reconsider alienation and think of it as "not loss but closure and contraction" (Lordon 2014, 146).

When reframed along the lines of contraction, alienation does exist in Desire, where features of "good work" (Hesmondhalgh and Baker 2011) abound. In fact, the abundance of features of good work accelerate alienation because as long as workers are given openness and creative autonomy, they may not have an issue with the fundamental logic of capitalism: value extraction and profit maximization. Yet, the story in this book will reveal how much of the joy and sociality derived from elements of good work are erased when the brutal fact that there is no job security hits the studio. In sum, even when one possesses most of the features of good work, alienation might persist if one's employment future is unclear.

If obsession with work constitutes the psychological dimension of alienation, the industry's risk-averse political economy yields another form of alienation, which I previously called the logic of one-dimensional creativity (Bulut 2018). In order to guarantee sales and avoid market risk, game workers produce sequels of the most popular genres, over and over again. This makes alienation inevitable. The remarks of a veteran developer shed light on how the industry's political economy reduces the joy derived from the experimentation associated with creative work: "Early games were just out of curiosity. People were just playing around. Then it was Pong and the market took over. Early games were about experimenting. . . . We don't see much innovation and experimentalism. Now it's commercially driven. They're not going to try new things when there is obvious demand for war games and gang simulation. You lose so much experimentation. Shareholders won't like it." The industry's political economic structure, then, is another fundamental factor in producing alienation by obstructing creative experimentation.

The alienation produced by the unequal regime of ludopolitics also has a contractual, material, and legal basis. Alienation in its legal sense "describes the transference of a thing from one person to another" (Stahl 2012, 283). Therefore, despite major differences between industrial production and game developers' tendency to see themselves as creatives, the following list attests to the materiality of alienation: waiving intellectual property rights through NDAs (nondisclosure agreements), the employment contract itself, lack of creative control over the labor process when subject to corporate demands, producing sequels to respond market demands, and not having input with respect to the future of the studio as experienced throughout the bankruptcy process (see chapter 7).

The materiality of Desire's workers' alienation became most visible when they met their new owners only to witness their disassociation from their own intellectual property. At the very outset of this meeting, one programmer, Matthew, who always struck me as a very confident and driven individual, said, "Thanks for buying us." This was a cathartic encounter since the rest of the studio passionately applauded him. Then, the new owners praised the studio for its successful record. But it was obvious that there was a certain level of anxiety in the room. Considering this exchange, one could think that Desire and their new owner, as two equal parties, had reached a consensual agreement. Nevertheless, the perception of their being on equal ground might be misleading because the game developers were not able to exercise full control over their intellectual property (IP) despite living "good lives." That is, the bankruptcy clearly meant that Desire's highly successful developers had no control over the fate of their own IP. It was Digital Creatives that had the right to negotiate Desire's future and ultimately sell it to someone else.

The unevenness of the ludopolitical regime between Digital Creatives and Desire becomes even more pronounced given that Digital Creatives declared bankruptcy right after Desire launched its most successful franchise and finally established a firm identity for their game. At this point, rather than celebrating, Desire's developers had to work even more to gain some time and provide immediate cash for their dying parent company, which desperately had to sell downloadable content for their game. The artist Ricardo and I chatted before he was leaving for the Bay Area. His remarks were telling: "OK, awesome, we got this huge hit. But now, we need to—holy crap—get . . . dumb downloadable content out right away because if we don't, the parent company might not make it another month. . . . There was a birthday party one of our guys had for his daughter. . . . We're talking about it. We should all be so happy and so proud right now, but everybody is just sad because the studio is just falling apart."

Ricardo's statement bears testimony to how game developers, who enjoy creative freedom at work, end up working as if they were parts of a machine. This is what liberal approaches to creativity and creative labor miss. By focusing on the mutual consent that defines an employment relationship, they forget that employment and intellectual property are deeply liberal practices and relations. They ignore how both employment and intellectual property are liberal forms of subjecting creative expression to the seemingly neutral language of the law (Stahl 2012, 9). However, following Carole Pateman (1988), we should understand employment not simply as a market exchange but a relationship established through a contract, which frames the "political fiction" of labor power. Pateman is critical of the employment relationship because it is based on a logic where the capitalist not simply hires labor power but the whole self and the body of the worker. This is possible because the whole employment relationship is constructed on the liberal idea that "I own myself as a property." Once my ownership of myself and my body is legally established, my rights regarding self-government become alienable. And when my body is defined as a property, the idea of unfairness in this exchange is canceled because it is assumed that I exercise full control over my body and the law treats everyone equally. Ultimately, employment produces an illusion where the owners and performers of labor look identical, even though this is not true. In other words, although Desire's workers create the video game, their parent company ultimately owns the labor power and the workers as the performers of labor (Pateman 1988, 2002).

Ludopolitics, then, politicizes the inequalities embedded in the labor process at Desire. It allows for rethinking the features of good work as political tools to extract value and render alienation pleasurable. So, the emphasis on autonomy and love as the complete opposite of alienated labor is knotty. As liberal practices and relations, both employment and intellectual property block our vision and constrain our analysis to the social-psychological perception of working subjects, who may very well be happy at work. Yet, independent of the perception of subjects who may quite enjoy autonomy at work, employment exists as an objective condition, giving us the political, legal, and contractual foundation of alienation. For instance, when I was discussing the precarious condition of testers with the human resources (HR) department, noting that they had been fired, the HR personnel said, "They were not fired but were let go." That is, HR was using a language of release, as if the termination of employment just happened, again pointing to the unevenness of the ludopolitical regime.

This unequal relationship may not look antagonistic at all from the perspective of game developers. As Kylie Jarett (2016, 78) taught us, there are forms of labor and relationships that can be both exploitative, coercive, and socially meaningful. That is, the playful nature of this employment relationship disguises coercion since the antagonism at the heart of this ludopolitical regime "does not require someone standing over the worker with a gun or some other threat of force" (Andrejevic 2013, 154). Rather, the coercion is materially derived from the untouched property relations between the developers and their new owners. In other words, individuals performing creative labor seem to possess a good level of ownership over their labor process, but property relations between cognitive capital and Desire's workers remain intact, the former having the final call in terms of the fate of the studio, the organization of labor relations, and the production of future IPs.

In sum, Desire's workers enjoy work in their playful workplace. While this seems to negate the question of alienation, in fact it has even more intense manifestations since autonomy in the playful workplace transforms one's life into work. At Desire, one sees various faces of alienation: psychological, political economic, and legal. However, in the regime of ludopolitics, their playful labor practices also rest on uneven global relations of production.

Ludopolitics at the Global Level: Hardware's Racialized and Gendered Materiality

Now, let's leave North America for a moment to zoom out and sharpen our understanding of the global dimensions of the ludopolitical regime in which Desire's exploited workers, the aspiring students in the college, and the avid play tester are still privileged actors. If it weren't for properly functioning game consoles, it wouldn't be possible for college students to play games and network about their dream jobs in privileged educational institutions. Nor would it be feasible for Desire to conduct play tests in the studio. That is to say, the prefix *im-* in *immaterial labor* can flash on and off only when the manufacturing of game consoles in Asian countries, primarily China, continues.

The less glamorous end of the ludopolitical regime becomes visible only when the system breaks down. In 2012, manufacturing workers in China protested their employment conditions, leading to disruptions at Foxconn, the Taiwanese firm that produces half of the world's electronic gadgets, including game consoles, tablets, laptops, desktop computers, and iPhones. Foxconn employs 1 million workers in China, and it enjoys land and infrastructural support thanks to its relationship with the Chinese state. Its smallest factory employs some 20,000 workers whereas larger ones employ 400,000 workers with little labor protection, leading to workers' resistance (Ngai and Chan 2012; Qiu 2016).

The geographical triangle of the ludopolitical regime is still missing a node, the one that is even more disciplinary and necropolitical: the extraction and recycling of materials used in our gaming platforms. The Democratic Republic of Congo (DRC) is the central location for extracting 3 TGs (tantalum, tungsten, tin and gold). Coltan (columbite-tantalite) is the ore from which tantalum is extracted. It is vital for consoles and cell phones due to its high heat resistance.

Contested and accelerated means of extracting such minerals in conflict zones lead to massive environmental degradation and loss of nonhuman life, rendering the DRC geopolitically unstable as it owns 80 percent of the global coltan supply (Maxwell and Miller 2012; Taffel 2015). These minerals and the labor behind them become visible only when the pleasurable consumption processes in the Global North are disrupted. In 2000, gamers expecting Sony's new console had to wait longer as there were problems with coltan supplies (Dyer-Witheford and de Peuter 2009, 222). Not surprisingly, game corporations like Nintendo or Sony have not taken steps to completely ensure the use of conflict-free minerals (Dyer-Witheford and de Peuter 2009, 224; Valentine 2018).

There are also geographies of e-waste to consider. Because game consoles and hardware are renewed every five to seven years, the "uncool" gadgets are dumped in Nigeria, Ghana, China, and India, where workers sort usable parts, working within poisonous electronic mountains to make a living by valorizing waste. Ghana especially is a prominent site of such hazardous work, where women living close to e-waste sites suffer from infertility and children are born with higher rates of birth deformities (Ryneal 2016, 216).

The dialectical relationship between the conditions of game work in North America and the highly material labor in Asia and Africa is an invitation to think critically about the unequal ground on which love flourishes. In the former, we find passionate college students who can network with their role models but are not even aware of the production cost of their beloved games. This indifference to the financial and social cost of production cannot be considered outside global relations of race and gender. That is, they are not just inexperienced students; they occupy privileged positions. Their passion lies not in the material infrastructures of hardware but in ludic experiences. Similarly, the "terrible" recommendation to "work for free" and the invitation to self-sacrifice come from the privileged middle-class position of white masculinity. This socially powerful identity enables one, as an authority, to be able to work for free and normalize it as a practical piece of advice to share with others. Therefore, rather than leveling the playing field, calls to pursue love at work only reproduces inequalities at the global level, where racialized and gendered bodies are either systematically targeted or forced to undervalue themselves within the ludopolitical regime.

Subjectivity is surely at work globally, and there doesn't seem to be an outside to global capitalism. The concept of immaterial labor is mostly sufficient to explain the reality at Desire but not so much the highly material, territorial conditions of labor in the manufacturing factories and mining fields of the Global South. So the question remains: Who gets to decide who plays and who works? Hardt and Negri's (2000) framework of a new stage of capitalism is useful but may ignore how this new stage involves an ecology of racialized and gendered bodies, nation-state policies, materiality of game hardware, nature, and the total inter-actions of all of these (Fuller 2005). The ability to code and design digital games means nothing unless relationally imagined together with the networked mate-riality of other laboring bodies and natural minerals. Contemporary capitalism functions not simply through the "disembodied" flesh of game players and game producers but also the disciplinary repetitious work and natural exploitation in the Global South. The more the racialized and gendered groups in the Global South are exploited, the more prosperous the middle-class white creatives in the Global North become, because, independent of one's good intentions, the latter's well-being is dependent on the other's exploitation, demonstrating once again the inequality undergirding the regime of ludopolitics.

The Cultural Logic of Ludopolitics at Work

A final way that the uneven regime of ludopolitics shapes production is through a particular logic that marks the boundaries of what counts as fun. Who gets to decide what makes a game fun? What kinds of inequalities are at work when a particular design and narrative logic of escapism is coded into digital games? Ludopolitics, through a specific cultural framework, conditions not only the terms of who defines pleasure and fun but also the terms under which they are imagined and circulated as professional discourses and practices.

What makes a game successful? If we measure success simply by sales figures, certain genres—like first-person shooters, war and adventure games, and urban simulations—come out on top. Given their content, such video games attract sharp criticism and raise eyebrows for their sexist, racist, and violent content. Desire's game content is no exception. As I am touring the studio, I see sexualized game content on the walls. I hear gendered conversations about the content of their games, which, in a different corporate context, would lead to intervention by the HR department.

How do these creative people, who never used a slur word in our conversa-tions, feel about the content they and the broader game industry professionals produce? What kind of professional ideologies are at work in producing contro-versial content that they don't let their own kids play? What rhetorical stances do they deploy to defend their work? What enables the lighthearted production of imperial games despite public criticism against their militarist, sexist, and racist imagery and narratives?

Responding to these questions necessitates racializing and gendering Desire's predominantly white-male labor force. The dearth of nonwhite workers at Desire is extremely noticeable. At the time of writing, less than 10 percent of

Desire's staff were females, who mostly worked at project management, human resources, and production. In fact, when I was interviewing the project manager Renata, a white woman in her forties, in a dark and very small room at the studio, I asked her why women mostly occupied these positions. She said: "Perhaps, they need women to control all that testosterone here."

We laughed, but this joke signaled the broader "diversity problem" in the industry, not dissimilar from other creative industries (Saha 2012; Warner 2015). Desire is part of a larger high-tech ecology suffering from a lack of diversity. For instance, except for Apple, with 13 percent, the percentages of black and Latino tech workers employed at Silicon Valley's largest companies (Facebook, Twitter, LinkedIn, Yahoo, Google) range between 3 percent and 4 percent (Working Partnership USA 2014). Under these circumstances, nonwhite populations are excluded from middle-wage jobs and consequently constrained to low-wage positions (security guards, janitors, grounds maintenance workers) with few benefits.

Compared with the Silicon Valley ecology, the video game industry, in contrast to its earlier days when game content excluded minorities (Williams et al. 2009), has at least made some progress at the representational level by introducing nonwhite and female characters, albeit in problematic terms (Gray 2014; Murray 2018). A larger problem lies with the workforce, though. In Canada, the United Kingdom, and the United States, nonwhite populations are the minority (Ramanan 2017; Sheikh 2017; Weststar et al. 2017). Only recently, an article about Riot Games, the producer of the global brand *League of Legends*, revealed the toxic "bro culture" and practices of gender discrimination in the workplace (D'Anastasio 2018). Riot Games responded with an apology, promising progress toward diversity, but the controversy and the ensuing walkout at the company once again pointed to the structural problems regarding institutional sexism and the failure of meritocracy within the industry.

In 2017, the BBC's Rahil Sheikh (2017) asked nonwhite game industry professionals: Does the video game industry have a diversity problem? The journalist and game developer Chella Ramanan answered in the affirmative, suggesting a "cycle of white, middle-class men making games that reflect themselves." Sitara Shefta, a producer at Dream Reality, shared a story where all of her colleagues chose white characters for the faces of a game they were making. Operating along more color-blind lines, Konami Europe's social media manager Asim Tanvir depicted a "very welcoming industry" where the real issue was more about just picking "the best talent" and putting "background and race aside." Kish Hirani, chairman of Black, Asian, and Minority Ethnic (BAME) in Games Network, acknowledged the problem, but for him, the difficulty stemmed from the lack of applications by "a wide enough range of backgrounds" (Sheikh 2017).

Both Riot Games' response and the BBC report on the game industry highlight diversity as the key problem. Yet perhaps diversity is not the accurate frame to use because it is, I argue, not a bug but a feature of the game industry. I propose to frame the issue not in terms of diversity, because diversity discourse can remain at the level of talk and fail to achieve concrete action by simply blocking the path to action (Ahmed 2006). I want to foreground white masculinity as the elephant in the room for the industry's dominant demographics. Unless we frame the term *diversity* in relation to concrete practices of inequality and within the larger context of professional ideologies and institutional cultures of white masculinity, forming an egalitarian workforce might fail.

To understand how race and gender inform production, I discussed controversial game content with Desire's workers. I asked: How do we understand the appeal of certain genres with questionable representations of race and gender? At the heart of Desire's workers' responses to such questions was a curious ambivalence, an ambivalence that both acknowledged and disavowed problematic game content. On the one hand, it was easier for them to acknowledge problematic representations of gender. They surely wouldn't allow their children to engage with the adult content they produced. However, race talk was more delicate.

Once, I was with Matthew and Chris in a studio meeting room. Matthew, a longtime employee and a person of color, was eating lunch and joining our conversation whenever he was not eating. Chris, a white man in his midthirties, had previously worked in California. He had dropped out of graduate school in computer science. As we discussed video game culture, I asked: What makes your games and others in the same genre fun and desirable in the United States? With a few pauses, Chris said: "It's an interesting question. . . . uhhh . . . A lot of it is letting out your inner child. If I was an eight-year-old but had to do things you want to do but then you actually are not hurting anyone . . . It's like, 'Blow things out—that's cooool! It's neat!' . . . The general freedom to do what you want to do is pretty big for a lot of people." I continued with this word "freedom" and directly asked what they thought about video game criticism that suggests how this powerful medium enables "identity tourism" (Nakamura 1995), giving privileged populations the ability to consume the Other without consequences (Leonard 2003). Chris agreed:

> CHRIS: I think there's a lot of that. . . . I grew in a suburban house. I didn't know any of that stuff. But you see it in a couple of movies. . . . Everything from *The Godfather* to *Goodfellas* to even more urban . . . I can't think of a movie off the top of my head.
> ERGIN: *Boyz n the Hood*, maybe?

CHRIS: Fantastic, something like that. People watch those, Hollywood already, and then being able to . . . And you know it exists, so it's a matter of applying something you don't know.

MATTHEW: A fantasy.

CHRIS: I think people like myself are so far removed from it, you don't realize the complete unlikelihood or inability of that to be even more conceivable, possible. Maybe you could just come from the bottom ranks and take it over, but anyone who's actually lived there—"That's ridiculous. You're gonna spend twenty years selling dope on the corner, and you're gonna get shot or go to jail." That reality has hit them so hard . . . but that reality hasn't hit me out in suburbia, riding his BMX. I don't know.

ERGIN: So would you agree that this is a hard culture to live in but is commodified and sold mostly to white male audiences?

MATTHEW: We're definitely playing off of stereotypes of that culture regardless of whether those stereotypes are actually true or not. It's a romanticized vision of what that culture is. And the truth is that culture includes a lot of nasty stuff.

CHRIS: We carefully avoid all of that.

MATTHEW: The truth is less appealing. . . . It's escapism.

CHRIS: It's complete escapism.

It took me quite a long time to set up an interview with David, a producer in his late forties. He was always busy. As we sat in a meeting room after having had lunch in a sports bar, he had a similar response to my related questions: "We do an excellent job of escapism for players." David is married with two kids and previously worked in California. He majored in philosophy and dropped out of graduate school because of his disagreements over tuition with the dean. His philosophy degree permeated his response to my question about what makes their games appealing within a context of U.S. decline: "I don't know if you're headed that way, but there certainly wasn't a conscious thought about what we want to do is an extension of opium to the masses . . . so that they're not focusing on the potential downfalls of America."

I also talked to Stuart, a white developer in his early thirties. To discuss his career path, he approached me prior to his departure to a new position in California. His role at the studio was managing gaming communities. As we met at the studio, the conversation came to the peculiar narrative and visual language of their games. He remarked, "We offend everybody. We go after men. We go after women. We go after fat, we go after skinny. We go after white, black, Asian, Latino. It doesn't matter to us. I think that's what allows us to get away with it. It's the fact that we go after everybody equally. We don't just do jokes that demean women. We do jokes that demean men." Then the logic of escapism seems to involve the freedom and strategy to offend all demographics equally, enabling the developers to "get away with it." I was once interviewing with the departing artist Ricardo, a white man in his early to midthirties. We also met in a conference room at Desire. With a digital arts degree from Ohio, he always wanted to do video games. He had worked almost seven years at Desire. His wife needed a change, so he was now leaving. As we discussed game aesthetics, he talked about the allocation of colors for certain characters. I asked him how they problematically chose certain, racially loaded colors for particular characters and ethnicities. Laughing somewhat in an ashamed manner, he said: "I've always kind of felt that was a little racist. So, I'm not sure where that came from."

Ludic Religiosity and White Masculinity at Desire

Where did it really come from? How do we understand this "unconscious" design choice and such rhetorical stances as "escapism," "jokes," and "equal opportunity offense" against all demographics? Kishona Gray (2014) details how private jokes painfully become public through the networked environment of Xbox Live. Discussing race and professional norms in the industry, Sam Srauy (2017) demonstrates how game producers resort to racial stereotypes to more easily communicate the game content with the target audience and ultimately mitigate market uncertainty. That is, beyond being simply a psychological issue, racism, in what Stuart Hall (1995) calls the "inferential" way, emerges as a rational tool to serve capital. Inferential racism, as Ricardo's statement reveals, shapes choices of colors, stories, and body textures of characters. Without necessarily thinking about it or overtly practicing racism, inferential racism insidiously permeates game design through beliefs or assumptions about the natural "look" of a particular demographics or "fabric" of a society.

I offer the term *ludic religiosity* as a dominant cultural logic within the regime of ludopolitics to unpack developers' consistent reference to "escapism" and highlight how such statements simultaneously emphasize the ludic mechanism of a game and downplay the ideological content of digital play. As a belief system, ludic religiosity justifies every game mechanic, problematic or otherwise, in terms of whether it satisfies a playful need on the side of either producers or consumers. Within this belief system, fun becomes the measure of what counts as a good game. If technology is the U.S. theology (Carey 2009, 87; Dinerstein 2006), fun is the theology of game developers, and it operates according to principles similar to those of territorial expansion based on technology and religion. That is, ludic religiosity draws on the implicit idea that production of game content is somewhat like operating within the utopic landscape of a "new frontier" that is completely open to experimenting with game mechanics and content as long as it's fun. Ludic religiosity justifies market dynamics that mostly cater to privileged consumers and work as a discursive shield by casting a blind eye to criticism of game content.

Ludic religiosity is enabled by the fetishization of fun, which is based on the practice of commodifying and consuming the Other, ultimately producing and circulating pervasive enjoyment. Therefore, ludic religiosity is not simply a technological phenomenon. It is implicated in the ideologies and everyday practices of white masculinity. Statements such as "this is just a game" are only seemingly nonideological circumvential ways of reproducing hegemonic whiteness and masculinity within creative production. Such rhetorical stances have a history. That is, the white masculinity that shapes ludic religiosity within the game industry is historically tied to racialized and gendered scientific production structures within the United States (Dinerstein 2006, 579).

Ludic religiosity renders invisible game developers' own positions of power derived from whiteness and masculinity. What counts as fun is shaped by unequal histories of racialized and gendered social relations. Many desirable commodities and narratives of popular culture have values about race and gender historically built into them. The market's "objective" measures of fun are not independent from established relations of race and gender. Yet these measures are also racialized in that they are mostly white and therefore invisible because the default visual culture is white. Despite being partially aware, workers cannot quite point to how whiteness informs their aesthetic decisions at work. As Richard Dyer suggests, "white people create the dominant images of the world and don't quite see that they thus construct the world in their own image" (Dyer 1997, 9). Due to concrete consequences of ludic religiosity, game developers fail to see the practices through which producing a game can at times mean the production of pleasure for whiteness, as well as the affirmation of white masculinity.

Ludic religiosity has also implications regarding how game developers think about ideology, technology, and society. The technological pleasure of what one can achieve with code and game design—"blowing things out," "letting out your inner child"—privileges game play at the expense of a game's ideological content and meaning. Reducing video games to fun means ignoring their political outcomes. Since experimentation with game mechanics itself is fun and provides escapism, any political criticism becomes meaningless. Under the hegemony of ludic religiosity, "What is fun for? What is enchantment for?" are no longer feasible questions one can ask because at the core of ludic religiosity is technology, not society. The uneven ludopolitics of who creates the terms under which one is able to explore the terrain and consume the identity of the Other is closed to interrogation. In that regard, the fetishization of fun and technique through ludic religiosity takes creativity and play out of their social context and constrains them to an individual level, ultimately reproducing the mastery of technology along racialized lines and canceling the possibility of rethinking fun in social terms. The cancelation of critique is not simply an individual problem as it is embedded within institutional networks that rely on a particular racialized production logic.

Color-Blind Production Logic and Institutional Cultures of Inequality

Game workers' ludic religiosity operates within the context of a so-called postracial United States. Postracialism is an idealized image of the United States, where race supposedly no longer matters in shaping and determining people's life chances. In this context, color-blindness is the dominant ideology, projecting a liberal imagination of this postracial United States.

The use of the notion of equal-opportunity offense to explain away controversial content has to be linked with the casual operation of a color-blind ideology, which, despite its egalitarian claims, produces discursive and material inequalities. There are two distinct ways through which color-blind ideology produces inequalities. First, whiteness by default is a source of power, the universal location where counting as a human being is centered. Second, the very ability to code and design bodily difference in a video game itself is symbolically valuable, but what is problematic is the politics of this cultural production. That is, color blindness enables coding skin color in immaterial ways and poking fun at everyone. Yet, as one offends everyone equally, the highly racialized and gendered relations supporting the visual (the game itself, software) and the material (consoles and hardware) infrastructure of Desire's production become invisible to Desire's workers.

What frames this color-blind rhetoric of equal opportunity offense is an abstract liberalism and the ideas it uses, like "equal opportunity," "individualism," and especially "choice," with its multiple dimensions (Bonilla-Silva 2014, 76). Developers choose to "go after" each and every group. When the developer Stuart underlines how they "go after everybody equally," he suggests that others coming after him are more than welcome. "You do it too. Others can offend me, not a problem" is one of the logical implications we can derive from Stuart's remarks. However, there are at least two problems. First, being able to offend others itself implies a position of technological, economical, and political power in the first place. Second, the courage to invite others to offend him and the implied ability not to take any offense suggests a neutral, raceless market skill that one can acquire. The fact that one can imagine oneself as unoffendable indicates a power relationship not independent from whiteness and masculinity.

There is also the domain of consumption, where Desire offers their consumers the opportunity to choose and shape their avatars as they wish. Therefore, a progressive market of avatars through which consumers produce and perform their freely chosen identities in a supposedly level playing field is ensured. Finally, the institutional framework of the game market is defined through the discourses of choice and responsibility. Desire's workers would tell me how games are institutionally rated before they are put on the market, and it's therefore up to parents to decide which games their children should play.

Discourses about economic value and creativity are all laden with racialized and gendered assumptions. The racialized and gendered structure of the games industry is based on uneven relations of global production. The privileged component of video games—the software—is produced by mostly white, male populations in North America, Japan, and Europe, whereas hardware is assembled in Asia. Imaginations and possibilities of good work with respect to creative/cultural/digital/immaterial labor all rest on gendered and racialized assumptions about humanness, which itself is situated within a broader global political economy. What makes Desire's creative workers more valuable is not simply an objective economic value derived from design, art, or programming but rather racialized and gendered global political economies within which their labor is valorized. The value of Desire's workers draws not only on networked relations of exploitation involving Asian manufacturing labor but also racialized and gendered conceptions about the very notion of creativity being seen as superior to manual labor. More importantly, manual labor in this picture is deemed to belong to a backward era, the imagination of which is also racialized and gendered. If we are to uncover how the industry keeps reproducing certain privileges usually coded as "the diversity problem," we have to consider the material totality of the unequal relations surrounding the video game industry.

Individual cases of racism and sexism are worrying, but what's at stake are institutional cultures of white masculinity and the political economy of a highly competitive industry that leaves very little space for reflexivity. The problems stem not from individuals but from systemic inequalities. It is not always possible for professionals to engage in critical practice in a work environment that pushes them to produce games that comply with existing norms. This, however, does not and should not let them, or any other creative workers, off the hook. Although game developers tend to downplay the political significance of their products, their work is one of representation, which, at the end of the day, is nothing but giving meaning to the external world, as well as defining themselves. One thing that they may start doing is simply to engage with the criticism of demographics they represent on the screen. Game studies and creative labor studies also have lessons to learn because play (enjoyment) and representation (text and ideology) are never quite separable. As Sabine Harrer (2018, 19) suggests, "the separation of play and representation, declared by the authoritative voice of academia, legitimizes a color-blind approach to racial relations in video games." That is, game studies should not underestimate the subtle but significant ways in which ideology informs play.

Reflexivity from the perspective of game developers and intervention by scholars is possible especially because ludic religiosity is indeed strong but not almighty. Rather, it is partial, contested, and fragmented. A contradiction, for instance, is that on the one hand, workers acknowledge problematic content but then justify it by describing games as sources of escapism. On the other hand, they strive for realism in a powerful medium that they define as a ludic source of escapism. That is, games simultaneously become a powerful and a serious medium, as well as an innocent destination for lighthearted escapism. And in fact, beyond these fragments of contradictions, there are also concrete moments, like Ricardo's admission, when they question problematic game content. More moments of such contradictions can emerge if the game industry welcomes the voices of subjects from outside its echo chambers. In sum, disrupting ludic religiosity is possible, desirable, and vital to move toward a truly equal world of play.

Conclusion

Love, as a supposedly internal and infinite resource, is at the heart of our working lives. For Kathi Weeks (2017), the corporate world's takeover of the emotions, first and foremost, suggests a propagandistic way to induce efficiency through responsibilizing the worker. Second, through mystification, the command to "do what you love" disguises overwork, self-exploitation, and domestic conflicts, which are inequalities all intrinsic to employment. Third, when workers are advised to pursue their passion, they fail to see commonalities with co-workers as they become "blinded to their generality as a class" as argued by Shulamith Firestone (1970). Weeks (2017, 48) then shows how love produces subjects from below "as a biopolitical project rather than a traditionally ideological one." Practices and discourses of love are not simply programmed into subjects. On the contrary, subjects act upon and practice love with different objects and within different spaces.

This is where I extend Weeks's work and offer ludopolitics to emphasize how this "from below biopolitical production" is surrounded by gendered and racial inequalities at the local and the global level, shaping the labor of love at Desire. Linked with the broader political economy, which in turn shapes labor conditions in the studio, ludopolitics enables materializing love and its frictions. No matter how privileged Desire's workers are, they can still be precarious and alienated. Frictions of love occur on many fronts. The moment Desire became successful and was acquired by Digital Creatives, the advent of bureaucracy bothered the creative workers in the studio. And the same Digital Creatives that brought precious finance to Desire could still drag the studio into uncertain waters during bankruptcy. Frictions of love are not limited to the workspace. They emerge in the domestic lives of game developers, as well. In summary, ludopolitics allows for visualizing how inequalities surround game development to which failures are endemic.

Imagined at a planetary scale, ludopolitics also unravels the global unevenness beneath the racialized and gendered relations of production. A racialized, gendered, and ecological take on game production enables us to write a global political economy of fun where there is an international division of not only digital labor but also pleasure. In privileged geographies and workplaces like Desire, governance relies more on neoliberal technologies that harness wellness, working, and living capacities of workers. Desire's workers' love toward work is cultivated from below within the networks of digital play. At Foxconn, the love is imposed from the top down as a banner in one of their factory saying "Heart to heart, Foxconn and I grow together" suggests (Ngai and Chan 2012, 398). That is, in locations that manufacture and recycle the hardware of our ludic worlds, technologies of subjection and despotic regimes of labor that mark and differentiate working subjects socially and spatially are more prevalent (Ngai 2005). Sure, neoliberalism permeates both Desire and Foxconn, but time and space are differentially managed and experienced in these spaces. Sleep, rest, bathroom breaks, and pace of work are differentially experienced in Desire and its global connections (Sharma 2011), conditioned mostly by where one fits spatially and temporally within our uneven regime of ludopolitics.

Ludopolitics also initiates a conversation about white masculinity. As a predominantly white-male workforce, Desire's workers can perform a labor of love. They can sacrifice in and beyond the workplace but only through their white masculinity, which covers the pleasure they derive from work. This particular masculinity in turn affects their creative work. That is, the narratives, art work, and characters they create are, consciously or unconsciously, gendered and racialized. So is the fun that they design and code in a game. Fun, pleasure, and escapism may sound like innocent words, but they all signify power and privilege. Just like love and work, fun is also socially configured and relationally composed. That is, one's escapism or fun can be someone else's pain. How one relates to fun, pleasure, and escapism depends on that person's racial history and gender position within the broader society. Therefore, the moment game developers declare something to be fun, they simultaneously produce a universalizing discourse and definition of fun, embedded within a privileged social location.

In sum, we can draw direct lines between different regimes of inequality in the workplace, in the household, and in the gaming industry's global networks of manufacturing and waste. Inequalities are endemic to the game factory, but the ones pertaining to Desire's own workers first contradictorily emerged when their market success was rewarded with acquisition by Digital Creatives. Achieving financial security thanks to this buyout by one of the major game publishers was a milestone for an independent studio. Yet it also led to disenchantment at work.

THE END OF THE GARAGE STUDIO AS A TECHNOMASCULINE SPACE

Financial Security, Streamlined Creativity, and Signs of Friction

When Desire was still an independent studio, it had to constantly struggle to find financial resources for their games. This anxious rush to secure funding came to an end when the publicly traded Digital Creatives decided to acquire Desire in the 2000s. This was a moment of relief and validation, as Desire's games were successful enough to draw the attention of one of the largest game publishers in the market.

This acquisition, however, brought its own problems. Digital Creatives' coming to the scene meant "a contradictory drama of expropriation" (Huws 2014, 111) in that the laboring capacities of Desire's developers became the parent company's property. Digital Creatives' acquisition of Desire produced what Ursula Huws (2014, 101) calls the "antagonistic imperatives" between creative workers and media corporations. While creative workers long for expressive spaces and creative recognition, companies have to streamline the labor process to mitigate market risk by strictly controlling intellectual property. When Digital Creatives bought out Desire, they did give the studio the creative space they needed. Overall, developers were happy as Digital Creatives brought a large amount of financial resources for better means of marketing and distribution. Yet at the same time, game developers' desire for creative experimentation collided with the newly introduced bureaucracy and the corporate demands that did not exist before. Indeed, as the experienced programmer Karl, who witnessed the transition, would underline, the buyout process was full of tensions in relation to autonomy and commercialization.

I was once interviewing Karl, who had worked at Desire as a programmer for more than fifteen years. He went to school in the area and had a master's degree in computer science back in 1992. That year, he met Desire's founders when he worked as a tester for their simulation company, before Desire became a distinct game studio.

The day before I met him at his new start-up company, I was at Desire and saw wine glasses that had been used at his good-bye party. Karl is a tall white man in his late forties. He described his departure as a "bittersweet" experience. He said that there were things he wouldn't miss about the game industry, and he had "made peace" with moving on. When I asked him what he'd miss, he underlined the "cool factor" and the "neat technologies" they worked with, but suddenly shifted to what he wouldn't miss. For instance, he wouldn't miss the long development cycles (more than three years of work on one single game) and being part of Digital Creatives. This was confusing for me because for a considerable amount of independent game developers, the major goal is to be bought out by a publisher. After all, that's what Desire—as what Karl would call "a total entrepreneurial studio"—had achieved. But despite realizing this goal, Karl had left, and a fundamental reason behind his departure was Digital Creatives.

Following Desire's acquisition, what Bill Ryan (1992, 2) calls "the corporate form of a capitalist cultural commodity production," emerged, and through a microanalysis of the political economy of culture at Desire, we can reveal the organizational and cultural tensions that emerged after Digital Creatives acquired the studio. This is important if we are to understand Desire's transition from a small studio of fewer than thirty people to a medium-sized studio with more than two hundred employees. Analyses of media mergers and acquisitions most often do not pay enough attention to the commodification of media workers' creative spaces, ordinary aspects of their organizational culture and everyday materiality (Whitson 2018), or their occupational identities within production (Weststar 2015). Therefore, the goal of this chapter is to shed light on the dynamics of "formatting," as a "form of creative control based on corporate attempts to confront the uncertainties of the cultural marketplace in a context of expanded production" (Ryan 1992, 160).

With formatting, the game developers felt that their communicative capacities were mainstreamed with the increase in red tape, which they did not particularly enjoy. In those days, the developers embodied what Karl called a "not invented here" syndrome, which caused frictions with project managers because Desire's veterans found it hard to understand the project managers' function. As the following narratives reveal, being bought out by Digital Creatives led to a contradictory situation where financial security also meant an increase in the size of the development team, the burden of a tiresome bureaucracy, and corporate demands mostly related to marketing. These were not always welcomed by the developers and led to antagonisms.

While the "not invented here" syndrome implies a gendered practice, it strongly hints at workers' desire for creative autonomy. The case of Desire's workers amounts to what would have been a dream come true for scholars like Daniel Bell, Fritz Machlup, and Peter Drucker. Through their "liberal-democratic theories of the knowledge workers" (Brophy 2008), these scholars would challenge Marxist analyses of labor and argue that workers' alienation would be terminated with the advent of office and computerized jobs. With its reinvigorated treatment of the labor process, Harry Braverman's (1974/1998) seminal *Labor and Monopoly Capital* contested Daniel Bell and others. Braverman argued that the streamlining and degradation of work under capitalism for surplus value creation had not changed under the circumstances of monopoly capitalism. White-collar office jobs were not exempt from Taylorist principles and could very well be subjected to calculation and degradation. In other words, in the age of white-collar jobs, the antagonism between capital and labor was far from being over.

Braverman's insightful perspective, if not the whole analysis, has been usefully deployed within the field of media and communication studies. Bill Ryan's pioneering *Making Capital from Culture* (1992) examines the dynamics of a range of issues, such as the star system, marketing, and distribution in culture industries. Mark Banks (2007) deploys the notion of "cultural work" to understand this kind of labor, primarily focusing on workers' subjectivities and arguing that these workers are frequently "openly antagonistic to these [capitalist] values" (184).[1]

These insights form the background of my analysis in understanding Desire's transition in this chapter. Yet the view of the artist as something of an anticapitalist producer—as exemplified in formulations like "art is incompatible with the imperatives of accumulation" (Ryan 1992, 34)—needs to be rethought. We know from historical analyses that artistic critique and rebellion have become central pillars of the new digital workplace (Barbrook and Cameron 1996; Boltanski and Chiapello 2005). Both the broader market forces and the gendered ideologies and practices of a start-up culture—high commitment to job, libertarianism, technomasculinity (Johnson 2018), and competitive individualism—are too strong to ignore in the formation of employee subjectivities. Game workers are hard to control and manage as far as their desire for creative collaboration is concerned. Yet at the same time, conditions of survival in the game industry, along with the cultural factors informing a particular work ethic, push the workers to voluntarily enter into relations with finance and stock markets. In other words, Desire's developers were not only decidedly not anticapitalist; they were more than willing to be bought out by a major publisher to secure financing.

This chapter documents the dynamics of what the game developers called "the trade-off" between financial security and autonomy. This trade-off reveals the interactions and struggle between what Raymond Williams (1977) calls the residual (read: garage) and the emergent (read: publicly traded/corporate) cultures, where frictions occurred since the market survival of Digital Creatives depended on its abilities to streamline creative production. Overall, Desire's workers did not fundamentally see a problem with it as they had wanted to be acquired by a major publisher in the first place. Yet the introduction of new organizational structures led to the advent of a more impersonal culture and inequalities, all mediated within a gendered context.

Changing Culture at Desire

The game industry came into being as a fruit of the research and development work carried out during the Cold War. Decentralized work cultures established during the Cold War, digital utopianism, rebellion, libertarianism, and the countercultural ideas of the 1960s have shaped the industry (Barbrook and Cameron 1996; Dyer-Witheford and de Peuter 2009; English-Lueck 2002; Turner 2006; Tyree-Hageman 2013). Entrepreneurialism is embedded in the game industry's DNA.

Nevertheless, being entrepreneurial-spirited is not enough for success. Competition is tough. While indie and mobile game production mean new markets, especially in Asia (Jin 2010), market success strictly depends on certain organizational, cultural, and technical capacities (Keogh 2015). Unless such capacities exist or are enhanced, failure becomes unavoidable. Although video game historiography mostly features winners, as opposed to failures, start-up failure in the console segment of the video game industry is not uncommon.[2] In that regard, Desire is a success story.

Becoming the flagship studio of Digital Creatives didn't happen overnight or automatically, though. On the contrary, Desire's story is one that is woven through precarity, ups and downs, and frictions. Being an independent studio means constantly working on demos and portfolios to build a relationship of trust with publishers. It involves compulsory networking under stressful deadlines. The struggle to produce good demos does—and did—involve crises when a publisher loses faith in a project, meaning that the developers had to find another publisher. That's what Karl would tell me during our conversation at his new start-up company, suggesting that not having sustained access to money would jeopardize business, leading to start-up anxieties: "Where is the next stream of income gonna come from? What is our next project gonna be? Because we are really busy, finishing the current one. We don't have time to start up something. There is gonna be this big gap where we have got nothing." Similarly, as we discussed in a focus group meeting with his longtime former colleagues at Desire, the experienced programmer Matthew emphasized how being bought out by Digital Creatives was a relief: "We were shopping around trying to find publishers. So it was actually nice now this feeling of, OK, we never have to go through that again. Right. And we don't worry so much about . . . if this one title doesn't sell, then . . . we are all out of jobs."

Financial security did yield major changes at the studio, though. The reason behind this massive cultural change stemmed mainly from the practical requirements of competing in the triple-A market, which necessitated mobilizing vast resources to facilitate cooperation and communication at Desire, now a new workplace. These novelties were manifested through three interconnected major nodes: workforce, space, and the broader culture.

First, Desire had to hire a considerable amount of labor force to create hours of game play to enhance the parent company's triple-A portfolio. The studio was now on its way to becoming an organization of more than two hundred employees.

This expansion takes us to the second dimension: spatiality. Managing this large workforce came with organizational and spatial restructuring. In organizational terms, Desire had to recruit project managers to oversee the work of the game developers for either harnessing their productivity or making sure they completed their tasks within deadlines. In contrast to the simpler setting in the garage days, the studio had endorsed a complex organizational structure comprised of such divisions as finance, human resources, project managers, producers, and assistant producers. In spatial terms, housing the large number of developers in Desire's original nest was no longer an option. Therefore, developers had to move to a modern commercial plaza, occupying two floors and leaving a visible impact on the city where the studio is based.

Finally, as the studio relocated with a considerably larger workforce, social relations at the studio were transformed. For instance, in the new context, employees started wearing name badges, meaning that a cultural shift was taking place.

Work Culture during the Garage Days

I once met Ronaldo, a tech artist, in a coffee shop. He is married with kids. In his midforties, Ronaldo is a person of color, originally from the suburbs of a city in the Midwest. He'd liked living in the suburbs and had been a happy kid. According to him, he had lived in an unusually diverse environment, as opposed to other suburban areas. His family had migrated from Asia three years before he was born.

His mom was a housewife. His dad started off as an accountant, and in the late 1970s, he quit. When he quit, the company gave his dad an Apple 2000 as a gift. Then, he started his own business as a computer programmer; Ronaldo claimed that kind of entrepreneurial spirit was to be found in both sides of his family. "He didn't want to count other people's money; he wanted to make his own money," said Ronaldo.

Ronaldo had worked long enough at Desire to reflect on the studio's transformation over the years. So I asked him to show me how it felt to work at Desire. He photographed some banquet tables sitting next to a vacuum cleaner in the studio's storage. The banquet tables and the space where they were stored were completely off my radar. On the one hand, the photograph didn't quite fit with the stereotypical image of a video game studio as a glamorous work environment. The objects were quite ordinary: brown banquet tables. And yet the affective ordinary social relations the photograph embodied are helpful to grasp the garage spirit and what the shift toward a more corporate structure entailed.

> RONALDO: It is significant because when we started the studio, those were our desks. . . . We moved around a lot. So we didn't have desks like we have here. We had a bunch of banquet tables, six and eight feet, that we would just move around so we could put our work out—like a computer and stuff. And I think, actually it wasn't until we moved into this building that we actually have what most people would associate with an office. Up until then, it was your thirty-dollar banquet table we had bought at Staples. And . . . guys would use those for a long time—until they broke basically.

Back when Desire was independent, the studio's needs—for instance, for fancier chairs—were kept at a minimum since the main concern was oriented toward getting the demo out and finding ways to secure new funding. Flexible and functional desks were just enough. Before the studio was bought up by the parent company, the president of the studio, Ronaldo said, would "get a truck" and the employees would participate in the whole moving process. Yet, as Ronaldo told, acquisition by Digital Creatives meant formal arrangements for relocation: "When we moved here, they had movers. It was kind of this big transition moment where . . . we are packing our stuff into boxes and they are being marked, shipping labels and everything. It was very professional, I guess . . . We didn't really do any of the moving ourselves." For Ronaldo, this was a "pivotal moment" that signified a "big disassociation point" since they were not in a position to move themselves. It meant the end of the garage culture: "But if you compare now to then, we were still pretty much like in a garage, which is kind of ironic given that what we used to work on is now sitting in a storage," he said.

If Raymond Williams (1977) was right in suggesting that "culture is ordinary," mundane objects and material practices bear the signs of how the garage ethos looked. When Desire was small and independent, the rituals for celebrations were intimately organized around close friendships and existing familial links. For instance, Karl mentioned that they used to have "parties in people's houses." He hosted the first Christmas party in his own house. Now the parties were organized in large bars or clubs where the personality of the host had disappeared.

The intense work rhythm of the garage culture was heavily gendered. The entrepreneurial garage spirit was sustained through the aspiring young male who was either single or did have a family where the household was mainly sustained by women who had to perform unpaid labor when their partners would be absolutely dedicated to their work. As Karl told me in his new start-up office, "all guys started off fairly either single or pretty close to it, no kids." Indeed, without the developers' dedication to crunch and willingness to put in extra hours at work,[3] the studio might not have achieved its flagship status, as Karl suggested: "It was just a personal sacrifice from a number of people and ridiculous hours that we pulled it off. I am not sure where we would be today, probably nowhere if we hadn't managed to pull that pedal off." "Pulling that pedal off" collectively in a small studio environment required everyone to be "all sort of in charge of the stuff" that they built.

I asked Karl how the programming culture looked when the studio was independent. Were they like hackers? Did they have a strong business perspective? Apparently, what defined Desire's spirit was not radical or anticapitalist seeds of imagination as is sometimes attributed to new media companies. According to Karl, the president of the company "was a great programmer but he was always equally great at business stuff." As he confidently put it, "they had a pretty solid grasp of the business ends of things that always felt like a . . . business, not just a bunch of hobbyists getting together hoping it works out." The entrepreneurial spirit was always strong. As Karl further told me, this aspirational attitude manifested itself among programmers, who had a "self-centeredness about them that they sort of know better than the next guy." These entrepreneurial and competitive programmers did indeed "love to just craft their code in a way that they like," which would constitute a conflict with the project managers, who wanted to be in charge of the completion of tasks in a timely manner rather than experimenting with code, art, or technology in general.

Ultimately, the culture at the start-up game studio was a mash-up of pride, ego, and technomasculinity (Johnson 2018) sustained by a distinct lifestyle. The creative ego and fetish for cool production was a major pillar of the materialization of the Californian ideology at Desire. Matthew asserted that the developers thought they were doing something that "nobody has ever done before" and they were "revolutionizing" technological production. Similar to new media and fashion workers, game developers were both the hip cultural workers and "the Stakhanovites—or norm-making shock workers of the new economy" (Neff, Wissinger, and Zukin 2005, 331). It was this entrepreneurial, youthful, and masculine culture that fueled the creative juices of the labor power in the studio. It was through such sacrificial practices that Desire caught the attention of Digital Creatives and resolved the issue of financial security for the company. At the same time, it was this same financial relief that enabled the production of large-scale console games, which in turn intensified an already extreme labor process. While the rush for finding publishers to sell demos was over, becoming part of a corporate structure required major cultural shifts and organizational changes, creating moments of dissent on the side of the developers.

With Financial Security Comes "Shades of Dedication"

What happens when financial security comes to a start-up whose future depends on the potential success of a demo? As the developers' accounts below reveal, a buyout event is never just an economic trade-off. It is a cultural process because acquisition by Digital Creatives rearranged how Desire's employees communicated and worked with each other. Now that they had more resources to compete with major franchises, questions about work ethic emerged. Because the studio immediately hired many more people to enlarge its talent pool for large-scale game production, the nature of teamwork shifted to the extent that employees' attitudes to work came under scrutiny.

During a focus group meeting with Ronaldo, Otis (nonwhite, designer in his late thirties), and Edward (white, programmer in his late thirties), Matthew said: "Back then, people in the company I think were just willing to go to really great lengths, unbelievable lengths sometimes, to really buoy the company up to . . . put the best foot forward. And now, it is a lot more corporate. It is a job now." According to Edward, the success of the studio stemmed from the chemistry of the people, who made the right decisions at the right time and at the right place: "I think we could have attempted the same exact games with different people and totally gone out of business. So the reason we are here now is because of the core of people who, at the beginning, were really, really dedicated." Ronaldo echoed both Edward and Matthew, pointing to how "there were a lot fewer shades of dedication" when they were independent.

Work, according to these remarks, was more about love whereas "shades of dedication" that emerged due to financial security had transformed passion into a job. However, the garage culture cannot possibly just be explained through love and dedication. Rather, the special work environment that Matthew and Ronaldo describe was constituted by an overlap of various factors. One of these factors was the smaller size of the development team and the peculiar culture and channels of communication it entailed. During the start-up days, everybody knew each other and hung out with each other. Besides, dedication is not simply a psychological asset or some intrinsic energy that every developer during Desire's garage days happened to have. Of course, they were passionate about games, but that wasn't the only reason. They were also precarious because they lacked financial security. Unless one worked hard for the project, there would no longer be a studio to be employed at.

In this focus group meeting, there was agreement about dedication, but what really produced the studio's success was a matter of contestation among these longtime Desire employees. Some emphasized precarity related to the lack of constant money flows, while others underlined the passionate work ethos. The latter group was more concerned about the loss of that "pure" dedication to work, as the following conversation reveals:

> RONALDO: Back then, everybody was dedicated to doing what we needed to do. Nowadays, because of the security, there is a lot more shades.
>
> OTIS: It is about the safety net. So it was depending on all of us to do our best as well as possible to keep us alive.
>
> MATTHEW: I do think that it is a factor, but . . . at least when I came on at that time, I wasn't thinking, "Oh, if I don't work my ass off, I am going to be out of job."
>
> EDWARD: No, I was too stupid to think that.
>
> OTIS: That is all I mean; what I mean is, the attitude came from the top down. Because the president and all those guys were like—shit if we don't do this and they've set an example, that made us want to do the same thing.
>
> MATTHEW: There definitely was a much stronger culture at that time. Everybody around you was working like crazy. And . . . you fell in line. And it wasn't something you thought about. It was just like, this is what everybody is doing, right?

Then, Desire's success depended on a constellation of factors including but not limited to passion for work. Material culture and practices, the rush to find financial resources due to precarity, and the existence of role-model creatives on the higher levels of the hierarchy all mattered. That the president used to be one of the "guys" whom a developer was able to see and interact with daily produced a feeling of camaraderie. Additionally, in a smaller organization where face-to-face communication is more common and feasible, it is easier to establish channels to create a rigorous work ethic and accountability, as Karl emphasized: "When you have a small team, you are more easily held accountable to your other team because you are all there together. John is not in the seat next to you. You kind of know what. But he is gonna tell you when he is gone . . . with the self-accountability thing."

Technomasculinity at Desire: Gendering the Work Ethic

How Desire's developers narrate their success during the garage days and frame the company's transformation following the acquisition process through terms like "shades of dedication" or "pulling the pedal off" call for a gendered analysis. I describe these practices through the term "technomasculinity" (Johnson 2018). Technomasculinity becomes visible through good command of computer knowledge, machinic manipulation, passion for games, antiauthoritarian work attitude, or ordinary use of language that bears the imprints of gendered imaginations and assumptions (Dovey and Kennedy 2006). Gamers' technomasculinity involves mundane forms of everyday sociability. This particular masculinity is often cultivated during childhood when somebody in the family—typically fathers—allow their sons to tinker with computers in order for them to become experts. Gaming's technomasculinities are also bred and practiced in the online environments of games, blogs, websites, schools, campuses, internships, and workplaces.[4] When coupled with discourses of meritocracy, the concept becomes a particularly powerful way to understand the dearth of female workers in the industry, as well as grasping why simply adding more women will not solve this structural problem (Consalvo 2008).[5]

There are various manifestations of technomasculinity at Desire. First, creative work itself is racialized and gendered. It assumes the white male as the universal subject with whom the practices of tinkering or hacking are predominantly associated. My discussions with many of the developers revealed a narrative where they emphasized family and early socialization and used the word "always" in terms of how they attributed a natural quality to themselves and games, emphasizing their attraction to and skill for game development as almost a biological feature.

Second, and relatedly, language matters. Words like *passion* and *love* are in fact euphemisms that operate as the infrastructure for technomasculinist ideology and practices. Desire's workers talk about their garage day work as if it was a calling, which defines the job as a religious commitment based on passion.

Third, technomasculinity is foundational to understanding the functioning of a given "community of practice" (Newbery 2013; Pyrko, Dörfler, and Eden 2017; Wenger 1998), where game workers think, learn, work, and imagine together, which are all gendered practices. That is, game development becomes a community not through an intrinsic quality that resides in one's heart but rather through the material practice of passion. How Desire's workers as a community of practice perceive the world also shapes their ethos. Their gendered conditions of work inform their cultural imagination. In that regard, technomasculinity acts also as a gatekeeper for this community of practice, providing the foundations of inclusion and exclusion, as well as determining the terms and boundaries of the proper subject in that community of practice.

Then, it is within the everyday work of technomasculinity in Desire that we should grasp the nostalgia toward the start-up days, where there were "less shades of dedication." This whole discourse performs identity work in that once a subject utters the words "I am dedicated whereas the new workers are not," this does something to the addresser and the addressee. These remarks define who an authentic game producer is, somewhat setting the foundations for a potentially toxic work culture since one is not authentic or passionate unless he or she is willing to stay at work past 5:00 P.M.[6]

Such identity work through the discourse of dedication creates cultures of heroism, in which stars are produced and worshipped by seemingly neutral terms, practices, and spaces, such as "battles," "love," "garage," "trenches," "just falling in line," and of course "crunch." Inspired by Hilde Heynen's (2012) notion of "mystique of architectural authorship," which explains how the field of architecture values gendered forms of creativity and genius, I argue that Desire's workers' narratives of dedication reinforce what one might call the *mystique of ludic authorship* in the industry, producing a mythical discourse around success and dedication that unfold in gendered spaces, such as the garage, where an economy of respect and innovation is cultivated (Fuller 2015; Melo 2018).

These narratives are in fact political statements. They give a particular orientation and twist to history, attributing a causality to how things unfolded in the past. In the narratives I explored above and the narratives to follow with respect to frictions with project managers who are mostly female, game developers foreground their efforts in dealing with hardships and target nontechnical staff's lack of creative expertise, which ultimately solidifies a masculine, self-made, and heroic creative mind-set.

As political statements, these narratives create and reproduce archetypes of the self-made game developer who survived thanks to his bravado. The archetype at Desire is not the loyal organization man but rather an entrepreneurial technologist who has endorsed a gendered risk-taking work ethic. Such archetypes are powerful because, through certain rhetorical and oratorical skills, they are able to "inspire awe, mystery, and romance" (Gill 2013, 334). That is, when Desire's veterans narrate their past, they are simultaneously drawing an archetype in terms of who they were and what the new aspiring workers should be like. And when one achieves an archetype, there is "a concomitant achievement of gendered expectations" (Gill 2013, 335).[7]

The ethos at Desire—namely, the "underlying attitude of a social group toward itself and its world" (Geertz 1973, 127)—unites workers emotionally and morally. We should critically reflect on this rhetoric of dedication precisely because how one produces discourses about passion, dedication, and creativity takes us directly to the regime of ludopolitics: Who can dedicate himself to work for innovation? Who can talk about innovation in the first place? Which locations count as spaces of innovation? And who defines what is valuable innovation or dedicated work?

It is precisely these elements of the technomasculine work ethic that formed the basis of the developers' frictions with project managers. As mentioned earlier, Desire's workers were very protective of their work practices, but there occurred a significant cultural shift when teams expanded to produce competitive triple-A games. Since the studio needed "warm bodies," as Matthew put it, a more bureaucratic structure was put into practice.

Signs of Friction: Larger Development Teams and Project Managers

My conversations with developers on various occasions suggested an almost elitist way of working and hiring practices in the studio. During the focus group interview, Matthew said: "If there was like, one person saying, I don't know about this guy, it was like, OK, we are not gonna hire him." Karl echoed Matthew, mentioning the not-invented-in-the-studio syndrome, an exclusive culture prevalent during the garage days. The developers were not always receptive to the introduction of new technologies and practices unless designed internally.

Yet a distinct change took place when Desire found itself having to produce one of its games for the new console generation. This required larger teams. To fill the empty spots, the developers had to loosen their elitist hiring policy, which, according to Matthew, had a "watering down effect." Karl defined this shift as a "culture-changing experience," as well as leading to a shift in work ethic: "As the teams got larger, when we hired more people, I think . . . the quality of engineers and artists and designers we had to hire because we ramped up so quick—that probably dropped. So, . . . over the course of having so many people work there, work ethic dropped. It didn't drop dramatically. But it became more varied. Let's put it that way."

When teams got larger and developers were dispersed across a larger spatial setting, a formal project management and producer system was put into place. The developers did understand that project management was necessary, but the need to quickly fill positions proved to be problematic. In the focus group conversation, Matthew said: "Half the people on Game X had never worked on a game before. And I think, because of that, they had to hire on all these project managers . . . to watch over everybody and crack the whip and say, 'This is what you are going to do now.' . . . There was no longer that . . . self-motivation to just really work hard."

While relations with the project managers gradually became smoother, a considerable amount of uneasiness emerged among the employees when the system was still new. The project managers were hired to control the "weaker employees," according to Edward, who considered himself to be "lucky enough not to be on Game X during all that time." For Edward, the first stages of project management were such that it turned this "really brilliant, smart programmer . . . youthful guy" into "the most bitter, cynical person ever."

However, for Ronaldo, the transition to a larger development team revealed other issues regarding how the acquisition affected the communicative aspects of the labor process, where experience and knowledge were constitutive: "My perception is that the big thing that happened was, Game X was when we became corporate . . . we experience that disconnection between experience and what we had to do. And because we had so many people, we couldn't communicate that experience to all the new people we had. We ended up replacing that with a management structure."

The discomfort caused by the project management was especially relevant for the longtime employees since it was an alien system to them. Considering some of the policies "draconian," Edward stated that the new system "became almost adversarial between the employees and the project managers." While "it did provide the guidance that people needed to some extent," it also limited the kind of freedom "for the kind of creative work" that they did. As Matthew mentioned, game workers particularly enjoyed being "able to switch tasks quickly and without having to constantly tell somebody else, 'This is what I am doing, this is what I am doing,'" and "establishing reports." At times, frictions were big enough for some workers to quit.

This is not to suggest that Desire's developers regard project management as pure evil, as our focus group revealed. For instance, while Ronaldo did agree with Matthew with respect to the constraining nature of project management, his experience with another studio assured him of the importance of such a structure, especially for his discipline, art. For Ronaldo, without a structure, the artists were "just going to run forever." He underlined the role for somebody to "play the parents" and urge the creatives to adhere to work schedules. The designer Otis, too, agreed that the trouble they encountered was due to the shift toward building a new game in a new generation of console rather than the imposition of project managers per se.

Edward was still more critical of the introduction of the project managers because they were "cracking the whip across the board." For him, not everybody needed to be told what to do and how. At the heart of Robert's critique was the fact that project management did not always understand organically how the game developers worked. For Robert, project managers acted in ways almost reminiscent of the labor process described by Braverman (1974/1998) in which capital aims to regulate each and every move and moment of labor and translate it into manageable and calculable steps:

> The project managers love the stamping widgets type people because it works directly with how their brains work. They can schedule and say, "You have got five widgets done today, great." But it was a real challenge to get them to understand, especially when it comes to programmers, there's a lot of work that is completely undefinable. It is like, you can say, "Well, how long is this going to take?" And you go, "I don't know, two weeks." And you just don't know, because you are inventing something completely new, or you just know in the back of your head this is complicated, and you are not going to know how hard the problems are going to be until after it's done, blah, blah, blah. So, yeah, part of the issue is like . . . getting the project managers not to just turn everything into a huge factory and understanding that a large percentage of people of the company work iteratively and incrementally and with heart.

As a tech artist, Ronaldo had a similar critique of the project managers' obsession with producing a measurable output in an ideally open, creative labor process: "They are saying, 'All right, what can you get done in this three weeks? We want something rough.' And what I have seen a lot of people struggle with is, they have this mind-set of, I want this and it doesn't match up with the reality of being in the business. And so they are like, 'Well, you want something rough, but it has to have like these five bells and these ten whistles, and I just can't get these five bells and ten whistles in the two weeks you want.'"

Interestingly, it was not just the core creative group of people that were vocal against the project management and Digital Creatives' involvement in creative processes. I once interviewed Stacey in her office. A human resources staffer in her late thirties, she would underline how creative people are "fickle," adding that "the

more specific tasks they're given, the less creative they feel." For Stacey, Digital Creatives' interventions at certain times, especially prior to shipping the games, would
expand "to permeate down to what kind of characters the studio made. The more
distracted people are from being creative, the less creative they are," Stacey said.

Ultimately, the switch to a streamlined structure and the introduction of a new
console system constituted a clash between the minds of the project managers and
the hearts of the creatives. While the longtime employees had previously enjoyed
the open channels of communication enabled by the smaller size of the studio,
they felt they were encroached upon by the advent of the project management.
As Karl mentioned, utilizing a technomasculine discourse, there was skepticism
on the side of the developers; they asked, "How are these nontechnical people
really gonna understand what we have to do?" According to him, the developers
sometimes even thought the project managers were "creating work to create
work." Unlike the younger members of the studio who liked the fact that their
work was "laid out," the longer-term employees had more resentment, and it took
a couple of years for the project managers to reach a somewhat balanced communication with these employees.

It was not just the project managers' attempts to Taylorize creativity that the
developers disliked, though. The financialization of production through the publicly traded Digital Creatives also reduced channels of communication and created frustration, leading to discontent.

No Longer Privately Owned: Stock Prices and the Frustration of Not Having a Say

The buyout process overall had come with financial security, and Digital Creatives
had not strictly intervened in creative decisions on a day-to-day basis, which was
overall a relief for the game developers. However, this did not immunize the studio from potential economic risks or future uncertainties. In other words, the precarity of the garage days had shifted gears toward a large financial structure.
While economic uncertainty is endemic to capitalism, Desire's uncertainty was
linked with the nature of Digital Creatives as a publicly traded company. Compared to private companies, public companies enjoy such advantages as external
financing, leading to potential growth and investment opportunities. This is much
harder to achieve for private companies. Publicly traded companies also have easier access to financial markets and capital for projects. On the flipside, publicly
traded companies have to share information with respect to their financial standing, as well as meet certain standards and listing requirements if they want to
remain feasible as a publicly traded company.

While the gaming industry is very competitive in general, the nature of being part of a publicly traded company created further tensions. In addition to losing some of the managerial control, Desire's future was now tied to a relationship with investors, whom Digital Creatives had to brief. Moreover, Digital Creatives had to impose certain scheduling limits on the development team so as to keep the promises to its investors and sustain a healthy company image. Belonging to a publicly traded company meant that "the company is going to have financial requirements at certain times that we cannot hang on to a game for too long, because we have to deal with that concept of publicly traded. We have stockholders to satisfy," Stacey, the HR staffer, said, expressing the contradictions of working with Digital Creatives.

Desire was one studio among many others that Digital Creatives had acquired as part of an aggressive buyout process. At the time of the acquisition, stocks proved to be profitable for the developers, whereas over time, the stock market watch on every developer's computer desktop ended up being a source of frustration. Low stock prices, over which, Matthew said, the developers "don't really have much control," became, as Ronaldo put it, "a water-cooler topic." In general, developers mostly disagreed with the management and investment decisions of Digital Creatives, because they believed that these decisions put Desire in a precarious position despite their record of success. What were the sources of the developers' frustration, then?

When corporations have disposable funds, it seems like a feasible idea to start investing for future profits. However, as some of Desire's developers put it, this led to an almost reckless growth period where Digital Creatives bought out "subpar studios" and did not make desirable investment decisions but rather rushed to enlarge their IP portfolio. "Why the hell are they doing this?" asked Matthew, in relation to some investment decisions at the corporate level. Responding to Matthew, Ronaldo expressed that their parent company "didn't have a plan for identifying the quality of the studios that they were buying." He further stated that corporate actually "should have shut" some of the studios "years ago." Matthew echoed Ronaldo, adding that Digital Creatives were "supporting all these other studios that are dragging us down." In this sense, being bought out by a larger corporate body meant that the studio would become part of a family where it did not always have a say in whether it wanted other siblings or not. Desire's contribution to investment decisions was absolutely zero. Depending on the conjuncture, the studio would have to share the burden and the joy of being in a family, which increasingly became a less joyful relationship to sustain.

In addition to the frustration with Digital Creatives' bad investments and the devaluing stock options, financialization became another obstacle to the communicative aspects of the labor process that game workers had previously enjoyed when they were independent. While Desire's developers did have a sense of the financial situation of Digital Creatives, they did not have access to information about finances or future plans precisely due to the publicly traded nature of the company. In other words, the initial financial relief that rescued the developers from having to constantly chase external funding later obstructed communication channels. It was impossible for the parent company to give specific information to the developers, which made them anxious regarding their own fate. During the focus group conversation, Otis jokingly asked me if an hour would be enough to discuss their thoughts about their parent company. When I said, "We can order whiskey," Ronaldo responded, "We might have to." In this sense, a cynical atmosphere had begun to permeate the studio, despite the fact that Desire's most recent game had done well on the market.

While frustrated and cynical, the developers were well aware that they had "no influence over what happens in corporate, whereas the decisions that happen at corporate affect us very much," as Matthew indicated. Despite owning the means of production and imagination, the developers had absolutely zero control over the means of making financial decisions, which at the end of the day defined the boundaries of the political control over the labor process. While the relative autonomy of creative production was not much violated, the larger framework of production was shifted. Karl would point to the numbers-driven nature of the publicly traded parent company in the sense that "it is very difficult for them to think any further out in three months, because it is about quarters, it is about the fiscal year. So . . . it is very spreadsheet, financially driven."

The lack of information that made the "end of the tunnel" invisible proved to be a burden for the developers. For Karl, lack of communication left the developers "in the dark" and made them "frustrated" because they wanted more information. When the stock prices hit some dramatic points, Digital Creatives would further want to intervene in production schedules at times, "to make the investors happy and show growth," and that was not necessarily what the developers wanted to do, Karl emphasized.

The Cost of Trade-off between Autonomy and Financial Security

Over the years, the thrill of the financial security stemming from Digital Creatives' buyout waned, if not totally evaporated, at Desire. Feelings of anxiety and precarity were transferred to a different level. Karl knew this so well because he had worked for the studio more than fifteen years but reached a point where he decided to leave. He said: "Being beholden to the shareholders is a very difficult and fine line" and caused a lack of control over the future.

In this sense, the injection of shareholder value into the studio can be understood along the lines of what one might call *intensified commodification*. Upon purchase, Desire developers' labor has become subject to the rules of corporate governance and stock markets. The stock market watch app on every developer's computer had become "an EKG to the global body" (Martin, Rafferty, and Bryan 2008, 124). Desire's workers were solidly integrated into capital and were put in competitive relations with their own sibling studios and blamed them for their "failures." The urgency to satisfy the investors caused an intensification of the labor process in which the developers suffered from frustrations and anxieties for not being able to unleash their creativity as they wished.

Moreover, feeling the pressure of the markets every day forced game developers to act increasingly *as* capital to extract more value out of themselves, since their success would impact the parent company's well-being, their own patterns of consumption, and their distinct lifestyles as part of the creative class. The feeling of indebtedness to the parent company and to one's own consumption patterns, such as home ownership, intensified the labor process, while rearticulating precarity into the new context of stock markets. This is why precarity needs to be considered beyond short-term job contracts. As an existential condition, we need to grasp precarity in relation to how Desire's employees increasingly began to see themselves *as* capital or indebted to capital.

At the beginning of this chapter, I mentioned that Desire's developers who witnessed the cultural shift following acquisition regarded the process as a trade-off between financial security and creative autonomy. While they did have concerns and fears regarding creative autonomy, the employees also enjoyed the conditions of financial security. They no longer had to rush to find funding for their next project. Fortunately, concerns about the loss of autonomy did not prove to be real. The employees at Desire were pretty much left on their own because Digital Creatives needed original titles, and overall, they were happy with the studio's past performance and production of original IP. At the same time, the transition also embodied the rationalization of what formerly used to resemble craftwork, creating a disjunction between the employees and the parent company. While the buyout process eliminated the financial insecurity intrinsic to the garage culture, it essentially moved precarity to a more financialized and networked level. Now what mattered was not only the concrete performance of the studio and the games it made but also the publisher, its network of studios, and the abstract performance of stock prices.

The ambivalent outcome and the perception of the buyout as a trade-off pushes one to rethink certain questions regarding autonomy within the labor process, because the discourse of trade-off serves to conceal the loss of control over the labor process. Although Desire became part of a more complex network of relations—fellow studios, marketing, and stockholders—it lacked access to crucial information to make sense of their future, feeling that they were "left in the dark." While the "average guy," in Matthew's words, used to know everyone in the studio, where the president was "just another guy," the new circumstances were radically different for the "average guy," who was now partially disassociated from other disciplines.

The language of trade-off reminds one of the liberal principles of the free market upon which the developers predominantly construct their occupational identities. The perception that there can be an equal and fair trade-off erases the history and material reality behind how Digital Creatives expropriated the developers' knowledge, information, and experience, turning it into private and financialized intellectual property. The discourse of trade-off presents nothing but the paradox of economic liberalism, which is "parasitic upon some preceding form of socialization" (Zizek 2011). The language of trade-off implies a realm of exchange that supposedly functions outside the regime of ludopolitics. However, since Desire and Digital Creatives encounter each other under asymmetrical terms, their trade-off is never a free or equal trade-off.

Desire's "debt" as a garage studio to the market was rearticulated into a more complex network of financial relations and ownership structures, which ultimately failed to eliminate precarity. When Desire agreed to be acquired by Digital Creatives, it confirmed the absolute transfer of control over finances to the parent company, which ended up managing hiring practices and deciding on the genres and shipping dates of games that were produced. And these, at the end of the day, are not just economic but political decisions. Ultimately, precarity was rearticulated into a bigger league of players, which had to find the right space to work.

3

GAMING THE CITY

How a Game Studio Revitalized a Downtown Space in the Silicon Prairie

The preceding chapter revealed the tensions between creativity and commerce as Desire transitioned from being an independent studio to a corporate one. A rationalized and streamlined creative labor process brought organizational shifts to the studio. Acquisition by a major player in the industry relieved the workers from the mandate to produce demos again and again, but this freedom also unleashed antagonisms and inequalities derived from Digital Creatives' imperative to rationalize production along its own financialized logics.

Although space is fundamental to understanding how people and companies work on an everyday basis, media studies scholars, with a few notable exceptions (de Peuter 2012; Kerr 2013; Rosler 2010; Ross 2007), have mostly ignored it. Companies surely search for skills and passion in the creative sectors, but space is equally important. When Desire was acquired by Digital Creatives, it had to relocate to a larger corporate plaza not just for organizational reasons but also to harness workers' productive capacities. To make sense of the outcomes of this move and the actors involved, I draw on historical-geographical materialism (Lefebvre 1991; Harvey 1990; Herod 2012; Massey 1994) and tell the story of how Desire's contingent relocation ended up revitalizing a dysfunctional downtown space in the U.S. Midwest.

Game City is worth unpacking also because smaller and medium-sized cities have largely been ignored in the global economy at the expense of major nodes (Sassen 2002). It's only recently that a number of scholars critiqued sweeping tendencies within globalization narratives and foregrounded how small to medium cities can very well be major nodes in the information economy by mixing entrepreneurialism with ideals of family, nature, and local practices (Larson and Pearson 2012; Luckman 2012; Waitt 2006).

Why discuss urban space in a book on game labor, though? First, it seems obvious, but, as an embodied practice, work takes place in a physical context. Therefore, even in the context of globalization, how workers exercise their labor power depends on the physical features, affordances, design logic, and limitations of a particular workplace. Second, spaces are arenas where workers struggle for recognition. The way a workplace presents itself is important for operations of symbolic power because places are not just a background story. They are *the* story that communicates ideas about social esteem, social power, and norms. Especially in the creative industries, they brand a specific group of workers as role models and communicate images and ideas of love and glamor across the society. Third, a materialist approach to space is indispensable because that's how we grasp the spatial dimension of the ludopolitical regime. Who can work in these workplaces? Which subjects are welcome in certain sections of a city? To that end, I take discursive and material inequalities at the urban level seriously (Peck 2005). Finally, space also matters as it casts social reproduction as a frame. Work is not simply about formal practices in a given workplace. It's about schools, hospitals, infrastructures, and leisure activities. In that regard, when we think about work in critical terms, we should not limit ourselves to the formal boundaries of the workplace, especially within the context of the "social factory" (Negri 1989).

In unearthing discursive inequalities, framing space as an actor in the contingent production of social life, and revealing the consequences of Desire's relocation, I use Henri Lefebvre's (1991) concept of the "production of space." While the concept emphasizes the continuities within a capitalist mode of production, it also allows for understanding space as active and productive. There is a double meaning to it: space is both produced and productive. The production of space implies not only the structural forces that produce space but also how space, with its historical specificities and material practices, *produces*, and therefore, is "a condition of future practices—a basis of making History" (Hay 2011, 122). An active, productive, and social notion of space underlines the importance of culture, signs, representations, imaginaries, and aesthetics in producing space, which in turn produces social relations, representations, and material practices. In this respect, Lefebvre's perspective is useful in rethinking the role of media and cultural industries in producing a particular kind of space and thus enabling the birth of the creative city in the neoliberal moment.

In our case, the transformation of Game City's downtown was contingent and historical rather than natural and therefore needs to be understood as the theater of hegemonic struggles over the iconography of the city (McCarthy 2011). The revitalization of Game City's downtown and the emergence of *micro-urbanism*[1] as a discursive strategy in branding Game City in the Silicon Prairie did not automatically emerge. A major catalyst in these developments was the relocation of Desire upon its acquisition by Digital Creatives. To grasp these developments, a materialist analysis of space is crucial to first dissect and then assemble the broader forces, processes, social relations, local particularities, and actors' practices in Game City. Only then can we assess the consequences of Desire's relocation, the emergence of public-private partnerships, and discourses of micro-urbanism. Combined, they all foster the creation of a smart, innovative micro-urban space where Desire's workers aspire to work.

Game City: A Small, Powerful Island in the Silicon Prairie

Incorporated in the second half of the nineteenth century, Game City is a quiet island in the Midwest. It's not a metropolitan setting but is close enough to various regional hubs. Historically, it owes its development to its proximity to communication and transportation networks. There is only one building that survives from the era when the city was incorporated. Since the late nineteenth century, brick structures, which house retail shops, banks, churches, spaces of entertainment, and government offices, have given the city its architectural character.

In the Midwest's Silicon Prairie ecology, Game City is an edge place for creative production. Signs of high-tech production are not easily detectable in the city. Its high-tech employment is less than 2 percent, but the quality and historical position of its high-tech legacy, due to its education and transportation networks, is outstanding. The list of historical innovations that the city originally developed and hosts today ranges from computer science and software to electronics, materials science, physics, and fine arts. The technology legacy attracts various companies producing farm technologies, flight simulations, and mathematics software. A major technology company still maintains a research lab in Game City. Various start-ups populate a research hub designed playfully like the corporate spaces of Silicon Valley. Therefore, the city legitimately brands itself as an alternative innovation destination outside the Bay Area and the East Coast.

The city claims to be one of the top start-up cities in the country, but when you drive ten miles out of the city, you are in open fields. In other words, although there is a relatively vibrant high-tech and start-up environment, the city is by no means absorbed into a network as, for instance, San Francisco is into Silicon Valley. But again, the city attests to how smallness is not adverse to creative production (Waitt 2006).

Studio Desire for one doesn't broadcast its presence right in the heart of the city. Although there is arguably a midwestern attitude underlying this modesty compared to the hypercompetitive ethos in Silicon Valley, Desire is invisible mainly because video game production is not common in the area. Despite the city's young population, there are only three other game studios, and none of them compares to Desire in size or advantageous location. Desire is so unique and precious to the city that when its ten-year lease of the plaza was up, city officials considered offering Desire $200,000 in incentives to stay. Owners of various downtown businesses, such as bars and coffee shops, also wrote city officials to emphasize how Desire was vital to a thriving downtown. In fact, Desire's workers spend around $400,000 in downtown restaurants to which they pay roughly thirty thousand visits annually.

Contributing to the downtown economy is not hard as Desire is right at the center of the city with easy access to various recreational spaces. Although a considerable amount of Desire's workers, including Desire's founder, have links with the existing educational institutions, employees don't typically hang out in spaces close to campuses. They prefer to stay downtown, where one can spend time in a bar, a brewery, an Irish pub, artisanal coffee shops, and restaurants (e.g., Indian food, pizza, fine dining, a tavern that caters to local taste) or visit vintage cloth shops, book stores, or a record store, all in walking distance. In fact, I did some of my interviews in these downtown businesses. Downtown is usually calm except for evenings and weekend nights, when it gets crowded and loud. Typically, the heart of the city where consumption takes place aims to be a multicultural setting although certain sections of the city are segregated along racial lines.

What is it like to work in a cool workplace in a small city? Desire's employees were happy overall, with some caveats. Chris, an artificial intelligence (AI) programmer in his midthirties had previously worked in California, and he did acknowledge that it was "not the sexiest place to live." What attracted him and other Desire workers to Game City, then? The network of good educational institutions was important, but a primary reason to work and live in Game City was cost of living and housing. Despite the fact that cost of living was 8 percent above the national average, one could buy a house at around $150,000–$200,000, whereas the prices in Silicon Valley ranged from $700,000 to $1.5 million. In fact, this was a major selling point when recruiting workers from elsewhere, especially California. The producer David, for instance, enjoyed his fifteen-minute daily commute and house with a yard, as opposed to his fifty-minute average commute and two-bedroom apartment in California. Chris now owned a house, the mortgage of which was lower than his previous rent in California.

Another attraction was having family in the region. In fact, in contrast to the stereotypical cosmopolitan creative class, Desire's workforce preferred to be close to their home in the Midwest. It's where their roots were. They'd grown up or gone to school there. They valued family and being close to extended family members. This was especially true for the older workers who had already had a taste of the tech-intensive regions. For instance, it was David's midwestern wife who encouraged him to accept the position at Desire and leave California.

Game City as a place also meant a particular way of life, involving a somewhat sustainable routine with easy commutes between work and home and easier access to outdoor activities. Unlike the culture and pace of New York or Silicon Valley, the relatively laid-back lifestyle attracted Desire's workers. In that regard, with its physical features and material practices, Game City reveals important distinctions between cultures of work and life, as well as workers' imaginations in California and the Midwest. Chris thought that "people in the Midwest live more outside their work. Have more of a home life whereas in California, their job is their life." From his perspective, people move to the Midwest to establish roots whereas in California, professionals will move as soon as they find a better house or job.

However, this particular lifestyle choice comes with challenges because except for those at Desire, there aren't that many game workers living in the city. It's hard for Desire's workers to network with colleagues and feel part of a production ecology that is conducive to alternative practices and imaginations. They are not necessarily stuck in Desire but do wish that the city hosted more game companies, more networking venues, more opportunities for the cross-pollination of techniques and ideas, and more talent. Although the educational institutions around are helpful for hiring new graduates, the company still finds it hard to recruit given the location. In sum, Desire's developers work in a quiet but powerful island in the Silicon Prairie. The community at Desire embraces "an alternative and locally improved reading of entrepreneurial identity, one that values home and family as much as occupation" (Larson and Pearson 2012, 255). An entrepreneurial spirit definitely defines Desire, but this spirit also takes pride in not sacrificing, or at least trying not to sacrifice, family life.[2]

Yet, given the calm Midwest atmosphere, Game City does aspire to reinvent itself as a micro-urban city that can attract members of the creative classes from elsewhere. This aspiration and imagination of micro-urbanism has become partly possible thanks to Desire's success and subsequent relocation. Yet, to understand how the *production* of Desire's plaza in downtown in turn *produced* certain practices and imaginaries, I ask: What forces and actors come together at a particular time through which Game City aspires to be a micro-urban space that houses arts and culture? Doreen Massey's (2008, 262) analysis is useful here because, as she argues, "what gives a place its specificity is not some long internalized history but the fact that it is constructed out of a particular constellation of social relations, meeting and weaving together at a particular locus." In that sense, we need to narrow down the question and ask: What are the historical peculiarities of the downtown where Desire is located? What kinds of imaginaries has Desire's relocation produced in terms of city branding? And finally, what does this revitalization mean in terms of the reproduction of Desire's workforce and urban inequalities?

Successful Games Revitalize a Dead Downtown

In the second half of the twentieth century, driving habits had changed Game City. Vintage buildings were demolished to open parking space downtown. But this was not enough to retain customers because consumers were able to drive elsewhere for shopping. To attract these fleeing customers, the city built a pedestrian mall downtown. This was a productive solution but only for two years. Businesses did not stay. Until the 1990s, downtown was something of a ghost town, although a few actors, including the city government, a health institution, a movie theater, and a newspaper, chose to stay.

The city management responded to the downtown's dysfunctional condition after 5:00 P.M. by successfully introducing a tax increment finance (TIF) district,[3] thanks to which a bank opened and a health institution expanded. The impact of TIFs became even more visible when city management recognized that the pedestrian mall was a huge mistake. For them, downtown's future was tightly linked with whether entrepreneurs would reevaluate the plummeting property values for their own purposes to ultimately create a vibrant service economy. In this sense, TIFs provided the institutional framework for the transformation of the dead town into a vibrant arts and cultural district.

A major event in the history of downtown and the relocation of Desire took place when a fire destroyed the space where the studio is currently located. This fire in the late 1980s devastated the department store that occupied the site at the time. Not being able to reconstruct the building, the developer had to sell it to Game City. The city demolished the remnants of the building and created a parking lot. It was through the TIF that this parking lot was sold to a real estate developer, who then built the plaza where Desire moved upon acquisition by Digital Creatives and is still located.

The construction of a plaza on this parking lot was historic. First, TIFs initially aimed to renovate existing buildings, and the construction of a new plaza was not a common practice. Second, since nothing else had been built in the city center for over fifteen years, the plaza was the first step in recreating downtown as a more modern and creative locale.

At the time of the construction, local press predicted that the plaza would have a phoenix effect on the area since it was really Desire's relocation that drove the $14.5 million building. The studio confirmed these expectations and ended up occupying more space than initially planned. As the game programmer Matthew and I were discussing the history of downtown, he said: "The president was thinking, we should be able to stay within the confines of this floor for the next five years without expanding, right? . . . This space, just this floor alone, was supposed to last us for five years. It's like . . . no."

Reactions to this public-private partnership were mixed. I once visited and interviewed Alan in his office. Alan is a city planner who specializes in economic development. He had started as an intern and ended up working for the city for more than ten years. He was very welcoming and answered my questions earnestly. In his late thirties, Alan was passionate about urban sustainability that involved both growth and preservation. He was honored to be part of the downtown resurgence, to the extent that he had a collection of photographs of almost every building in the city. Alan was particularly fond of the public-private partnership involving Desire, because "not only were they coming with the building, but they were coming with the business, the game studio, to the table." Impressed by the "youthful employees of the game studio," he hinted at the bias toward creative jobs by saying that "those kinds of jobs are exactly the kind of jobs that we love to see here" since "they're the ones that will keep the engine going."

Not everybody was happy, though; some city residents feared losing their parking permits. For instance, going through the local press reveals that a business owner accused the city of thinking that the game developers were more important than her business. While supportive of the game studio's relocation, another business owner underlined how she could have arranged her business plans accordingly had she previously known about this development.[4]

Desire's relocation, which was initially a political-economic negotiation, in turn generated other developments and produced new social relationships and cultural imaginaries. The construction of the plaza transformed downtown into a lively place comprised of luxurious residential spaces, offices, hotels, and restaurants. At the same time, this institutionalized public-private partnership enabled the advent of new actors and imaginaries invested in the active branding of the city. This is important because these new actors are now actively imagining and working toward the production of a micro-urban space, the catalyst of which has been the relocation of Desire. However, in addition to Desire, there have been two other major actors in this process: a real estate developer and the city. Their discourses about how the city should evolve and position itself have proven to be more than just words. In fact, both the real estate developer's and the city's discourses and urban imagination should be seen as important tools that simplify political relations by selectively creating a narrative about how Game City should project itself into the future (Fairclough 2006, 18).

Creativity Is Not Just a Discourse: The Rise of a Former Hippie as a Real Estate Developer

During an interview with HR personnel at Desire, I saw one of Richard Florida's books. I asked about it and, to my surprise, learned that Florida's book was introduced to Game City through the initiative of the same real estate company that had built Desire's plaza. Not surprisingly, the real estate company's website posits Florida as a leading force behind its philosophy.

The CEO of the real estate company—Bill—is a New Yorker and moved to Game City in the 1990s, only to witness the death of the downtown. He transplanted his work and life experience in New York to the Midwest. His first entrepreneurial initiative was a record store, which was followed by his real estate business. As I talked to him, I discovered his passion for music, culture, and creativity. In an office that looked more like an artist's work space than a real estate office, we discussed not only real estate but also global music.

He was very welcoming and, with a confident voice, described how he felt so proud of the urban developments he had spearheaded, transforming a dysfunctional downtown into a vibrant place. Also a member of the steering committee of the Downtown Plan, Bill was influential in resolving the recruitment and retention problem that Desire faced upon acquisition. The idea of building a plaza came up during a conversation between Bill and Desire's former president. The president had concerns about the future reproduction of the company and told the real estate developer that he "had no problem with a steady flow of engineers out of school, but after six months to two years, they would tend to go somewhere else." This conversation convinced the real estate developer to take action and talk to the city:

> The president [of the studio] said, "I'm leaving town. I'm gonna have to leave town, and I don't want to. I want to live here." So I went to the city, and the city had financing programs in place, TIF programs in place, taxing increments, financing to allow . . . to subsidize the upside-down nature of real estate downtown. And when I went in, I said, "Look, I've got this done in three months, because [of] a whole host of reasons

[related to acquisition by Digital Creatives and the mandate to remain competitive], this guy [might have to] leave town." And they [the city] said, "We'll make it happen." And for them, this is validation.

We discussed some city residents' concerns about whether the public-private partnership was problematic. Denying that Desire "got a deal" from the city, Bill emphasized the positive economic and cultural impact they had made in downtown. He underlined how his "hippie" past informed the philosophy behind both the construction of the plaza and his company. For him, the plaza mattered a great deal in terms of representation and style because when he'd first moved from New York, downtown was "dangerous" and deserted. That had to change, and the relocation of the studio was a catalyst. "Maybe," he said, "it's part of the human condition. If you're cool, doing something cool, you'd like to be . . . around people saying that you're cool." The following remarks make the relationship between the productivity of space and subjectivity even more clear: "So, bringing them downtown, let them walk around like lords of the universe down here. I never thought of this before, but . . . during the heyday of Wall Street, they called those guys 'masters of the universe.' They're sort of masters of a certain universe. . . . You know, I can come in in shorts and work. And if I'm in the art department, I can wear leather and spike my hair, and I get paid fifty grand a year."

While Desire's downtown presence was the first product—a very successful one—of the real estate company, the coolness associated with the creative class became a pillar of the company's branding strategy. On its website, the company regards sustainable urban development as closely related to "responsible corporate citizenry." As the company website further suggests, its clientele is decidedly the creative class, without whom communities "cannot survive." The company's vision is to create a neighborhood in which the members of the creative class are willing to "work, play, and live." Through this imagination, they invite their clientele to invest by buying or renting residences and workspaces located at the heart of a vibrant downtown. As part of its branding strategies, Bill deploys the narratives of its residents, who unanimously emphasize the convenience of the luxurious residences and workspaces in a cozy downtown environment.

Due to the success of the plaza and other developments downtown, Bill has been featured in local press with specific reference to Richard Florida's theory of the creative class. For instance, one of the local papers published a feature article on the revitalization of downtown. The paper interviewed an academic who underlined the importance of uniting art with economy so that local artists could thrive and network. The article also foregrounded Bill and his downtown developments as the driving force behind the declining crime rates and flourishing businesses in downtown. Bill, according to this press article, was the mastermind behind the growth of downtown employment thanks to the relocation of the studio.

In sum, the relocation of Desire not only revitalized the downtown but also *produced* new imaginaries with respect to constructing luxurious developments, condos, and office spaces in a formerly decaying downtown. Nevertheless, the real estate company is not the only actor to imagine and build this micro-urban area. Game City, especially after the successful partnership with the real estate company, has embarked on a set of activities to consolidate the trend in revitalizing the downtown along the principles of public-private partnerships, a direction set out in its Downtown Plan, a strategic document that envisions a future for the city.

How the Downtown Plan Imagines the City

Having accomplished a major step in revitalizing the downtown through Desire's relocation, the city management engaged in another initiative, the Downtown Plan, to further consolidate and institutionalize transforming Game City into a creative city. The plan was particularly keen on public-private partnerships, whose members formed a steering committee, an alliance of local elites, including Bill, the mastermind behind downtown's transformation.

In preparation for the plan, the committee organized fourteen meetings and conducted interviews with social actors ranging from social service organizations to realtors and property owners. In various workshops, the committee designed five different scenarios through which participants envisioned the downtown's future. From these five scenarios emerged an ideal blended scenario where the emphasis was not only on buildings but also people, culture, diversity, and different sets of activities that would create a vibrant downtown. The plan underlined that a successful city center needed the creative energies of residents and therefore had to consider their desires and interests. The plan proposed public-private partnerships as a remedy to the lack of gathering spaces for the creation of such urban relationships. The cultivation of these urban relationships would require the construction of spaces for a public plaza and open spaces oriented toward families and festivals, and activities of different sorts, such as ice skating and concerts.

Discourses, language, and definitions matter. Once the relocation of Desire proved successful, a new imaginary emerged. In that regard, Desire's plaza is not simply a physical or political-economic entity. It signifies distinct values about the creative class and creative city. It embodies different kinds of evolving materialities, social relationships, imaginations, and representations. Overall, the Downtown Plan does important discursive work as it imagines and struggles toward a social space, constructed through public-private partnerships as important cornerstones of the "creative cities script" (Peck 2005). It is a political script that blends entertainment, involves local actors and flavors, and centers arts and culture.

Needless to say, this is a hard task. The promotion of art stands as a particular challenge, which the plan proposes to resolve with the right partnerships by incentivizing the allocation of a place for artists to work and live. This, of course, depends on economic resources. The plan mentions the need for a cohesive branding strategy and new funding opportunities mainly because TIFs as a precarious urban revitalization strategy have a political expiration date. It is this looming expiration date that pushed the city to invent a new partnership—the Game City Center Partnership—which I examine next.

A New Local Partnership: Branding the Micro-Urban City, Educating the Consumer-Citizen

In an age of austerity, local and regional governments have to generate new resources to build urban infrastructures and attract new investment. The recognition that TIFs, unless extended again, will at some point expire forced Game City to devise alternative funding patterns. To construct a city that also supported creative lifestyles, two viable options emerged: micro-urbanism, a term deployed by the local elites, and a concerted and institutional effort to build public-private partnerships to generate funds, market the city, and educate its citizens via media shows and smartphone applications to boost consumption and entertainment downtown.

Micro-urbanism is a branding strategy to appeal to the creative and intellectual classes who may prefer a more manageable lifestyle to living in the global urban centers. This is a lifestyle much different than one encounters in New York, San Francisco, or London. It involves relatively shorter commutes, as well as easy access to recreational spaces and activities. Game City has them: museums, blues venues, film festivals, and an international guitar festival. The existence of an elite public high school, major educational institutions, and influential entrepreneurs is also important in the micro-urbanism discourse. In short, local elites invested in branding Game City use such keywords as smart, innovative, and micro-urban to shape the city's future.

This discourse may sound like a mundane branding strategy, but my interviews with Desire's workers confirmed Game City's capability to appeal to and retain a segment of the creative class. That is, not all creative workers aspire to work and live in large metropolitan spaces as prescribed by Richard Florida. On the contrary, Desire's developers enjoy their small but smart city as it is possible to find things to do and, more importantly, buy houses they can afford. In Game City, they can raise families away from the chaotic and expensive environment of the larger creative hubs.

The local elites behind the discourse of micro-urbanism are not the only ones struggling to rebrand the city. City management also concentrated its efforts by founding a public-private partnership, the Game City Center Partnership. In April 2011, the city council reached an agreement to boost connectivity across the three prominent business centers in Game City. Through this partnership, the city aims to gather smaller business organizations under one umbrella so that they can operate more smoothly and evolve into a sustainable and strong identity. The larger objective is to promote the city regionally and nationally.

In the initial stages of this partnership, the city provided infrastructural and labor support by offering an executive director position. This executive director would be responsible for mapping business in the city, informing the residents of various local urban developments, running a website, offering advertising opportunities for members, carrying out public relations, and ultimately branding the city as a venue for working, playing, and living. The executive director would be "loaned" to work twenty hours per week for a year for the Game City Center Partnership, whose budget ($50,000) would be met through the Food and Beverage Fund.

As a 501(c)(6) not-for-profit organization founded through a merger of the Downtown Association and another business group in the city, the partnership is up and running, right across the street from Desire. In an interview, the executive director stated, "We have money to put towards these promotions and branding our downtown and the micro-urban community." The partnership's executive director is a city planner; on the city's website, he states that he is happy to see that the town is growing to be more than the stereotypical silent regional small town.

Indeed, through a (new) media operation, the executive director and the partnership are doing their best to wake up the micro-urban city, educate its citizens, and acculturate them to certain material practices. Game City Excitement, for instance, is a program produced by Game City Center Partnership. As a media production, it is dedicated to marketing downtown. In its first episode, the uniqueness of downtown is underlined through its opportunities for leisure activities and having "over 1,100 seats" for potential visitors. Underlining the transformation efforts, the program also introduces its audience to downtown retailers and restaurants, some of which position themselves as businesses that serve "local food." A restaurant chef, for instance, highlights the nice aspects of being in a small place and the opportunities it provides. In Game City, this chef can mingle with the local farmers, which he wouldn't be able to do in San Francisco. In its edutainment efforts, the program asks questions of its viewers about the city, such as "How many outdoor seats are located downtown?" The second episode of the program focuses on a local bookstore and a historical movie theater as major nodes in the arts and culture network. Indeed, the second episode is particularly dedicated to educating its public and creating a sense of history that cultivates the micro-urban feel. This marketing assemblage also includes information regarding smartphone applications, described as "the connection between you and the stores you love in Game City." In the third episode, the focus is again on restaurants and cafés, some of which Desire's workers frequently visit. One of the restaurant co-owners specifically mentions Desire, with which they do business.

In the third episode, the Guild of Public Artists stands out as an important actor within the arts and cultural district. Formed in the late 2000s, the guild is engaged in, among other activities, increasing the presence of public art in the city. The support of the city is described as crucial for this endeavor because it is the city that pays for the installation. The guild brought twenty-nine sculptures in three years, thirteen of which are situated downtown, by both national and regional artists sponsored by Studio Desire, Bill's real estate company, and a few other public institutions and private businesses.

Aside from the guild, 999 East is another important actor, involved in producing the arts and cultural district. With its mission "to cultivate creativity" in the area, the organization sees art both as a "vehicle for social change" and "a catalyst for economic development." It is really an umbrella organization to connect artists with each other, with the community, and with businesses and to advocate arts in the region. The city and Game City Center Partnership are among the major partners in this organization. It provides space for local artists to display their work on traveling billboards, thereby creating a mobile gallery experience.

Consequently, a constellation of material developments, practices, and discursive forces inform the emerging micro-urban scene, which thrives on the aestheticization of urban experience and commodification of arts. Businesses, arts organizations, and the city collaborate to produce a micro-urban space, which in turn produces modes of urban experiences and consuming identities. It is a complex set of transformative relations within which the relocation of Desire had a historic role. In this assemblage of neoliberal forces and practices, the hegemony of the public-private partnership needs to be emphasized. To promote and market the city, the city has undertaken the initiative to allocate staff and funding for the Game City Center Partnership to evolve into a sustainable and coherent organization, deploying both old and new media to incorporate city residents and artists into the micro-urban experience as actors and consumers. The extent to which such benign endeavors obliterate questions of urban precarity and exclusion, however, is dubious.

The Spatial Dimensions of Ludopolitics: Instrumentalized Creativity, Precarious City, Unequal Citizenship

When Digital Creatives bought out Desire, they had to move to a larger place, the infrastructure of which was established through a public-private partnership. Once this project was successful, the city began to imagine constructing a playful downtown, which would ideally appeal to the creative class. As Bill, the CEO of the real estate company, said, this success served as a "validation for the city" because it enabled the maintenance of a creative workforce right in the heart of the city center. Out of these contingent developments emerged a partnership that now invites city residents to come, shop, and dine downtown.

A dead downtown for over ten years shifted toward being an arts and cultural district with a major focus on creativity, now imagined as a micro-urban space. In his analysis of Amsterdam and its desire to be a creative city, Merijn Oudenampsen (2007, 173) uses the metaphors of hardware (the infrastructure) and software, the city's cultural "programming." Desire's developers, as the hardware, were influential in terms of constructing the infrastructure (production of space, where production literally refers to the building of the plaza). They were at the same time actors within the broader constellation of the micro-urban experience (production of space, where the term now refers to how that plaza actively produces the space along with cultural meanings, social relations, and representations) and in this respect became the software behind investments in art festivals, arts organizations, and the Game City Center Partnership. Desire's developers, with their capacities and desire to both produce and consume, emerged as crucial local actors in terms of reinventing the city where they work, play, and live.

How is it, then, that local actors are so willing to construct new micro-urban, smart, creative cities? One explanation behind the quick adoption of creative city policies across the globe is that they are low-risk and relatively low-cost endeavors (Peck 2005; Ross 2007). However, this readiness to implement the "creative city script" (Peck 2005) is laden with contradictions and inequalities. Because "nothing is forever" (de Peuter 2012, 92), cities will still be precarious in a highly volatile and flexible economy despite the relatively low cost of creative city policies. As Jamie Peck (2005, 767) sharply puts it, creativity strategies "empower, though only precariously, unstable networks of elite actors, whose strategies represent aspirant attempts to realize in concrete form the seductive 'traveling truths' of the creative script." In other words, the material and discursive seductiveness of the creative city discourse can only achieve so much.

There is a broader social problem regarding the creative city discourses and practices, though. Despite their emphasis on grassroots and local flavors, creative city policies often instrumentalize creativity, fetishize the artist as the entrepreneur, hierarchize particular valorizations of creativity, trivialize nonurban centers that support metropolitan areas, homogenize cultural forms, prioritize middle classes that are highly racialized and gendered, and end up being used as "a discursive weapon to further problematize non-middle class values and peoples" (Edensor et al. 2010, 7). To put it bluntly, the "creative city script" is biased in terms of gender, race, and class (Mosco 1999) since it privileges the city's ludic function at the expense of a more democratic urban design.

We cannot predict how Game City's downtown might turn out in ten years. We do, however, know that Game City is by no means Vancouver, for instance, or Montreal. As Canada's oldest game development hub, Vancouver employs 3,500 workers and 140 companies. Montreal houses the French video game publisher Ubisoft's biggest studio with 1,800 employees. With their public infrastructures, facilities, and tempting tax incentives, these locations, especially Montreal, are able to attract firms from the United States and Japan, thereby giving rise to the so-called Montreal model for the rest of Canada and other countries around the world (de Peuter 2012, 89–90).

Nevertheless, while we cannot predict the future, we can conclude by making at least two arguments. First, discourses have material outcomes. The transformation of downtown has been the result of an amalgamation of various actors and processes that include Richard Florida's discursive influence, the physical relocation of the game studio into the heart of the downtown, and the emergence of a decidedly entrepreneurial city that aims to revitalize itself and turn its city center into an arts and cultural district with a micro-urban feel. The relocation of the studio not only created an economic transformation but also a cultural and governmental one in which the city repositioned itself as an entrepreneurial entity. Second, the public-private partnership as a form of urban governance privileges consumption in the bar and restaurant economy, as the promotional posts from the Game City Center Partnership's Facebook page confirm. While there is nothing essentially wrong with how a dying urban space is revitalized, the terms under which certain actors, discourses, and imaginaries get to be invited and others are excluded is worthy of critical consideration. When the urban space turns into a playground where consumption identities and practices are displayed, political questions regarding who can participate in these spectacular economies emerge.

In sum, the unequal spatial dimensions of the ludopolitical regime in the video game industry matter in terms of who can work, live, and dine in certain sections of the city and who are excluded from such practices of citizenship. Who are consulted when important urban decisions are made? Who are left out? What might urban citizens have to say when such vital and political decisions are made (Rushkoff 2016)? Designing cities consistently and exclusively in line with the imagination of neoliberal urban planners and real estate developers will reproduce the exclusionary urban practices of eras that well predate the age of micro-urbanism. Unless local residents' access to and fair use of the city is established along inclusive and egalitarian lines, the residents of Game City, or any city for that matter, will remain shoppers and tourists in their own city. They will be remembered only during restaurant weeks and summer festivals. In that regard, the video game industry and the broader high-tech ecology in which it thrives need to pay particular attention to the unequal spatial politics they purport (D'Onfro 2018).

Desire's relocation resolved some of the spatial and organizational issues that emerged upon acquisition. However, problems were far from over, because Desire was no longer a small studio where developers were able to easily communicate with each other and retain the vision of the project they worked on. Once the studio moved to its new location with its expanded workforce, the management had to devise temporal and spatial strategies to harness self-regulating and communicative subjectivities ready to passionately work in the highly competitive triple-A market.

THE PRODUCTION OF COMMUNICATIVE DEVELOPERS IN THE AFFECTIVE GAME STUDIO

Titanic was only one metaphor among others that game developers used in describing their work. For instance, roller coaster, as a metaphor, came up in a conversation I had with Theodor, one of Desire's art directors. Theodor was a big fan of superheroes and a very calm and kind man. Before becoming an art director, he had gone to school in the region and studied civil engineering. Then, he studied fine arts, focusing on painting, which led ultimately to a BFA. Following college, he was involved in sales and graphic design before he started his job at Desire. Before being promoted to the art director position, Theodor served as an environment artist. In his early fifties, Theodor had been at Desire long enough to witness the organizational changes described in chapter 2.

As we sat on the patio of a coffee shop, Theodor described the ups and downs of game development. He emphasized how love was crucial for survival in the industry to the extent that he recommended that I should ask other developers if they loved what they were doing. Theodor believed that if they did, then it would mean that they also could "ride the roller coaster, because game development is a roller coaster."

Following Theodor's advice, I discussed love at work with Siva, a project design director. In his midforties, Siva always struck me as a joyful worker. When he laughed, you could hear him from afar. He had previously worked in a PC company, working on games. This was then bought out by Microsoft, for which Siva worked for nine years. Having worked in Seattle, he then applied to Desire and found a position and relocated to "raise [his] family around family." His love for video games was so deep that he was very upset when Roger Ebert challenged the aesthetic qualities of video games. He was very frustrated with how society perceived his profession and the attendant inferiority complex in the industry. He was now very happy to see how video games were competing with the movie industry. When describing his passion for the profession, Siva said he loved working at a place where one of the common questions was "what if?" Such questions pushed them to think outside the box and imagine things differently. Over time, these questions would produce something cool, behind which a collective effort lay. As he discussed his interactions with art and programming, he used another gendered metaphor: parenting. He said: "I've got two kids, OK? It's almost like having a baby. You watch it grow; you watch it start off incapable of doing anything. And then it learns more, and it learns more, and you try to guide it and so on and so forth and finally end up doing [something] you're proud of."

"Fighting battles" was another analogy that developers used when describing game production. Despite being part of the same "army," developers also fought battles against each other in order to win their collective war against the competitors. I was talking to Silvio (forty-three years old, white) at the studio before we had lunch at a Japanese restaurant for our interview. After high school, Silvio had worked in different industries, including white-collar IT jobs and blue-collar positions like pizza delivery, warehouse, and janitor. When he was working as a content editor in online banking, he got sick of his job and quit. At the urging of a friend, he took a position in design testing in a game company and loved it. He knew he "had to get into the industry." He borrowed some money and went to Vancouver Film School. He was "top" in his class. During a Game Developers Conference meeting, he met a worker from Desire who also went to the same school in Vancouver. He hyped Silvio to Desire, which ended up hiring Silvio three months before our interview.

The love of games along with the wish and pressure to do something that one is proud of leads to battles. Once, Silvio was changing some game features. An artist objected, saying, "No, no, no, no, that's been signed off. You can't change it; it's gotta be this way." However, Silvio wanted to implement those changes. The other artist was against them mainly because he was "overloaded." Silvio lost the battle due to practical reasons: "The boss in question at the time was on his side because he's gotta worry about deadline pressures. He doesn't want to add work to anyone. I don't want to add work to anyone either, but the game play just sucked."

Such battles were at the core of my various conversations with the veteran programmer Matthew. He often highlighted how programmers' many encounters with other disciplines—particularly management—involved convincing others about the open-ended nature of programming. As I interviewed him and the AI programmer Chris, Matthew said: "There is a tendency for nonprogrammers to view programming as assembly-line work. Really, this can only be done for the simplest of tasks. For projects of the size we work on here, it's simply impossible to plan out work with that degree of certainty beforehand." Chris agreed: "When working on enemy behavior, for example, it takes a lot of changes to get something that feels intelligent and threatening. It is not a simple process that can just be translated; it is an idea and making an imagined outcome."

These gendered metaphors—roller coaster, parenting, fighting battles—reflect the dynamics at play within technomasculine work cultures. With their vertical loops and intense movements, roller coasters do have some thrilling and some other undesirable effects. Parenting, especially for mothers, is a tough experience but can also be rewarding. Although militaristic in content, fighting battles suggest the adrenaline-driven, competitive nature of game production, which can also be joyful as a highly collaborative practice.

The tension of participating in such an emotional labor process, involving passionate and at times opinionated workers, is partly alleviated by the reality that developers are united by the shared materiality of one force: love. A survey I conducted with Desire's 109 developers confirmed this. 36 percent of the participants *strongly agreed* and 28 percent *agreed* with the statement "working in the video game industry has always been my dream job." It wasn't just about money, Matthew said. For him, nobody really got rich by simply working in the game industry: "A lot of that is internal. It's just passion for games. We love games. . . . That passion—it has to come internally. And I think that's what drives us to put [in] these insane hours."

These metaphors reveal two central dynamics. First, game development is a highly emotional practice. Desire's developers demand unrestrained schedules and reject mandates on their creative labor processes. Second, as developers long for creative self-expression at work, this leads to commercial clashes with management because Desire itself is situated in a risky business field and has to abide by production schedules that are crucial for the success of Digital Creatives.

Then, the question becomes: When one's work is fraught with not only such creative battles but also heavily depends on a "vocabulary of love" (Gill and Pratt 2008, 15) and a compelling desire to experiment with technological systems, how does management regulate this evasive workforce and ensure productivity within a somewhat fluid and networked labor process? This problem became obvious again and again throughout my conversations with Desire's management. As I talked with them at the studio, I witnessed their "rants" about creativity, as the management put it. Once, the conversation addressed directly the anxiety at the heart of many creative workplaces: measuring productivity and maintaining employees' drive. Management had to make sure that the game developers "feel more driven to get their work done." "We are not getting anything out of this forty-hour-week, sit your butt in a chair," said one manager. "Because I can manage everything but productivity."

While no easy task, managing productivity and cultivating driven workers is not impossible, and Desire's management has been able to harness the temporal, spatial, and subjective dimensions of both the workplace and the labor process to maintain productivity. They are well aware that value in the game industry is best realized by investing in the developers' bodies and enhancing their imaginative capacities.

To succeed as a studio, Desire *has to* make work time so flexible that it actually becomes infinite. Therefore, with respect to time, I consider what Desire management called the "impossibilities" of a forty-hour workweek in the game industry and the dynamics of a policy shift toward a flexible work environment. For success, playful workspaces have to be designed, as well. I address the question of space by examining the construction of Desire as a playground in which objects and activities of play are abundant. Finally, the studio has to invest in developers' laboring subjectivities. Specifically, Desire needs to cultivate a particular type of developer who works on her or his communicative and linguistic capacities. For the studio, broadening channels of communication is vital to enhancing a labor process that is fundamentally fueled by tensions and love. Since game development is full of both positive and negative emotions, such as joy and frustration, Desire organizes training sessions to construct communicative subjects. In these sessions, an "intellectualization of intimate bonds" (Illouz 2007, 34) occurs where workers are encouraged to reflect on their communicative capacities, as well as communicate and express themselves so that the peaceful maximization of surplus value is guaranteed. Collaborative creative production at Desire thrives by instrumentally capitalizing on developers' feelings and interpersonal relationships.

Discussions of emotions with respect to immaterial labor have mostly remained at a theoretical level (Hardt and Negri 2000). Excavating the role of emotions at work is essential if we are to materialize immaterial labor. I asked developers to show me how it felt to work at Desire as a playful workplace. They were free to take photographs of any object or space and use them to talk about their feelings. Their photographs are not in the book, but I will describe them in detail. Deploying photography is methodologically productive because immaterial labor is not only performance *by* the self but also performance *of* the self within highly aestheticized and individualized cultural economies. In addition, photography gives life to objects and spaces that are invisible to the researcher. Relations of work that are lost in and between these objects and spaces are revived. Thanks to photography, how bodies work and move between such objects and spaces becomes intelligible to the researcher. The following narratives will reveal emotions that emerge in and outside the workplace and demonstrate how they are located in between the game developers' bodies and the office chair, the blank wall, the computer, or a crack in the parking lot.

Emotions at Work

When I asked game developers to show me how they felt as they worked at Desire (Warren 2002), I was mostly expecting to receive images of glamor that reflected the dominant imaginations and representations of game development. I was wrong. The photographs taken by the game developers reflected quite ordinary objects and invisible spaces.

The first volunteer was Michael, the studio's design director at the time. Michael had a degree in English literature. He was interested in playwriting, for which he enrolled in a master's degree in Ireland. Following that, he came back and entered a PhD program at the University of Minnesota in theater historiography. He had finished two of the three preliminary exams and moved to where Desire was located. He was planning to work on his dissertation from afar since his wife had moved there. He worked at some teaching positions, but at some point, Michael decided that he was "tired of being in school and the academic lifestyle" because he "wanted to write plays not scholarly articles." At the time, Desire was looking for a writer. Michael applied and was hired in 1998.

Michael brought a photograph of a blank office wall to discuss his emotions about work. While taking the photograph, he had sat on a chair as if he was positioned to lead a meeting at a large table. This table was big enough to seat ten people. In front of him was a keyboard and a remote control. As we went to this meeting room to discuss the photograph, Michael said that the white wall was a "canvas" on which they projected other images, carried out a teleconference, made a presentation, and organized a meeting. As he emphasized, "there is nothing interesting or inherently interesting in and of itself," but for him, it was still "a space of potentiality." He said:

> We are . . . creating things out of nothing; we are . . . creating these experiences and these desires before people even know that they had them till they started playing the game. I picked this room in particular because that's the room where we have—every Friday morning from ten until twelve—this process we call studio design groups. . . . Each group is also focused on coming out of the process with some kind of a deliverable, something that can be shared with the entire group. . . . How do you

create a cohesive design culture at a studio when everybody is . . . out doing their own thing, their project stuff, and doing their project work? Creating a space and opportunity for people to . . . get together and talk about their experiences and their thoughts about design.

Looking at Michael's photograph makes one assume the role of the design director. The empty white wall, which meant nothing to me, was where the desires of many other designers clashed and materialized or sometimes failed to do so. It was this wall on which affective and competitive encounters between developers took place.

The art director Theodor also kindly shared some photographs with me. One was his office chair right in front of his desk. The desk had a computer screen, a mouse, a speaker, a keyboard, a development kit, and a drawing tablet for his art work. Many Post-it notes floated around his desk. I asked Theodor what made him choose an old office chair. "I was joking with my wife because I was telling her about this project, and I was like, 'You know, I spend way more time in that chair than I have in furniture in our house,'" he said. And the more he described the workplace, the clearer it became that game development was indeed a "roller coaster" involving "constant influx," where one got "five hundred emails a day, or more, in certain times." He continued:

> Everybody needs to talk to you, or they need to just be able to. Just because you're on an email list, people assume that you've read and understand everything that's on there. I do the same thing. You know, you get cc'd on lots of things. Because, just in case, you cc something that's out of whack, you've gotta jump on: 'Hold on! I didn't realize we're doing this.' So, that's what I mean. When you look at Desire, it seems so laid back. You just walk around; people are . . . working at their desks, talking or typing. But then, I think there is this kind of other internal portion of, Desire, where it's just like this frenzy of activity.

Theodor's office chair signified a lot more than just some ordinary seat. It was an invisible space in which a lot of work was buried. Also, Theodor emphasized, it was the only thing, along with his mouse pad, that had not changed throughout his employment there, signaling the immense amount of change endemic to workplaces like Desire. He said: "My mouse pad and my chair have not changed. My chair is actually a little bit falling apart. And those are the only things . . . It's not like you get assigned to an office and you're gonna be there forever. You're gonna move and move and move."

Theodor then took us out of the workplace, full of cables and technological devices, and showed me the photo of a crack in the parking lot. I was stunned. A crack from the parking lot ground? Theodor patiently explained:

It didn't really occur to me until I started thinking about this, but we had a meeting at two in the morning. I don't know . . . It was a couple of months ago. We really needed to get something by 10 A.M. the next morning. We're just gonna keep going until we're done. I'm sure other people do that. . . . It's just the way it works. There's this certainly association with the games industry that it's just part of the way it works. So, I wanted to get a picture of the parking lot at night. That's kind of what I wanted. You will see it at night. There are certainly people who have done crazy nights and certainly other game industry stories . . . things like that. I've done, I feel like, my fair share of crazy late nights, as well.

Again, an invisible and in fact unimaginable space had been integrated to cultures of overwork, where the crack evoked Theodor's stories of doing his "fair share of crazy late nights." Theodor was the most generous of all the developers who volunteered for this project, taking photographs of Desire's balcony, as well as chairs of a coffee shop where he and his colleagues took time off from an emotionally and bodily taxing labor process.

Finally, one artist took a photograph of his computer screen, which he described as his canvas, where he worked all the time. This canvas was also the material space that kept reminding him how much work he had to do, as well as other work dependencies that had to be completed before each milestone. Again, the computer screen is perhaps the most ordinary object one can encounter in a game studio or any other modern workplace. Game developers work with them, but their importance goes beyond what workers do with them. We should understand the computer screen and various kinds of software installed on it as agents of work that *do things* in the world. The artist's computer screen displays a list of pressing tasks and information about what tasks other members of the development team are completing. It is a sign of temporality as well as a sacred space that protects the game developers from the external world. The computer screen emerges as the space of immersion where feelings and moments of joy and frustration are accumulated.

Creative workplaces are engaging. They have to be. Nevertheless, what moves the laboring bodies within and outside the field of creative production cannot simply be reduced to glamorous objects that are increasingly the norm across creative workplaces. The tensions of an intense labor process are also embodied in ordinary objects and spaces that researchers may not always recognize. It is through the capture of such ordinary objects and spaces that we can grasp the flow of ordinary working lives, the material practices of working bodies, and the energy that these objects and spaces yield within an affective economy (Ahmed 2004; Bennett 2004; Thrift 2008).

In addition to the images presented above, the game developers also took photographs of a table on a balcony and a table outside a coffee shop to reflect their moments of escape from work. They came back to me with images of Pop-Tarts and coffeemakers from their office kitchen to point to the centrality of food to the studio culture. A momentary freezing of these ordinary objects enables us to observe the roller coaster in slow motion. It becomes possible to recover the emotional and subjective aspects of riding the roller coaster, which are either buried within objects or leak to spaces outside the studio.

"With Great Power Comes Responsibility": Flexible Work Temporality

On the agenda of my first meeting with Desire's developers were not only success stories to celebrate but also problems to eliminate. One major concern of the developers was crunch, but management mostly complained about overcommunication, a result of too many meetings and too much communication in general. This was an obstacle to productivity. The solution was a flexible work environment policy. In this flexible context, game developers—except for testers—were required to be present at the studio for only two hours. As long as tasks were completed on time, developers were free to work any time they felt creative. While they had practical reasons to be at the studio more than two hours and pretty much worked their regular hours anyway, the new policy gave them the freedom to go jogging during the day, take their kids to school or the hospital, or simply not work if they were not feeling creative.

Through this new policy, management aimed to address the peculiar difficulties of measuring, capturing, and harnessing the productivity of immaterial labor within digital networks. Almost all my interviews with management ended up with their targeted efforts to construct a diffuse work temporality: "How do you stick that [creativity] into a nine-to-five job, forty-hour-a-week job? It doesn't work in my mind. . . . People have creative moments. They might have them home; they might have them anywhere. Well, we want to keep that. We want to enjoy that. At the same time, we have to also make sure that dependencies and communication happen." Creativity indeed did take place outside usual workplaces and moments. For instance, the programmer Pipa once told me that he found himself coding as he was taking a shower.

In addition to overcommunication and concerns with respect to measuring productivity, crunch was another factor behind the switch to a flexible work environment policy. That's what the lead designer Robert, who has been making games since 2002, underlined. Robert had a degree in fine arts. A year after graduating, he started his position at Desire as an animator. Then he became the lead designer of their major franchise. For him, the new policy was devised "as a response to the company's first attempt at large-scale game production, double the size of their previous games." The policy was a way to address this big expansion in the scope of production. Robert said: "In the old days, it was always managed by hours. Are you in chair for fifty or sixty or eighty hours? Eighty hours was always the worst. It's like you can't do more than eighty hours, and it's counterproductive. Overtime—it's just not healthy. What we want to do is we are not gonna be able to get away from that. We are gonna have to ask for more work in a short period of time. That's just life. That's what our business is about."

Desire's developers welcomed the flexible work environment policy. The senior developers in particular enjoy these spaces of freedom mainly because they have been embedded within production networks long enough to embody institutional and professional knowledge. With a neoliberal and technomasculine tone, Matthew highlighted how the policy got "team members personally interested and invested in the welfare of the project." For him, such a work environment "supports and nurtures developers' natural desire to produce good work," and identifies the few "underperforming individuals" who "wither" and "fail without constant oversight." For him, "getting rid of people who cannot self-manage is actually a twofold win: not only are you eliminating a subpar performer, but you are also eliminating the cost of managers having to constantly watch over that person's shoulder." Robert also pointed to the ameliorative functions of the policy: "If they do fail their goals, then they're directed on how to change their behaviors or the appropriate repercussions occur to make sure the issue isn't repeated."

Not every individual can easily handle this flexibility. I once talked to James, a programmer who was laid off in 2011. We met in a coffee shop. He had started his job in 2006. With his friends, he went to a game developers' conference and attended a party that Desire organized. He did some networking and then applied for a position. Before the interview, he was given a test, the questions of which he didn't find quite relevant to what they did for their jobs. Ultimately, he passed the test, took the phone interview, and was invited to Desire for the final interview and started working there until 2011.

During our interview, I felt his discontent regarding the content that Desire produced. James didn't seem to have the dominant technomasculine attitude. He was also critical of the strict IP regime in the industry and firmly believed in sharing in creative production. As far as flexible work environment policy was concerned, he said: "It required me to exercise more self-control because I technically didn't have to get into work until 3 P.M." Perhaps he needed more oversight, an issue that Matthew didn't seem to think was necessary.

In short, management's cure to Desire's organizational expansion was the flexible work environment policy, which would ideally push developers to "feel more driven to get their work done." The goal was to capture surplus value through a diffuse temporality by granting autonomy and freedom to developers. It was also a pedagogical exercise involving the self-responsibilization of employees, who had to be on top of their tasks and schedules. The policy signaled a "stronger cultural change," where, as Matthew said, quoting Spider-Man, "with great power comes great responsibility." The ethical dimension of the policy was notable; productivity was defined as a matter of moral and individual responsibility. Seemingly "undermining" the expertise of project managers and empowering developers, the policy had relieved management of the responsibility to "babysit" the developers and invite developers to "take control of [their] lives," as indicated by the management. The flexible work environment policy, however, had to be accompanied by a spatial strategy: turning Desire into a playground.

Desire as Rebellious Playground

Desire is invested in providing a playful work environment for its workers. From their website to its interior offices, the studio promises and materializes an open, communicative, and personalized environment without cubicles. The desks and offices are fully customized, housing various items ranging from canned food to alcohol, family pictures, and game posters signed by the team. From the entrance to the farthest corners, the studio welcomes you as a rebellious playground. The posters of games produced since the early days of the studio are on the walls. The studio displays its historical record of production to foster pride.

Rooms where developers hang out, chat, and share ideas are comfortably furnished. Some rooms are flexibly constructed to perform such different functions as mobile video conferencing or presentations. There are showers in the studio for the use of developers during crunch or after jogging, also possible thanks to the flexible work environment. Certain days of the week are designated for special kinds of breakfast; free coffee and soda are constantly available. A kegerator with a joystick tap serves the developers when they crave beer. Drinking is an important cultural aspect of Desire; beer is served during team meetings on Fridays. If there is a new employee joining the team, he or she is welcomed with a big round of applause. Important milestones are celebrated with food and drinks. Food is particularly important during crunch. Holiday parties are organized, sometimes in the form of potlucks.

Developers are free to play games during their lunch breaks or simply when they feel like playing a game. Especially during crunch, playing games can be motivating for workers, who are reenergized before they go back to work. The studio has a game library, which can be used for research. Employees can check out films for inspiration, as well. There are arcade machines in the studio. I witnessed workers' passion about board games, which they play in designated spaces. The studio also has a poker table for those who love card games. Nerf gun wars do take place in the corridors.

These cultural practices in Desire's laid-back work environment constitute the "new spirit of capitalism" (Boltanski and Chiapello 2005). Work is so spectacular that it doesn't even look like work. It's fun, dynamic, and *feels* different than industrial work with its hierarchies, tedium, and dirt. Desire welcomes and celebrates a certain level of chaos and informality precisely because informality, communication, and playfulness potentially increase productivity in the context of creative production (Virno 1996, 15). By allowing recreative diversions and investing in the well-being of its workers, Desire incorporates even the most mundane characteristics of social life into production and amplifies life in a workplace that is no longer different from a living room, full of conversation, laughter, or leisure.

Such features of "good work" then become an integrated strategy to both control and harness the creative labor force. Seemingly two opposite actions— controlling and harnessing—converge to produce subjects who happily work long hours and do not say, "God, I have to go to work today," as Stuart told me when he described the spatial strategies of game companies. It is imperative for the management to turn the studio into a spectacular workplace, a "home away from home" (Albom 2013), to which they want to come back and keep working even when laid off, as a tester once said to me.

Learning to Perform Communicative Labor

Aside from the temporal and spatial practices of flexibility and playfulness, Desire's management is also invested in cultivating communicative developers based on an in-house training program. The goal of this program is to train a workforce that can quickly adapt to the changes demanded by management in an intense labor process where work blends with sentiment. Specifically, Desire at times acts very much like an MP3 player, where "the sequence of production can be varied at will" (Sennett 2006, 48). For instance, especially during the production of demos (for the media, the parent company, or the Electronic Entertainment Expo), developers form a smaller team to produce what the studio calls proof of concept (POC). POC refers to a vertical slice through which developers prepare a demo of the larger game and ask for a green light from the parent company.

The specific POC I examine below was scheduled for a visit from Digital Creatives. To produce a demo that would satisfactorily meet the expectations of the parent company, particular developers were realigned with new, different tasks. The routine production process was disrupted to prepare an outstanding demo for the visitors. Management constantly reminded the developers that the goal was to ensure that the visitors from the parent company would "walk away . . . feeling impressed," as the producer David put it in a POC meeting. To that end, a smaller team was formed. This team would work closely within an intense schedule. While this initial team consisted of about forty people, the studio could "add/ remove people as needed." In a way, POC represented a kind of state of emergency, because, for those developers working on it, POC work would take priority.

The first meeting started with icebreakers and jokes, but some exchanges quickly revealed its stressful and complex dimensions. One seemingly insignificant but pressing issue, for instance, was where the developers would work. Were they going to use the regular software or a spreadsheet for tracking tasks? How and when would the actual tasks outside the domain of POC be completed now? It was obvious that developers were excited but also nervous. The remarks of a developer made this clear: "All I wanna know is how much stuff there is left for me to do."

Another POC meeting was particularly telling in terms of the extent to which communication and developers' communicative capacities are vital to game development as a roller coaster shaped by passion. When two artists raised their objections about the scope of the new milestone, the producer David responded by saying that they were focusing on details. Then, the following conversation took place:

> ARTIST: No, these are not details but rather have to do with both the interior and the exterior.
> DAVID: [*A bit frustrated*] Plans change, Dominic; things change.
> ARTIST: OK, you drive it. Let's talk about it offline.

There were other creative clashes in the same meeting. Matthew said, "We're told PlayStation 3 is important and then told again that we can't have it. It is frustrating." David responded in a somewhat angry manner: "It is also frustrating to me when I hear people saying that they don't care about it." This was followed by another intense exchange between the lead designer Robert and an experienced programmer. When the programmer said a few words about the design department's work, the following conversation took place:

> ROBERT: Was there a critique of design?
> PROGRAMMER: The last time I checked critique was fine.

The programmer Pipa later confirmed that "this was not the best meeting" as "sometimes meetings do get tense like that." In such an emotional labor process, where tasks rapidly change, employees might lose sight of the project's broader vision unless efficient communication is established. Game development, as an assistant producer said, is "more of an orchestrated chaos; people working simultaneously on different missions and activities." In the middle of this chaos, the developers can get "overfocused on what they're doing" and not tell their colleagues what their needs are. This is why management wanted "people to care about the people around them."

How does one develop a culture of caring across game developers who ride this stressful roller coaster? Desire's response to this has been to implement an in-house training program called Crucial Conversations. Rather than simply being a top-down ideological drill, this program is aimed at improving the linguistic and communicative capacities of game developers so that they can handle intensities, tensions, and disagreements in an emotional labor process. The language and exercises of this training imagine communication as beyond simply exchanging words. Rather, as argued by Eva Illouz (2007, 19), communication is "a technology of self-management relying extensively on language and on the proper management of emotions but with the aim of engineering inter- and intra-emotional coordination." In fact, communication becomes inseparable from the laboring capacity of game developers, who are required to enhance their affective and linguistic capabilities to the maximum level, mainly because at Desire, as an informational workplace, communication and labor have become one and the same (Brophy 2008; Marazzi 2008, 17).

Crucial Conversations—also the name of the book assigned to the workers—is designed to train the developers to handle intense and necessary conversations and "clearly communicate" what they want. The training addresses those "crucial conversations" that the developers have with "opposing opinions, strong emotions and high stakes." For this training, participants read *Crucial Conversations* (Patterson 2002), watch videos together, discuss them, and engage in individual and group exercises. The studio teaches its developers to discover their natural tendencies and, for instance, ask: Do you get angry or shut yourself off during crucial conversations?

The first step in answering this question invites the developers to learn to get unstuck. According to the training, there is a scale within which human beings operate during such crucial conversations. This scale is between silence and violence. The developer should figure out where he or she stands on this scale and then work on his or her communicative laboring capacities. Apart from working on the self, the developers are also invited to focus on the "pool of shared meaning," which is about "trying to get information from yourself and others." Having crucial conversations doesn't necessarily mean one has to reach mutual agreements all the time. Rather, it is meant to ensure that everyone "contributes his or her two cents." "Anything less than total candor shrinks the shared pool, saps motivation, and dumbs down decisions," the tutorial says. Again, participation and communication become the motor of the labor process.

During the training, a video illustrated how this concept of "shared pool of meaning" worked. In this video, a boss was asking an employee to fulfill a task within an unreasonable amount of time, when the employee had already made other work commitments. This example sparked conversation about labor practices in the industry because the scene and the story were familiar. The HR staff in charge of the training somewhat naturalized this, saying, "It is the industry." The following advice, based on the training manual, was not to leave the conversations no matter how unreasonable the demands might be. The reason was straightforward. Leaving conversations or avoiding them is affectively and financially harmful to the health of the company and relationships within the team. In fact, having those conversations saves "over $1,500 and an eight-hour workday for every crucial conversation employees hold rather than avoid" (Patterson 2002, 13). In sum, being a good game developer was not just being restrained in emotional situations; it required having the right communication skills required by the profession. As a game developer, one had to also regulate her or his emotions because emotions, as the training underlined, burst out for reasons of survival rather than contributing to the shared pool of meaning or improving one's communicative labor power.

Crucial Conversations also aimed to teach developers to overcome their fears of being shut down, because in a creative environment, a fluent team had to be willing to challenge each other and not take criticism personally. As illustrated above, that was the message between Robert and a programmer during one of the intense POC meetings, where the latter reminded Robert how "critique" was essential to game development. In addition to providing critique and not taking it personally, Crucial Conversations taught the developers various skills in becoming effective and emotional communicators. These skills included "starting with heart, learning to look, make it safe, master my stories, state my path, explore others' paths and move to action" (Patterson 2012). Mastering these skills, the developers were told, would help them fix problems on the spot and enhance *communication as labor* and *communication with others*. The training taught the developers that they themselves were the best person to work on since they could change themselves. By regulating their emotions, they would be able to work on their own behaviors and learn not to blame others, thereby avoiding the production of toxic cliques at work.

The developers I talked to found the training useful. I visited the studio design manager Otis in his office. He told me that it was a good learning experience since he worked with a lot of people in design and it was important for him not to fall into the "sucker's choice." He practically benefited from some of the skills when he had a conflicting situation with another designer. For him, the training was useful also because people in the studio really needed to learn to "be vocal with the right people" and give constant feedback to each other. The training underlined the importance of constant questioning, critiquing, and being proactive when it comes to tasks and work processes, where there might always be alternative ways of doing things. He posed a widely applicable question: "Is it the best way to accomplish the high-level goal we're all trying to achieve?" Warren, a self-taught artist, drew attention to how the training was influential for teaching the skills to be a good team member since "no one here works in a bubble." "Being plugged in" is important, and the training taught him "where to look." Thanks to the training, he was able to effectively communicate with a fellow artist who was furious when he thought he was being overtasked.

Thus, as a pedagogical platform that targets the communicative and emotional capacities of game developers, this training serves a couple of functions in maintaining a smoothly working, profitable roller coaster. It invites game developers to constantly reflect on themselves in their ordinary work-related exchanges. In addition to working on their selves, the training puts a distinct emphasis on the shared pool of meaning and teamwork, ultimately asking the workers to think of their communicative and linguistic capacities as capital that needs to be monitored and invested in. By positioning the worker as "an active economic subject" (Foucault 2008), Crucial Conversations encourages Desire's developers to manage both their own emotions and other team members precisely because emotions, capabilities, dispositions, and affective relationships in a development team are all imagined as a form of capital to work through and invest in (Virno 2004, 12). In the name of collaboration and teamwork, Crucial Conversations ultimately targets the productive capacities of language and communication.

Desire's success has heavily relied on the construction of a flexible temporality, affective spatiality, and communicative subjectivities across the developers. To survive, Desire has to manage, measure, and harness the productivity of its employees. These practices—a flexible work environment, a playful workspace, and the in-house training program—reveal a strategic investment in the well-being of the game developers as the glamorous workers of the contemporary informational economy. Game developers are advised not only to display and communicate emotions but to also integrate these emotions into production. The developers are encouraged to become subjects who are proactive, self-responsible, passionate, flexible, and good team members. This self-regulation, however, is not imposed from above but rather activated through the discourses, spaces, and practices of freedom. In this sense, it is not that Desire's developers are simply duped; rather, they are active subjects who come into being through cultural practices that unfold in affective relations, spaces, flexible work policies, and digital machines. It is through the powerful constellation of these material forces that language, communication, and subjectivity all converge into labor, from which the extraction of surplus value is ideally maximized and rendered fun. Ultimately, what we are witnessing is an intensification of generalized and socialized creative labor.

I began this chapter by presenting the art director Theodor's metaphor for Desire as a roller coaster fueled by love. While this love became materialized in his office chair, it at times got buried within the invisible cracks in a parking lot. However, the actual space where this love is buried, enabled, and reproduced is the developers' houses, where their partners, with their classed femininities and domestic labor, sustain a whole studio.

REPRODUCING TECHNOMASCULINITY
Spouses' Classed Femininities and Domestic Labor

Right before the Christmas break in 2012, I was at Desire to interview Dan. It was a calm day. One could feel the holiday joy at the studio. Workers looked relaxed as they were enjoying snacks and beverages scattered around the studio. A white man in his early forties, Dan had started his career as a 3-D modeler in 1995. Around 2000, he joined a start-up where they had the budget for only three artists, which forced him to learn the roles of multiple positions. This ultimately turned Dan into a technical artist, his current role at Desire.

Dan was the only male in a family of four. He played a lot of games, whereas his wife was "not at all into video games." He was trying to get his daughters into video games, and his wife was "kind of grudgingly" letting him do that. During our conversation, Dan told me that when he worked at the start-up company prior to Desire, his wife resented how Dan would go and "hang out at the fraternity house for eight to ten hours" while Jill, his wife, would "go do her accounting job every day" and make less money. Dan did acknowledge his wife's point, saying, "From the outside looking in, I can see that, and we certainly did have fun." But at the same time, he would respond to Jill's criticism by proudly embracing the industry's technomasculine ethos around "working in the trenches": "Especially at the start-up company, we never missed the milestone; we never cut a feature. We worked our butts off at that little company."

On the one hand, Dan was hearing Jill's criticism regarding the technomasculine work environment in game development, which Jill likened to a "fraternity house." On the other hand, neither Jill's criticism about the gendered workplace culture nor Dan's former mentor's warning that he should do "absolutely no work" on Sundays and devote "his entire Sundays to the family" could help Dan put a clear boundary between work and life. Unfortunately, Dan confessed, he was "not there yet."

Dan's lack of presence at home brings us to the unequal politics of social reproduction outside the studio, because at the end of the day, somebody has to reproduce the laboring bodies of these "men in the trenches." In the case of Desire, women perform unpaid labor in a variety of ways: cooking for both the partner and his colleagues, taking care of the kids when daddy is gone, or bringing cupcakes to the studio during crunch to cheer people up. These activities reduce the costs that would have otherwise been undertaken by the studio. Such activities also ideologically reproduce the heterosexual family. Perhaps most importantly, these reproductive activities normalize the technomasculine work ethic and discourses of passion in the video game industry.

Interrogating the politics of Dan's "not being there yet" necessitates an understanding of how Dan's and his colleagues' passionate working lives are reproduced in the domestic space. To that end, I interviewed partners of ten developers (all white, eight married, two in a relationship, all working except for two) to answer the following question: What kind of classed femininities reproduce technomasculinity at Desire?

Scholars of video game studies have tackled the question of gender and sexuality by examining gendered forms of labor regarding hardware production and promotion (Huntemann 2013), postfeminism and indie game production (Harvey and Fisher 2013), queer gaming practices (Ruberg and Shaw 2017), industry's attempts to attract more female gamers through essentialized perceptions of womanhood (Chess 2015), and representation within game content (Alloway and Gilbert 1998; Downs and Smith 2010). Others have addressed the need to go beyond representation in gender analysis due to games' medium-specific features (Daviault and Schott 2015). Nevertheless, except for the infamous EA Spouse case, the reproduction of the industry's labor force has barely been scrutinized (Dyer-Witheford and de Peuter 2006).

A critical perspective on what happens at home when Dan and his colleagues "work their butts off" is important because love at work has a social cost. Deconstructing individualized and psychological notions of love and rethinking video game production through the lens of social reproduction requires examining the materiality of the domestic space, because as Silvia Federici (2012, 33) suggests, "far from being a precapitalist structure, the family, as we know it in the West, is a creation of capital for capital, as an institution that is supposed to guarantee the quantity and quality of labor power and its control." Desire's developers' homes are in fact factories where the workers, in this case developers' partners, produce human capital for Digital Creatives. In that regard, there is a dialectical relationship between the developers' technomasculine work cultures and the exploitation of domestic labor behind Desire's workforce. Cultures of overwork in the video game industry are in fact rendered tolerable thanks to the mobilization of women's emotional capacities at home (Reay 2004).

Exploitation of domestic labor is nothing new (Dalla Costa and James 1975; Federici 1975; Fortunati 2007; Jarrett 2016). However, compared to Silvia Federici's account of the witch hunt that expelled women from the public sphere, the field of game development as organized in Desire is different. First, most of the women I talked to are working and therefore not constrained to the domestic space for their livelihood. Second, the exploitation of women's domestic labor is exacerbated by the new communication practices that terminate the line between the workplace and home (Gregg 2011). In the digital age, women's emancipation from domestic work is still an unrealized goal. What Arlie Hochschild (1989) calls "the second shift" is still there and in fact coexists with the "fourth shift" of the post-Fordist economy (Adkins and Jokinen 2008), within which the sexual contract is being redefined and technologically mediated in numerous ways (Adkins and Dever 2016). Third, Desire's workers are different from their fathers. The women I talked to told me how their partners tried to share domestic work. They were willing to help. Finally, these men hold glamorous positions. In class terms, they are the envied subjects and desirable role models of the information age. With their valuable technical expertise, they are the "superdads" (Cooper 2000). That is, performing domestic labor is partly alleviated by the fact that video game development is a cool job with such perks as international travel. In sum, there are different, if not completely new, aspects of how women's domestic labor is exploited in the context of Desire.

The classed subjectivities of women can simultaneously be an exploited resource (domestic labor) and a symbolically legitimate form of cultural capital (the good, caring, compassionate middle-class mom). Their subjectivities are classed because in contrast to working-class women, these women are able to mobilize a relatively large amount of support and resources during crunch. For instance, in addition to relying on external family, they have the time to take their kids to a park so that they can see their fathers, who can briefly take a break from work. These strategies require time and certain forms of knowledge, capital, and capabilities to mobilize in the first place.

What is particularly important is that these classed subjectivities intersect with femininities that are ambivalent and flexible (Skeggs 1997; Vijayakumar 2013). While these women endorse the neoliberal rhetoric of choice and aspire toward a relatively glamorous middle-class lifestyle, they also mobilize a critique of the exploitative work practices and technomasculine production logics. These classed femininities are ambivalent and flexible because although these women don't necessarily critique the heterosexual family unit, they are willing to confront how their reproductive labor and emotional capacities are exploited by the industry. That is, the subjectivities of these women are never static because class and gender constantly and ambivalently intersect in everyday life.

Here, I define class in terms of how subjects are inscribed value within a given society. In continual formation, class is dynamically "produced through conflict and fought out at the level of the symbolic" (Skeggs 2004, 5). So, on the one hand, class is about the present and involves a struggle around how respect is redistributed in that present. That is, the women in this chapter are the respectable partners of the desirable subjects in our ludic economy. Respectability is a fundamental marker of their classed femininities. It shapes their desires and how they speak, act, and classify themselves and others (Skeggs 1997). On the other hand, class is not simply about the present. It goes beyond how respectability, salaries, or economic possessions define the present. It's also about everyday cultural practices of hope and imaginations that temporally extend beyond the present and toward the future through aspirations (Hage 2003).

The women in this chapter practice hope in their everyday lives. They refuse to be seen as powerless because they are able to suggest alternative systems of value, work, and life. Their identities are not simply limited to the position of being "the caring" woman. They are also classed agents who struggle for power in a symbolic economy. They are not just objects through which the industry or game developers accumulate capital. These women have strategies and are in fact also capital-accumulating subjects. For instance, when one of these spouses speaks fondly of the technical skills that her husband will pass on to their children, that implies hope and a strategy of cultural capital accumulation.

Again, these classed femininities are ambivalent. On the one hand, they undertake extra labor that they regard as personally fulfilling and important for the unity of their relationships. On the other hand, this extra labor is to be situated within the circuits of capitalist production since it produces not only use value for maintaining the relationship but also surplus value for the studio by reducing the potential reproduction investments to be undertaken by Desire. At the same time, even if these women are exploited, they are not only resources of domestic labor but also invest in a classed future flavored with the promises of the glamorous profession of their partners.

The classed femininities of Desire's developers' partners become visible in various ways in their everyday lives. On the one hand, game development's glamor partly alleviates the burden of women's domestic work. On the other hand, developers' partners still reproduce an entire workforce and industry especially during crunch. Women's domestic labor is further intensified because mobile technologies increase game developers' 24/7 availability. Nevertheless, developers' partners, perhaps even more than their husbands and boyfriends, are quite vocal against the industry's technomasculinity, the discourse of passion at work, and the precarization of their very own middle-class lives related to the reality of working for a publicly traded company. Although these women were overall not unhappy about Desire's treatment of its developers, they still had a more skeptical view toward passionate work, suggesting that the association of love with work needs to be taken with a grain of salt. The narratives of these women reveal how developers' love at work is not necessarily an intrinsic but a material force rooted in the gendered regime of ludopolitics.

Glamour at Work: "What Male Wouldn't Wanna Get in and Make Video Games and Say That's What He Does for a Living?"

Despite their criticism regarding Desire and its male-dominant workplace culture, the partners of the game developers I talked to almost unanimously emphasized the "cool factor" associated with their significant others' jobs. The first person I met to discuss how developers' partners experienced game industry's intense work practices was Jill. In her late thirties, Jill worked as an accountant. At first, she wasn't quite sure how her thoughts would be of use for me. But we managed to secure a time after 5:00 P.M. and met at a coffee shop. The first thing she mentioned was how she was "very proud" that her husband Dan had "found a niche" in the industry and was on the board of directors of the Game Developers Conference. When she told others that her husband made video games for a living, the response was immediately, "Oooh, that's cool," to which Jill replied, "I count money. Yeah, he has the cool job."

I also talked to Isabel, who was married to a longtime Desire employee. I reached Isabel via email, and it took a couple of days before she was able to get back to me. As a forty-year-old stay-at-home mom, she took care of the kids and attended various charity-related activities, but she graciously agreed to an interview. She apologized for skimming emails in her phone, but it would take time for her to get back to them on the computer, since she had to share it with three children who played Minecraft along with their dad.

This was a very emotional interview. Isabel had met her husband back in college. And as she was describing their college days and her partner's involvement with work, Isabel burst into tears. She got very emotional as she described the time she saw the poster of a game that her husband had made. Isabel was very family oriented. She was glad that her husband had "great skills and computer knowledge that he could pass to [their] children."

I also had the chance to talk to Mary (white, midthirties), who was married to a project manager. She had a PhD and was looking for a job. When I asked her what it meant to be married to somebody in the game industry, she told me that her "nephews absolutely love it." It paid "well"; the benefits were good, and ultimately, they had "a nice lifestyle" tied to the good salary.

The issue of lifestyle came up in almost every conversation. I met Sabrina in a coffee shop located on the outskirts of the city. With a degree in environmental communication, she had been working as a public program coordinator in the city for about five years and dating an assistant producer—Vincent—for two years. In fact, Vincent was fired just a month after they first met. For Sabrina, the coolness of her partner's job was very important. "They throw great parties," she said and added that Desire's reimbursement of taxi fares for the Christmas party was terrific. The fact that Desire allowed Vincent to travel a lot and sent him abroad to promote their game was a major perk, and thanks to this, Vincent "interviewed on Paris TV." Dating Vincent, Sabrina got to hear "behind-the-scene stories" and was able to appreciate "how deep video games are."

I once interviewed Mona, again in a coffee shop. She had met her designer boyfriend when they played softball a year ago. Before meeting him, Mona didn't know much about the game industry, as there was no game studio where she grew up. She found game developers "kind of nerdy" as they were "big into electronics" and they had to have "state-of-the-art technology, an iPhone and an iPad." She mentioned how her boyfriend knew people in the movie credits or music albums as he went to school with them. She also emphasized how her boyfriend and her colleagues were proud about what they did and said things like "that feature was something I came up with," giving hints of the technomasculine work practices. Like Sabrina, Mona too enjoyed the "awesome parties" and overseas trips. However, she was also at times frustrated. "I want for one day that people ask my job, I say middle school math teacher and people react, 'Oh my God, that's amazing,'" she said, adding teachers "barely get anything." In sum, these narratives reveal how women were happy that their partners were doing something they loved and were also impressed by how the studio compensated their partners' labor with material and symbolic benefits.

But then, perks like free food, flexibility, and fancy offices have been around for some time in the new media industries. As Sabrina underlined, new media companies like Desire have to make the lives of their employees enjoyable by, for instance, throwing "great parties," especially because their employees work so hard. However, Desire also specifically organizes various meetings and activities for the spouses. Surely, Desire cares about these women, but at the same time, organizing special events for the spouses reveals the political dimension of what these women mean and do for the studio. Desire, in other words, has recognized how valuable these women's domestic work has been to its own success and workers' well-being. It is imperative for Desire and the industry in general to please the hidden workforce—women—to maintain profitable business practices, because, as the EA Spouse case revealed, the domestic space "may be the terrain of a social struggle" (Federici 2014, 87). Women's refusal of domestic work can significantly shape the future of the industry, demonstrating again how social reproduction is a valuable tool in expanding our intellectual horizon to grasp these perks beyond the framework of governmentality. Parties, overseas trips, and flexible work environment policies for the workers themselves can help only so much because practices of overwork, which adversely affect the domestic space, are not easily avoidable given the persistence of crunch, new communication technologies, and the enduring technomasculine work ethos.

Gendering Passion and the Cost of Cool: "It's Kind of Like Being a Single Mom"

In his discussion of crunch and passion surrounding game development, Casey O'Donnell (2014) argues that cultures of overwork spring from workers' immense joy related to the significant amount of discovery and self-reflexivity associated with work. While he does acknowledge the unfavorable working conditions that the EA Spouse case revealed about the video game industry, his otherwise convincing explanation of the ongoing adverse practices through "secrecy, closed networks of access, and use of the state to discipline those networks" (20) partly misses the gendered dimension of passion, or what he calls the "deep hack mode" (161). Understanding creative work primarily through "being driven" limits our focus to the singular experience of game developers and their consciousness rather than a materialist approach based on gendered relations of class. Explaining the persistence of passionate work primarily through the notion of being driven might be dangerous. As Karen, wife of the artificial intelligence programmer Pipa, reminded me during our conversation at the studio: "I don't think that they think they work too much. Their wives think otherwise." In that regard, gendering "the deep hack mode" is critical.

Throughout our conversations, the first disadvantages that developers' partners named were "crunch" and "the odd hours." Even though the partners did not necessarily rant about Desire's work practices and were generally happy about Desire's more-or-less predictable crunch schedules, they unanimously emphasized the invisible labor that they undertook during crunch.

I met Gina through her husband, Ronaldo, a technical artist. She was a tall woman in her early forties. Gina's critical thoughts about game work came like big ocean waves every time she opened her mouth, partly because Gina was professionally involved in IT services and considered herself to be "pretty much a history of the internet." Because of her history in IT work and through her marriage to Ronaldo, one of the longtime employees at Desire, she witnessed the different waves of crunch at the studio.

Gina had a witty and gendered analysis of the industry. She considered the video game industry to be a "young, single, nerdy male industry, which means I got nothing better to do anyways." She remembered that during the early days of Desire, her husband and his colleagues "would sleep at the office and they would not come home for three or four days. And they would only come home to shower and make sure the cat was still alive, maybe."

Gina's description of crunch revealed how "passionate work" was experienced differently across genders. I asked her "what happens at home when studio crunches?" And she jokingly said: "Well, it is a good thing you ask to me because he sure as hell wouldn't know—he is at work. I am a single parent. . . . But yeah, it is like living with a roommate, a college roommate. It's like we see him occasionally. . . . 'Hey, yeah, I remember you.' . . . There is this person who lives in our house, and we occasionally catch glimpses of him, or there might be . . . socks in the hamper, and I didn't put those there. Oh, there's a cereal bowl; he must have had a snack before he went to bed."

Like Gina, Isabel was married to one of the longtime employees, but she seemed to be more tolerant toward crunch than Gina. She witnessed and helped with Desire's evolution. I say "help" because during the early days of the studio, Isabel at times would cook for her husband and his colleagues, who "would work around the clock, come, eat, hang out." Isabel found this to be fun as she "was glad to see them." Yet at the same time, her husband's passionate, hard work would sometimes cause "resentment," and she "would be so hurt." At the end of the day, however, Isabel's love and the sacrificial labor would overcome feelings of resentment: "I would have given up anything to do that [marrying him]. And the most important thing for me was he has to be happy with what he's gonna be doing. Because he can be very serious, solemn and grumpy. And if he is not happy at work, that comes home."

I interviewed Judith via Skype. Married to an assistant producer, she was working as a principal at the time. They had two kids and were living in a relatively big house ten miles away in a different city. Echoing Gina and Isabel, Judith said: "It's kind of like being a single mom and working full time. And that's not his fault. It just makes it hard on everybody when he is so busy." Even though the flexible work environment policy did help, crunch was not Judith's "favorite time by any means."

Emma used to be a teacher in California and quit her job after her husband, the producer David, was offered a position at Desire. Emma was the only woman I was able to interview in their house. As we were doing the interview, her two kids were playing together. Their scattered toys, along with an Xbox in the living room, revealed the hard work of being a stay-at-home mother. Emma's experience of crunch depended on geography and the status of her relationship because when they were living in California, they were not married but living together. Life in California meant long commutes. Her first crunch was very hard because she was "used to seeing him in the evenings and on the weekends. And he had a very long commute." Crunch was still hard for Emma in the current context, but she found it relatively easier now that they were living in a more manageable city and she was a stay-at-home mom.

These partners have developed various strategies to endure crunch. The primary strategy has been the inevitable deployment of domestic labor. Before laying out the specific forms that this unpaid labor takes, it needs to be underlined that performing unpaid labor is not temporally limited to crunch. Women start performing extra labor, for instance, from the very moment they consider relocating for Desire. Although others have not specifically mentioned it, this was the case for Emma. Before they left California, she emailed back and forth with other women whose partners worked at Desire. They exchanged information with respect to cooking, parenting, schooling, seasonal things to do, and other issues traditionally considered to be women's responsibilities.

When it comes to crunch, the "unity of the family" is the overarching ideology that organizes women's performance of domestic labor. Back in the day, for instance, "at the weekends I would drive and meet him [her husband, then boyfriend] for lunch so that we got to see each other. It was a month or two of not seeing each other. It was very hard," said Emma. This was when she was a teacher. After moving and getting married, Emma quit her job to become a stay-at-home mom, bringing kids into the equation: "I would take my daughter, pick him [her husband] up at work. We would go have lunch at the park. My daughter would play with him, great time of her day. It was even better than letting him come home for dinner. We did that almost every day during crunch time." Of course, the unity of the family under consideration here is a middle-class family, involving classed cultural practices and affordances, such as being able to quit the teaching job, drive kids for a play date with the dad, and the informational infrastructures and class investments that enable such practices.

Emma was aware of these class privileges. As she emphasized, this was "a luxury" because she wasn't working. Thanks to her class privilege, she was also able to take the kids to their grandparents "so that he [Emma's husband] could focus on work, and I was able to be with the kids." Unpaid domestic work is not simply about arranging and implementing these practicalities. There is much quasi-therapeutic consoling involved in helping the game developer partner go through crunch. As Emma said, "For him, it's more like personal stress. With us, it's more about me encouraging him, 'Take time for yourself. Make sure you play racquet ball. Don't worry about that person or thing. You're doing your job.'"

Although crunch is not as much of a burden for the unmarried couples without children—such as Sabrina and Mona—"the odd hours" and crunch did have an emotional impact on all women. Married or not, partners of all the game developers deployed similar strategies to sustain the relationship, such as seeing their partners at work or scheduling dates for lunch or dinner. In sum, when men passionately worked at the studio, it was women as the invisible domestic workers who kept the emotional budget and infrastructure of their relationships, ultimately supporting a whole industry through various strategies and means.

"Even Though He Is Home, He Is Not Really Home": When the House Becomes a Factory

In addition to crunch, Desire's employees' partners brought up "presence bleed," the novel, exciting, and pressing ways that work intrudes in our everyday lives beyond the regular work schedule and the formal workplace (Gregg 2011). Working from home was like a necessary evil. Women considered it to be a double-edge sword tied not only to new information and communication technologies but also the developers' passion for video games and the necessity to play video games for research. While the amount of and reason for working at home varied across developers, the partners of the developers had complicated feelings regarding homework.

As a teacher, Judith herself was used to the idea of working at home, but her partner's relationship with online technologies required more of his presence. "At times it's beneficial, but other times you can't get away from work. I think it would be nice at times just to be away—completely away from work," she said.

I talked to Patricia twice over email. Her case was different from all the other women because her programmer partner had been working from home for quite some time. They were living in a different city, meaning that home was the primary workplace, which allowed Patricia's husband "to help out and spend time" with the family. This particularly worked well during crunch: "Crunching from home does allow for him to take breaks to spend time with family that he would otherwise not get if at an office." Yet the spatial flexibility becomes a disadvantage "simply because he is always at his office," making it harder to get him "to quit work and move on to family activities." Despite the favorable flexibilities it introduced, working through virtual private network (VPN) posed major problems for Patricia:

At times I feel it is great that he is working from home because he is able to spend time with our son, and he is able to help me out. For example, if I need to go to the gym, doctor, or run an errand, he can watch our son; in that regard, it works out great. Before we had a child, there was no real advantage for me to have him working at home. His job now seems more ingrained in his life now. He checks his emails often, and it seems a bit—for a lack of a better word—insensitive at times. . . . I have often tried to discuss with him that he does have a life/responsibilities outside of work. I have the biggest issue with him having 24/7 access to his job on the weekends, holidays, or vacations. There has not been a day that I can remember that he has not done some type of work. . . . I try to explain to him that holidays and vacation time are supposed to be spent relaxing and not working. He just does not get this.

Patricia was particularly bothered by her partner's readiness and passion to work and thereby ignore the family: "I think he gets easily sucked back into work now that he has constant access to his job. Yes, it bothers me a great deal that he has constant access to work. It feels at times that work is his priority, and time with his family is something that happens if he gets a chance." Gina, who has professional IT experience, shares Patricia's feelings:

It's annoying especially on weekends. We had to make a deal that if the kids are awake, the computer is off. I can't stop him from checking email or doing things on his phone; he might as well have the goddamn thing grafted to his hand. You will never have his complete attention unless you demand it. I understand the need to work from home occasionally (probably better than most spouses as I'm in the IT industry myself and have been for years, and on call since 2000), but it can get strained. Still, better at home than at the office because then I'll occasionally be able to see his face/spend time with him.

For Gina, the blurred temporal dimension of work is a serious problem. "It's annoying as fuck and stupid on our part. Just because you can be available 24/7 doesn't mean you should. . . . How can you call it a weekend when the week never ends? How is it a vacation if you're on call?" she said. Rather than liberating the worker, working from home seems to have leaked passion outside the workplace, colonizing the most intimate spaces in the lives of these families. Due to the ubiquitous connection practices, alienation now defines not only work relations but also intimate relations. For instance, Sabrina's assistant producer partner Vincent "works a lot from home" because "it is easier for him." During those times, "even though he is home, he is not really home," she said.

Given Sabrina's statement, the contemporary context has obliterated the distinction between home and workplace, turning the lives of the game developers into a factory (Negri 1989) where every place and moment is a candidate for value creation. When the game developer is outside the studio, work still continues but only on the condition that domestic infrastructures are arranged in a gendered manner. So, while working from home does have advantages, it also integrates intimate relations directly into the labor process, since spouses too have to rearrange their spatial and temporal practices to accommodate the demands of an intense and diffuse labor process. Yet women are not silent about how work invades their private lives.

Women React: Critique of Technomasculinity, Insecure Work, and Labor of Love

It varied in terms of intensity, but the critique of the industry as a "fraternity house" was not an uncommon thread among the developers' partners. Jill called it "a fraternity house because in the fraternity they do have to do schoolwork, but there is a lot of horseplay. There is a lot of Nerf gun, and there is a lot of not-work-related conversations that happen." Having witnessed her partner's employment at different studios, Jill said that while different workplaces have different cultures, "the frat house mentality carries through."

Just like Jill, Gina regarded "the video game industry as a whole very much a boy's club." She agreed that while the population at Desire over the years has changed, where "it's a lot of middle-aged married men," "the industry as a whole hasn't." Isabel concurred with Jill's perception of the fraternity house, "except it's a maturing one." She also thought that the playful work environment was necessary as it "keeps an artistic or open, light environment that they need after as hard as they work."

Partners' criticism of technomasculinity was not restricted to the spatial limits of the studio because it leaked beyond Desire. When families from Desire get together, developers at some point form their own gendered space, "talk shop," and move toward the console, as a developer's partner indicated. "They talk a lot about what they're doing," Sabrina said.

In addition to technomasculine work practices and their leakage into socialization spaces at home, these women also criticized the precarization of their middle-class lives despite their partners' passionate work and their own reproductive labor. They were not happy about the insecurity related to the parent company's financial position. When Digital Creatives first bought out Desire, "it was good," and "we benefited from it," but later the situation "got worse and worse," said Isabel. While she was overall confident that her partner's position at the studio was "very secure," she highlighted that the "last two years have been wavy."

For Mary, who was looking for a job, the decline of Digital Creatives "was very stressful." Even though her husband's job paid well and the benefits were good, the fact that "you need to be the best" in the market to survive was a point of concern as consumers in a financial crisis were much more selective in their purchasing habits.

When I asked Mona how she felt about the declining financial conditions, she pointed to "job security." Finding her partner's job unstable, she said: "Teaching is a very stable career. I have tenure. With him, any studio can close any time. He's been at studios that closed down. Two times in the past he had to travel across the country." Mona continued, saying that her partner was "OK with that" as he had "the mind-set" and was "open to that." While not necessarily accepting the idea of uncertain working and living conditions, Judith said, "I feel like we've been on this roller coaster before. We know that this industry has ups and downs. We've seen the good times and the not-so-good times." Isabel considered the industry to be "a meat grinder."

I once met Emma in a park. It was the beginning of summer, and she had organized a play date with another spouse from Desire. As we sat on the grass, her kids kept coming from the pool, where they were entertaining themselves. After she reminded her kids that I was Mr. Ergin, who had previously come to their house to discuss their daddy's work, Emma commented on Digital Creatives: "I will say it's frustrating hearing about bad decisions Digital Creatives has made. Because it sounds like, gosh, they need to get their act together. The studio has their act together. Why can't Digital Creative get their act together?" Like Mary, Emma also initially assumed the game industry to be recession-proof, but her opinion changed over time. She now saw that the crisis "did affect Digital Creatives because people didn't have disposable income" to buy all the games they desired and had to be more selective. That is, the financial crisis was looming over the industry, and the effects of precarization did not go unnoticed in developers' houses.

Game developers enter the industry aware that it is a risky environment. Partly, it is their love for video games that keeps them in the industry. But according to their partners, passion and love may not intrinsically be healthy, and critique is necessary. I was interviewing Karen at the studio. Her husband Pipa kindly introduced us and left the room so that we could talk. The first thing Karen said about Pipa was "He's very analytical" as she discussed why they decided not to relocate to Canada when they were offered a position there during the days she interviewed. They had made a list of things to figure out for the kids, their dance classes, and other activities. As a family of five, they found the offer to relocate to Canada "insulting." Without a college degree, Karen was the most concerned among the women about the precarization of their lives. You could feel this anxiety based on how she detailed their strategies for shopping at the cheaper grocery stores. Karen was also the most critical woman when it came to pay and the long hours. For Karen, "when you really think about how much he works, like hourwise, he makes like nothing." Her criticism about the positioning of love as a prerequisite for employment was sharp:

> The love of it is a problem. Actually, you can almost love your job too much. Because he is here all the time. And that's expected. It is extremely expected. You are expected to come in early, stay late. Come in on Saturday. Come in on Sunday. Work from home. And when you are not working, you should be reading about games. If you are not reading about games, playing games. If not playing games, looking, buying a new game. You have to be constantly in the game world. Otherwise you'll be left behind. For the home life, that's a problem. Because it's too much. There's no time left.

Jill and Isabel also raised important questions regarding the gendered dimensions of love at work across creative industries. Still operating within the boundaries of a traditional family unit, Jill said: "When you are dying, do you really care that your title was VP, or do you care that you have a wife and children?" Isabel, also operating within the limits of the heterosexual family, agreed, demonstrating compassion for an average single worker in the industry: "I just don't think that's healthy. I think they need some outside interest. You need to get out of the office. That will save you. It's hard if they're single. And they're young. They'll never meet anyone." Both Jill and Isabel's remarks operate on the dichotomy between love toward work and love toward a significant other and a family, preferring the latter to the former.

Going back to Kylie Jarrett's (2016) useful description of unpaid domestic work as both a source of exploitation and a socially enriching experience, partners of game developers are critically aware of and react to conditions of self-exploitation. Rather than simply naturalizing gender roles, they reflect on what necessitates their domestic work and critically address it. They disapprove of how the perpetual production dynamics in the industry significantly affect and lead to precarity in their lives. Perhaps most importantly, while enjoying the status associated with game development as creative work, they are critical of the instrumentalization of love and passion and point out how the drive for work might be too infinite a resource to deploy.

Just Live with It?

The journalist and gamer Nicole Tanner (2011) once wrote an editorial for IGN (the video game and entertainment website), where she used to work as an editor. Titled "The Real Housewives of Game Development," the editorial unsurprisingly starts off with a discussion of the EA Spouse case:

> Since this case was settled out of court, it's hard to say for sure whether EA was legally doing anything wrong, but this whole event has led to a growing tide of angry wives (unfortunately game development is still largely dominated by men) jumping on the bandwagon and berating companies for what is actually pretty standard process for making a game. As the wife of a game developer myself, I'm starting to become skeptical that these women are really more concerned about creating a fairytale life for themselves than they are about supporting their husbands' dreams.

While it is hard to understand how and why settling a case out of court would legally clear any party of wrongdoing, Tanner's prescription to other housewives of game developers was crystal clear: "it's time for the industry spouses to stop complaining and start supporting." EA Spouse is not the only case Tanner mentions. She refers to another letter written by a Rockstar employee's wife and depicts that woman's tone in the letter as "the sort of shrill whining you'd hear on the *Real Housewives* television shows."

Tanner's main point is that stress is not specific to game development and is in fact involved in every profession. For her, game developers are paid well, and once salaries are above a certain amount, they are exempt from overtime. Having laid out the legal context, Tanner then moves onto the core of the issue: love and meritocracy. "Most game developers wouldn't put up with the long hours unless they really, really love what they're doing," she writes. She knows this firsthand because Tanner's husband is a game developer, whose "passion is apparent whenever he tells someone about his current project." In Tanner's narrative, love and passion pay off because in their "13 years together," her husband "has moved from entry level designer to senior programmer, and we've seen our share of crunch times." Tanner does accept that she doesn't particularly enjoy crunch but then adds: "That's OK because this isn't all about me. I knew what I was signing up for."

As Tanner concludes, she has both good and bad news. The bad news is that "very few games actually get substantial amounts of either resources or time," and "crunch is practically guaranteed." The good news is that one can "learn how to take crunch times in stride," as well as stop "banging our [game developers' partners] heads against the wall trying to change capitalism." The solution is not giving up on trying to reduce the hours for an improved work-life balance. For Tanner, "real life work balance cannot be defined in the number of hours spent here or there. It's the quality of those hours that counts."

In Tanner's somewhat classist narrative, perseverance seems to have paid off, but the extent to which this meritocratic dream is universally achievable is questionable. For instance, the wife of a game developer who used to work at 38 Studios in Rhode Island has a completely different story. I say "used to" because 38 Studios filed for bankruptcy in May 2012. In June 2012, this woman wrote a letter to the prominent gaming website Gamasutra. In the letter, she expressed her frustration about 38 Studios, for which her family abruptly moved to Rhode Island at the end of December 2011. They had to live in a hotel before they were able find a place of their own. Her kids were out of school until they found one. At some point, they did find a place and put their kids in their schools. However, only in their sixth month, her husband was laid off.

It soon became clear that this adverse situation had been anticipated by the executives, who kept promising the employees that they would be paid. In her letter to Gamasutra, she wrote, "Am I angry? You bet! I have been taken for a ride and am having to take a handout from the government for the first time in my life." Despite blaming 38 Studios for the situation, she then wrote that her "husband is interviewing daily thanks to an amazing industry trying to make up for what has happened" (Gamasutra 2012).

As an articulation of love, anger, exploitation, and hope, this disgruntled woman's letter has useful lessons for thinking about the relationship between the game industry and the women whose partners work in it. Perhaps rather than simply recommending to "stop complaining and start supporting" the husbands, there might be other ways to talk about the role of domestic labor in relation to the game industry. One useful strategy could be to insistently acknowledge that capitalism historically relied and still relies on women's labor for maximizing profits. For one, as this chapter demonstrates, women already support their husbands' work in the game industry—a lot. Another useful strategy might involve deconstructing the connections between domestic labor and the industry's libertarianism. Some women are deeply aware of this and are very critical of how the libertarian ethos renders the social and gendered dimensions of creative work invisible. Gina says:

> Here youth is king. It's youth and it is individuality. . . . It's up to me; I did it all myself, never mind the fact that I got financial aid and I had health insurance through my company, and my parents bought me groceries while I was in college and did my laundry. . . . No, I'm a self-made man. . . . And a lot of the problems, especially among like programmers and among the more engineering and scientifically inclined

people who, the intelligently savvy, professions . . . It's like, I'm too smart to have to rely on other people. Programmers sit in a dark room, by themselves, for hours and hours and hours, and they sink or swim by their own skills. As far as jobs, never mind that, . . . they might consult manuals or ask online or . . . have an IRC chat room they go to when they get stuck on a problem. No, it's me; I've done it all myself; this is my job; this my work. So they don't realize that . . . maybe if we banded together, we could . . . maybe get better hours if we decided.

These remarks are striking. Gina deconstructs the creative-genius myth in her struggle against the ideological pillars of libertarianism. She reveals how game developers' talent is in fact materialized on an unequal regime of ludopolitics that capitalizes on women's emotional and infrastructural capacities. Gina also suggests that collectivity, rather than individualism, can be a solution to the industry's structural problems.

Surely, this awareness at times goes also hand in hand with a neoliberal rhetoric of choice, legitimizing exploitation and alienation related to passionate work and crunch. For instance, as we discussed her husband's working conditions, Judith would say, "It's something you accept when you go into. That's the kind of choice you're making." It is right at this point that a reflexive intervention becomes possible and mandatory. If one is willing to frame game developers' working conditions as one of "individual choice," how willing are we to think likewise regarding Tanner's observation that very few companies give games the resources and time they need? Are they simply making a choice when allocating the resources and time to their workers? Or are they not passionate enough about their workforce?

One can make educated guesses regarding corporations' intentions, but that is not the point. One thing is clear. Desire owes its success partly to its developers' spouses' invisible labor. Behind the joyous moments players spend with Desire's games lay women's unacknowledged work both inside and outside home. It seems the unequal ludopolitical regime inherited from the media industries of earlier decades has not made much progress in the context of digital labor. Oppressive continuities with respect to gender outweigh progressive ruptures.

GAME TESTERS AS PRECARIOUS SECOND-CLASS CITIZENS

Degradation of Fun, Instrumentalization of Play

Nathan Peters (2013), a former video game tester (quality assurance, or QA), once wrote an article for the gaming site Kotaku. Entitled "Don't Sign That Contract," this piece received about a thousand replies, and due to its impact, it was also featured on the prominent Gamasutra site. In his article, Peters gave aspiring video game testers and developers some sobering advice: "Never accept a job as a contractor." Peters's story is informative in terms of highlighting the hierarchies, pains, and pleasures of video game testing.

First, perhaps even more than core development, video game testing perfectly fits the "do what you love" mantra. To a certain extent, game testing truly blends work and play and is a dream job for many. As Peters wrote, "who wouldn't want to play video games for money?" Second, video game testing constitutes a viable entry point for young (and older) people to find employment in the competitive video game industry, especially if they do not have the formal skills or educational credentials required for the more creative positions, such as programming. Peters, at the time when he worked for the development of *Halo 4*, "had no degree to speak of." He was aware that he "had to start back at the bottom of the ladder," but he was also confident and hopeful that if he "could get [his] foot in the door, within a year, whatever studio that hired me would realize that I would be quite an asset for their audio team." Having sent his résumé to more than fifty studios, Nathan Peters finally got an in-person interview at Certain Affinity in Texas. The studio hired Peters, whose first three months were "an absolute dream come true"; "the atmosphere was killer, laid back and super friendly."

Peters's remarks regarding the cool and laid-back work environment remind one of *Grandma's Boy*, the comedy movie about a thirty-five-year-old video game tester (Alex), whose life passion is to secretly produce his own video game: *Demonik*. In his Kotaku piece, Nathan Peters did not mention any secret projects, but he did have the hope and desire to become part of the audio team at the studio. And just like how Alex in *Grandma's Boy* worked on *Demonik* during his spare time, Nathan Peters too voluntarily blurred his work and leisure time. "Once, I worked an entire weekend on a voluntary basis," he said.

Given Peters's positive description of the work practices and work environment at Certain Affinity, one is left wondering why he ultimately calls "the gaming's contractors to strike" by not accepting the terms and conditions dictated by the game industry. Here is his answer: "It was like being Jon Snow or Theon Greyjoy under the Stark roof. Yes, people may talk to you, or relatively like you, but you are not accepted." Fans of *Game of Thrones* will understand what it means to be Jon Snow both under and outside the Stark roof. And even though fans of Jon Snow were all thrilled that he was revived by Melisandre, testers in the gaming industry may not be as lucky.[1]

As immaterial labor par excellence, video game testing blends work and play. The activity of play is not wasteful; on the contrary, it is highly productive in economic terms. Being an avid video game player is a key asset for finding employment as a tester in the industry. Testers develop their major employable skills through play and the blurring of both waged and nonwaged time (Charrieras and Roy-Valex 2008; Cote and Pybus 2011). Nevertheless, the experience of QA workers at Desire is a lot more intense than what we see in *Grandma's Boy*. Even though video game testing is an enjoyable stepping stone in the industry, it is a precarious position. Due to the perception that testing is a low-skill job desired by many young gamers who want to enter the industry, wages are depressed. The existence of an aspiring reserve army of testers outside the studio renders the employed testers at Desire a lot more expendable than the core creatives, thereby evoking sentiments of "second-class citizenship" similar to Nathan Peters's Jon Snow metaphor.

In chapter 4, I documented the work experience of video game developers as the exemplars of communicative laborers for whom there exists difficulties in control, management, and measurement of productivity. These game developers, I have argued, constitute a type of workforce for whom affective workspaces need to be constructed to harness their creative potential and capture economic value. As opposed to the more privileged and skilled developers, video game testers are decidedly younger and work under highly joyful but even more precarious conditions.

Understanding the precarious experience of testers is particularly important because what is missing from theoretical examinations of immaterial labor (Hardt and Negri 2000; Lazzarato 1996) is precisely their own account of this form of labor. In the first place, as Rosalind Gill asks with respect to new media work in Amsterdam, "what are we to make of someone who says they love their work and cannot imagine doing anything they enjoy more, yet earns so little that they can never take a holiday, let alone afford insurance or a pension?" (Gill 2007, 9). Second, except for a few studies (Briziarelli 2016; Bulut 2015), video game testers are barely visible in the field of game studies. Third, discussions of precarity in media industries have neglected the multiform nature of precarity (de Peuter 2010) or created a very dualistic picture where one ends up with either "technobohemians or net slaves" (Gill 2007). I thus foreground the experience of video game testers not only because they deserve it but also because precarity in the creative industries is a lot more complicated than what has been suggested so far.

In documenting the "playboring" (Kücklich 2009) experience of testers, and following Harry Braverman's (1974/1998) discussion of the separation of design from execution in industrial production and his concept of the "degradation of labor," I introduce the concept of degradation of fun to address how passionate gamers are alienated from play and develop a more selective and instrumental way of engaging with video games. It is evident that video game testing is a decidedly temporary position appealing mostly to young people, who are passionate about video games, have fewer occupational skills than game developers (a.k.a. the creatives), but enjoy being compensated in terms of the symbolic capital of having a cool job and access to the communicative networks of play.

Testers do what they love and hope that their temporary position will serve as a stepping stone into the industry, provide upward mobility, and lead them to better careers, such as full-time testing or programming and design. It is through what Lauren Berlant (2011) describes as "cruel optimism" that testers endure adverse working conditions where their passion for video games sometimes ends up being an obstacle to realizing this love. Reminiscent of how young and aspiring citizens struggle to find and hold onto glamorous positions in various media industries through aspirational labor in fashion blogging (Duffy 2017), hope labor in social media and sports blogging (Kuehn and Corrigan 2013), or apprenticeship labor for producing user-generated content (Shepherd 2013), game testers operate along the lines of what one might call the pendulum between dream job and dead-end job. When the youthful nature of the job is combined with the fact that performing this job requires relatively fewer occupational skills and can even be learned on the job, the outcome is degradation of fun, labor precarity, and the preservation of a large reserve army of labor. This depresses wages, disciplines the workforce, and limits the potential for organizing, precisely because testers, as one of them underlined during a conversation, feel "fortunate to have a job" in a highly unstable economic environment or even prefer this temporary—but still cool—job to jobs that come with higher wages and benefits.

Laid-Back and Surveilled Playbor Process in the Tester Pit

The tester pit is where QA employees test video games. It is a densely seated room where testers work with their development kits. Dim lighting is the norm in the tester pit; the testers want it. Yet the dense seating stems from the unequal structure of the labor process. Testers are more expendable than core creatives, so they are seated in a crowded workspace as opposed to the more spacious ones populated by the developers.

Yet there are other factors that alleviate such inequalities in the tester pit. There is a lot of joking and laughter. Some of the formalities and demands of regular workplaces are missing in the tester pit. One can see posters of games on the walls. There is a hoop for the testers to organize free-throw competitions during work. When I was in the pit one day, I saw a Nerf gun and asked the QA manager what that was about. He said that it belonged to a former employee and began shooting other testers in the room, causing some spontaneous laughter.

As the location where professional work values meet laughter, the tester pit is also the location where people are called by either nicknames or last names. It is not uncommon to see testers walking without shoes. The tester pit in some sense is an extension of the dorm room. As Cirose, a female temporary tester, put it: "This place becomes *a second home* at times and people have felt comfortable, or tired enough, to sleep overnight in the studio. . . . There are bathrooms equipped with showers that many employees frequently use before work and after and often during lunch. Many play sports or go to the gym during lunch" (emphasis mine). It is not uncommon to see canned food, beer, snacks, or soda next to development kits. Just like the dorm room, it is a setting where people work, play, and live. For instance, when *Call of Duty: Black Ops 2* was out, I was invited to a party in the tester pit where some of the testers played their favorite game in multiplayer mode, commented on the new aspects of the latest iteration of this major franchise, and enjoyed snacks and beer left over from an earlier party held during the day. As some testers were playing *Black Ops 2*, others were working on their project right next to them.

At Desire, testers are considered a support group as opposed to the core development team. During my time at the studio, there were ten permanent testers. The rest of the QA team was employed on a temporary basis, and their number fluctuated depending on the demands of ongoing projects. Even though testers were defined as a support group, Desire's developers did value them as a "key resource," as it was emphasized during a training session I attended. Testers' role in the studio was to help release a relatively bug-free game, or at least as bug-free as possible.

What kind of a job is video game testing exactly, then? The analogy between video games and websites that Eric, a permanent tester in his early thirties, made was useful in terms of defining the scope of testing a game for consoles. Games of earlier times in the history of video games would be a website of ten pages, whereas contemporary games produced by Desire are a "million page [website], even though, it may not be extreme." There are many complexities in terms of how artificial intelligence works in contemporary video games. In that regard, game testing is like "coming in and figuring out many different puzzles," as Eric said. And as it was emphasized during a training session for new testers who had previously worked at Desire and now were being rehired, figuring out these puzzles "can be a fun job, but it is still a job." Testing is structured along the lines of the capitalist labor process. As opposed to the friction-free workplace mythologized in mainstream accounts of the creative economy, the field of testing is not a free-floating playground. On the contrary, there are managers, supervisors, and strike leads.

Apart from this workplace hierarchy, there are guidelines, workplace codes, and attitudes that frame how testers should work. After the testers are given tasks with respect to what they should be testing, they need to be able to "put what [they're] doing in words," or else they are "just playing." In this sense, the blurring of work and play makes it necessary for testing to be defined in some specific ways so as to make this form of labor quantifiable and accountable toward the completion of specific goals in a limited time, thereby confirming scholars' criticisms of immaterial labor with respect to immeasurability (Caffentzis 2011; Dowling 2007; Hearn 2010).

Desire too deploys certain strategies and technologies to measure testers' productivity and surveil their actions in a laid-back work environment. A software program is used to streamline bug reporting and make the labor process quantifiable. Through this software, the studio collects and organizes information about bug reporting, bug severity, action taken, and bug status. This software enables all employees to see the status of bugs and the priorities to address them. In this sense, the software acts like a technology of surveillance and registers everyone's work rhythm and productivity. Similarly, testers use spreadsheets where they report what missions they go through and when.

In addition to the formal and technological means of productivity monitoring, Desire resorts to more informal ways to surveil QA personnel. Even though

QA managers are not directly working with the testers, intermediary managers, such as strike leads, simply wander the tester pit to see who is really working or "dicking around." Testers also compete against each other, which ensures productivity through peer pressure and play. Melissa, a temporary tester, said: "It's lighthearted, it's not serious at all, but there is this sense of . . . other people are keeping a track, keeping track of other people at the same time. And usually at the end of the day, we joke around about who won for the day."

Peers can also report each other to their managers via their in-house chat system. Physical proximity matters, as Cirose mentioned: "It's . . . almost your neighborhood watch kind of thing. The person sitting next to you, if they see you doing nothing all day, they'll probably get on their nerves. Like every now and then, if you see someone just sitting on Facebook all day, which some people do, usually, I am pretty sure people will tell the strike leads."

Measurement of productivity also depends on what kind of testing is being done. When it comes to art testing, it is the bug numbers that determine the productivity of a tester. Sometimes, testers will compete and "brag about" their bug numbers. For an employee involved in multiplayer testing, gameplay testing, or rendering, it is the quality of the bugs rather than the quantity. In the latter case, the process is more complex than just providing a screenshot of the bug; it requires the tester to break the game to understand "what's causing this, how often it happens," or in which console platforms it happens. Being able to address these bugs requires testers to engage with game crashes and their complexity.

Aside from these tactics to monitor productivity, what I learned after attending the testers' training sessions was that disciplining a fluid labor force working in a laid-back environment required cultivating the "right attitude." Even though the tester pit is a fun place to work, having the right attitude while communicating with core developers is crucial. The testers have to be "constructively destructive." A desirable tester is one that can learn to break the game in creative ways, communicate them to developers, and inform developers about what impedes play in the game. In such a communication-intensive labor process, language is very important in terms of ensuring the smooth transmission of bugs and problems. Using the correct tense; giving accurate information regarding problems, actions, and locations; making complete sentences; and avoiding "I" (because it sounds accusatory) are crucial skills to possess as a tester.

Mainstream accounts of creative industries mostly present a picture where open offices enable a democratic labor process and a participatory work environment. Even though this is true to a certain extent, the level of QA's creative input as a support group is limited. Their ideas are valued but do not always have a great impact. While they do verify the state of the game and communicate this to developers and producers, it is the producers who decide on the direction of the game or which bugs to prioritize before fixing. At later stages of game development, game play, standards, and compliance are prioritized over art bugs since, for the game to be shipped, it needs to be playable and not crash.

My conversations with QA revealed how their support group status upset them not only in terms of monetary benefits but also because of not being able to participate in creative processes as much as they wished. Moreover, because they are a support group, QA is not able to fully benefit from the flexible work environment policy, because their status and location within the broader labor process requires them to be "available to be there for people," as I was told during a QA training session. This is not to say that the testers are not allowed to enjoy this policy. Rather, their flexibility is limited by their position in the labor process. As hourly and nonexempt employees, in the past, testers had to use physical punch cards to log their hours. Currently, they do this electronically but still cannot work from home like the core developers. Such limitations subject them to a more regimented labor process. In that sense, the immateriality of creative labor and its fluidity do not apply to the testers as much as it does to the core creatives.

Ultimately, the regulation of the labor process in the tester pit relies on a hybrid combination of formal procedures and cultural aspects that pertain to a playful workplace. Quantification through a software system and spreadsheets and the gaze of and competition with peers ensure a disciplined and productive workforce. Having won a brutal "hunger games" among a large reserve army of labor, testers find themselves in a competitive environment where they monitor themselves in terms of bug numbers and quality. The intensity of the labor process increases even further during crunch. In this respect, while the labor process entails moments of creativity and fun, it also includes repetitive and mind-numbing tasks. The playful environment alleviates the feeling of a more regimented labor process, but precarity prevails.

Precarity of Desire's Testers

As I have argued in this book, I consider precarity to be a hegemonic form of employment reinvented by the capitalist classes in their response to the crisis of capitalism rather than a brand-new feature. But it is also an existential experience at Desire. Moreover, precarity is not uniform and is constituted relationally through various processes, such as ownership of different levels of cultural capital and occupational skills, blurring of work and play, and swinging between pleasure and pain (de Peuter 2011; McRobbie 2004). In this sense, the precarity of testers is more acute than the precarity of the core development team. Then what conceptual framework do we have to understand the precarity of this marginalized workforce at Desire?

Within the context of the creative economy, Greig de Peuter (2010, 2011) suggests three personas within which precarity is embodied: the cybertariat (Huws 2003), the autonomous worker, and the precog. Within this trio, precog, a term derived from the struggle of an Italian activist who attempted to unite precarious service workers and cognitive labor in the media and education, is useful for illuminating the experience of temporary testers. As de Peuter (2011, 5) vividly describes, "the precog, in its bid to cope, can adopt dispositions that make it not only a victim of post-Fordist capital but also a model subject of it." Precogs are characterized by the following traits: "self-driven, passionate, commitment to work; willingness to work for nothing; perpetual and personally financed reskilling; habituation to material insecurity; obsessive networking, bold enterprising behavior . . . the precog is a pragmatic adjustment to flexploitation" (de Peuter 2011, 6).

In the case of Desire's testers, precog is conceptually powerful precisely because testers operate along the lines of hard work and play and epitomize the individual who aspires to get a permanent job in the industry. As self-driven workers, testers also bear witness to the demystification of play. On the one hand, they suffer from uncertain futures, but they also enjoy the laid-back work environment and greater financial compensation when they work overtime. They swing between zones of video game testing as a dream job and a dead-end job, embodying both pride in the profession and a simultaneous awareness of the hierarchical nature of their labor. Enjoying their compensation in terms of symbolic capital as they are doing what they love, testers see themselves as decidedly different from blue-collar or low-paid service workers. On the other hand, although they aspire to become members of the core creative team one day, they do not belong to that privileged club.

With their inconsistent and intermittent work histories, testers epitomize the most vulnerable workforce in the studio. However, they remain completely committed to their work. Even when targeted as part of a massive layoff in 2009 (86 out of 102 were made redundant), they kept working until the end of the layoff day because there was a lot to do. This was especially depressing, as tester Melissa noted, because just before the layoffs, the studio was aiming to expand the number of permanent QA positions. Unfortunately, many testers' dream of a permanent position was devastated by the layoffs, and full-time employment was taken off the table. Testers' condition of precarity is now so entrenched among them that when Digital Creatives filed for bankruptcy, they simply "shrugged it off," as Andy said, because they were already used to layoffs.

A major factor in testers' enduring precarity is their relatively young age. The testers I talked to have irregular work histories; they have worked in quite different types of jobs, sometimes doing "anything to get by," like George, a temp tester. Similarly, they had attended various educational institutions to boost their skills and sometimes had to drop out of school. Some temporary testers sustain their lives by being roommates with their colleagues. The testers can also choose to relocate and move back and live with their families when laid off or reward themselves "with a break and play[ing] a lot of *World of Warcraft* and enjoy[ing] the amazingness called unemployment [termed, 'funemployment' by QA]," as Cirose once said. Being single reduces the burden of temporary employment. Further, the youthful camaraderie in the tester pit enables the testers to get through crunch, during which they have an ethos of almost being in the trenches.

With the material culture and experience of youthfulness, the testers both maintain their pride in their work and endure the hardships of job insecurity. While such insecurities are increasingly familiar across many media professions, degradation of fun is specific to the testers as part of the pain that demoralizes these particular workers and undermines their passion for their job.

Pain in the Pit: Degradation of Fun, Instrumentalization of Play

Across Desire, video game testers were the most vibrant group of workers in terms of engaging intensively with video games, playing them, and talking about them. But the question remains: What happens when play becomes work and one plays video games for play tests and earns money? One inevitable response is: awesome, no complaints. Yet at the same time, video game testers suffer from physical pain during crunch, since they work long hours for months due to the instrumentalization of play. While financially compensated well thanks to overtime, they may not always have a social life to enjoy their financial returns.

Second, and more importantly, as the line between work and play is blurred, symptoms of what I call degradation of fun occur because play in testing is subjected to time discipline and regulated by tasks laid out by managers. The notion of degradation of fun is inspired by Harry Braverman's (1974/1998) discussion of the separation of design and execution and Adorno and Horkheimer's (1944, 48) critique of leisure under capitalism. I define the various manifestations of degradation of fun in the following ways: translation of play into quantifiable tasks, long work hours, precarious working conditions, repetitive tasks, stratification in the workplace, and the inability to "purely" enjoy video games outside of work.

The concept of degradation of fun illuminates how testers' passion about video games is contested vis-à-vis the hegemony of precarity in the profession. The repetitive nature of the job—doing the same task, running the same mission, reviewing the same characters, over and over again—sucks the fun out of work and encroaches on play outside of work. When play is regulated through time discipline and corporate priorities, testers' passion for games is inhibited. Moreover, in their private lives, testers are encouraged to play to keep up with the industry or critique the games they play and therefore cannot have as much fun. In addition, precarious employment, constructed as a repeated process of layoff and rehires, contributes to the degradation of fun as testers keep hoping that their temporary position will ultimately pay off as upward mobility and more desirable careers, like full-time testing or programming and design.

One major symptom of degradation of fun occurs through an instrumental approach toward play. As the training sessions I attended revealed, to count as effective testing, play must be translated into tasks and become quantifiable. Capital deploys technology to streamline labor and ensure surplus value extraction. Additionally, testers' playing habits outside of work become more selective or instrumental since play becomes a tool for keeping up with the industry. While testers are still passionate about games, they go home, play games for an hour, and then, like Ricky, are "ready to do something else." He said, "You play the games differently; you're no longer just having fun; you found yourself to a degree testing, in terms of, you always trying to find—oh, what would this do? How can I break this? . . . It just kind of changes the way you play video games. That's the biggest downside." Play becomes purely instrumental to keep up with industry trends, as a QA manager once told: "I used to be that person who used to play games a lot at home. I still play games at home, but I go home now, and I play games to keep myself up in the industry."

The relationship between instrumentalization of play and degradation of fun can be better grasped within the context of crunch. While there are strategies and practices that reduce the pain of crunch, the meaning of leisure is radically transformed when play becomes (over)work. Over the years, the joy of playing games at home is diminished, as seen in the case of George: "I have absolutely no doubt that the amount of hours you put into one game will diminish your desire to play others. Forty hours in a week, you might be able to get away with it. But the seventy hours a week, you just go home. . . . I don't even wanna look at a computer screen. Just stare at the front door, just because it's not a computer screen."

While testers may look forward to coming to work at other times, crunch is an exception. It is the crystallization of pain in the tester pit. There is undoubtedly the masculine pride of being in the trenches. Nevertheless, pain, bodily and mental, outweighs pleasure. Crunch comes with both nice paychecks and mandatory, long hours. As much as the mental and physical toll of crunch is alleviated in the playful culture of camaraderie, social life simply does not exist. Cirose said: "Well, gosh, crunch is really mind numbing. . . . We had no social lives, absolutely none. . . .

We're getting better paychecks, but it didn't seem to compensate for the lack of a life you have." And Ricky agreed: "It really affects your life outside of work. You kind of don't have one." Responding to my question "How was life during crunch?" George echoed Cirose and Ricky: "You don't have one, you don't get one. I had huge paychecks, and by the time I got laid off, I had all this money because I would go home, go to bed, wake up, shower, go to work, go home, go to bed. And that was my life for like seven months and just don't have time to spend any money."

For Andy, crunch is "a necessary evil," but it won't be easily fixed. Crunch is the time during which game testing physically hurts. Employees feel like doing more physical activities, such as "playing Smash Brothers, air hockey, going downstairs, walking around the block," to alleviate the physical and mental pain. Andy said: "I'm so passionate about it but at the same time, like, just like ten minutes. I wonder if I'd get fired for ten minutes. I'll just tell them I'm taking an extra break, and I'm going to lie down on the carpet. I mean, really, mentally, you start to consider, what would I give just to take a quick nap? I remember people talking about going into the bathroom and like locking the door and like falling asleep just like sitting down on the toilet." And Eric said: "While working here, I have developed a respect for working outside. Because I don't get to see nature that much anymore."

Therefore, degradation of fun refers to the processes that ultimately reduce one's passion for games. Employees other than QA also experience degradation of fun. For example, artists and programmers told me they did not even want to look at a game that they worked on for so long. However, in QA, there is too much exposure to the game itself, where work is structured to break the game in every possible way to ensure it does not crash after being shipped.

Degradation of fun is at its extreme when testers need to work on sequel games or games that one does not necessarily enjoy playing. The production of sequels is not uncommon in an industry in which production of new and original IPs means risky investments, and studios want to create reliable and established titles. Many employees told me that, no matter how much the stories within the games change, they would prefer working with different titles rather than repeated iterations of the same titles.

Finally, and related to their roles in the labor process, degradation of fun is evident in the tension between IP ownership, creative decisions, and QA's inability to have much of an impact on the labor process. David says: "Whenever the corporate does something, it's probably gonna piss me off [*laughing*] because they always seem to do it outside of a passionate perspective." "The distinction between passion and wanting something out the door to make money," in David's words, diminishes the fun at work because clearly the corporate decisions are more tied to scheduling and finances. Whereas the parent company or even developers have more of an impact on the broader production process, testers are the archetypes of passion in game production. When corporate decisions override the testers' aesthetic judgments and priorities, the pleasure they derive from work is diminished and leads to major frustrations and a feeling of lack of control over the playbor process.

It is evident then that the meaning of play is radically transformed as far as video game testing is concerned. While testers do develop tactics and come up with creative ways to alleviate boredom stemming from repetitive work, the instrumental approach reduces play into quantifiable tasks. This in turn affects how testers play games outside work. They either become more selective about what they play in their free time or they play games to keep up with the industry. These dynamics are even further exacerbated during crunch, which comes with meaningful financial returns, but this may not mean much because of the lack of a social life outside work. The degradation of fun along the lines of an unevenly structured labor process ultimately emerges as a major way in which precogs feel the pain of their labor. However, it is not the only form of pain. Testers' pain is partly caused by the existence of a reserve army of labor as a disciplinary force regarding wages and work hours, all consolidating precarity.

The Reserve Army of Labor of the Hopeful Testers

When I was discussing the persistent reality of layoffs in the lives of testers, human resources stated that they were not actually layoffs since the testers knew from the beginning that this would happen and that they would be "let go." Through what conceptual tools can we understand this interpretation that a layoff actually is not a layoff? In the unequal regime of ludopolitics, what enables this language of a supposedly equal trade-off between a powerful studio and precarious testers?

The concept of reserve army of labor is useful to understand the material conditions necessary for the ongoing precarity among testers. When labor is increasingly deskilled due to technology or if there is a surplus population that can easily replace the employed population, layoffs can be used as a threat, leading to overwork and superexploitation. As David Harvey (2010, 275) argues, and as we can apply to the case of the testers, "agreeing to work overtime sometimes becomes a condition of employment." Indeed, when interviewing for a testing job at Desire, candidates are alerted to the fact that they will be crunching and are asked whether they are fine with that. Passion, love of the job, and willingness to work overtime are integrated into the dynamics of surplus value extraction.

The construction and material experience of game testing as a cool job is an important contributing factor to the preservation of a large reserve army of labor. It is the nerd culture in the tester pit that appeals to the testers; it is a lighthearted environment that people look forward to coming back to after they have been laid off. It is a "once in a life time opportunity" where "you're not doing retail, no customers to deal with," as Cirose mentioned. Indeed, when asked to elaborate on their work experience in the studio, testers would constantly compare testing to other jobs that they previously worked, such as at factories or restaurants.

In comparison to these traditional blue-collar or service jobs, testing involves a lot of communication. Steven, who defined himself as Grandma's Boy due to his relatively older age, said: "Especially like in auto plants and stuff, where . . . the division of labor is so very specific . . . The only time I would ever talk to the other guys that were further up the line who are making parts . . . I had almost no contact with anybody." The communicative capabilities within testing and the symbolic capital it brings, then, are important for the surplus population of testers, who prefer a temporary job without benefits to a full-time job with benefits.

Perhaps the most crucial dynamic with respect to the reserve army of labor is the relative lack of skills[2] needed to become a tester. This is precisely why one of the potential paths temporary testers take during unemployment is to finish their degrees or get relevant ones in the field of game production. As the QA manager once said: "You have to be very highly skilled to be a programmer. You have to have a lot of education. You have to know what you're doing, the experience. Again, you need the experience in QA . . . but it's something that we can teach people. . . . We can hire someone and then teach them to be a good tester." David made a similar point with respect to skills: "When it comes to QA, they aren't very selective to begin with. Just because, you know, like you said it was temp position and because there was a huge pool in that, most, most quality assurance testing that they want doesn't require a lot, doesn't require like a high quality of work here." George confirmed David in terms of the relationship between the reserve army of labor and depression of wages: "If you have larger pool of people to draw from, you can lower the wage because eventually someone is going to be desperate enough to take the job."

Thus, when coupled with the construction of testing as a cool job, the symbolic capital it brings, the relative lack of skills required to perform the job, and the existence of educational institutions nearby, the reserve army of labor becomes a useful analytical tool to understand how precarity persists as a mode of being across testers more powerfully than core developers. In a highly competitive environment where many young people want to get a job in the industry, having a job makes one feel fortunate, and this in turn weakens the bargaining power of the worker and disciplines him or her, as well as habituating testers to overwork. Ricky's remarks are telling: "One is that there's lots of people who want to do what we do. And two is, there isn't really a required skill set to get into the job. So . . . anyone who has any desire to do the job has a chance, at least can compete for it. . . . Those two factors, I think, combined to keeping the wages low and . . . the attitude that we're replaceable or . . . a little bit not as important."

Then, it is not a coincidence that the studio keeps records of previous employees and rehires productive testers when they are needed again. In this sense, while testers are expendable, preserving one's future value depends on how passionate and productive one is during temporary employment. Having the right attitude helps. Testers make sure not to burn bridges and remain active on social networking sites to seek reemployment.

Reemployment is indeed a possibility. At the same time, the possibility of moving outside QA or becoming full time is quite limited; wages are depressed. Still, it is that hope that keeps the testers' aspirations alive. When I asked George, a temp tester, why they do not look for alternative and more stable careers, he said that it was "the hope that there's an end to being a temp." As hopeful as they are, testers feel expendable.

Sentiments of Second-Class Citizenship

When I started my fieldwork in the tester pit, I got an email from the QA manager, who wrote, "I know we are awesome, but are you sure that you want to spend that much time with QA? The other disciplines might have more impact." On the one hand, it is hard to read this as an expression of the expendable nature of QA employees. On the other hand, there is definitely a feeling of underappreciation among QA, particularly with respect to expendability and deprivation of the benefits granted to full-time employees. Being hired when needed and then laid off, only to be temporarily rehired when projects ramp up, is of major concern to temporary testers.

While they accept the fact that there are not enough full-time positions in QA, they do not refrain from expressing their disenchantment. Moving out of QA into the more creative position of writing, Tim compared his new position to QA, where he said he felt "like a grunt worker, just another worker." Ricky shared Tim's sentiments: "The fact that they brought me back says that they recognized that I brought something to the table. So in that, coming back was a little harder to come as a temp. And you definitely feel a little bit underappreciated when people are doing the same thing as you and they have obvious benefits. And then you feel a little bit . . . like a second-class type of person." Cirose's feelings were not different: "I was informed in August that I would be among the group to be let go in December, so I can answer your question very genuinely. It was shock. My morale has dropped since August. I feel unappreciated, expendable."

Cirose's situation was even aggravated by the fact that her layoff deadline was extended, which she considered to be "a cruel joke" especially because she thought she was doing well in terms of bug counts. While the accounts of discontent are mostly about feelings, disenchantment is not restricted to emotions. It is intricately related to material (in)security. When I interviewed Andy and asked him what it meant to be a temp employee, he straight out said, "It's awful." He now had to pay for "health insurance out of pocket," whereas this was not the case when he was full time prior to being laid off in 2009. Apart from insurance, temporary testers are deprived of some other benefits (e.g., buying games cheaper) that only come with full-time employment. This undoubtedly paves the way for sentiments of second-class citizenship. Andy said: "Here, the phrase 'second-class citizen' is used a lot. I definitely agree with the sentiment. Regardless of their ability or their efforts to try and make it very fair and very like level, you can't help but feel like you are less valuable."

The feeling of expendability is further intensified because of the skill gap that the testers have in contrast with other contract workers (such as artists) at the studio, who are also hired on a project basis but with different terms and conditions. Andy said: "Contract workers in other departments feel like mercenaries. They're elite and they're hired on to this one task. Whereas contract QA feel a little bit more like serfs. . . . They're just sort of . . . pushed into the position. I guess there is a lot of demand for their job. QA is looked upon as a very untrained field as opposed to any other disciplines."

When becoming full time was still a possibility prior to the layoff in 2009, feelings of expendability were entrenched through the reviews that came every six months. If a tester were regarded as desirable, then he or she would become full time. If management opposed, it would take another six months to go through review. For Andy, who was full time before he was laid off, these reviews "felt really terrible" and "felt like they were kind of holding a carrot in front of you and leading you on."

As the financial situation of Digital Creatives deteriorated, I met with testers again to understand what this meant for them. The financial downturn of the parent company had accentuated the expendability of the testers.

> DAVID: If the corporate was to sell off the studio to somebody else, who knows if that other . . . publisher or whatever would keep the QA group with the studio.
> ERGIN: Right. So the fact that things are rough for the corporate means that this core group may not be here forever?

CIROSE: We would probably be one of the first to go . . .'cause we're more expendable than the developers . . . We've been laid off before. . . . There really is no job security in QA.

Job insecurity and the feeling of expendability is so entrenched among testers that when Digital Creatives filed for bankruptcy, they barely cared because, as Andy said, "Worst case scenario, I'm fired again. So what damage can they do?" The auction week, for Andy, was not "an atypical week" because "that's always something that's on the table." In that sense, having been laid off before had immunized Andy toward potential layoffs. This is not to say that they didn't care about the outcome of the auction. On the contrary, the temporary testers wanted a small publisher without its internal QA to buy their studio so that they could keep their jobs.

Being expendable, then, seems to combine with the carrot-stick reality and works through the desires of the employees who are so passionate about games. Testers are aware of the large—*and younger*—reserve army of labor, which is always a threat to their position in the studio. When aspirations to belong to the full-time club are not realized, disenchantment prevails. While sentiments of second-class citizenship are sometimes communicated to management, the conditions of temporary employment hinder the realization of creative dreams that the testers have nurtured within affective networks of digital play since they were kids.

Can the Jon Snows of the Industry Unite?

Precarity as a condition is not new within the history of capitalism. Capitalism, in fact, as a system produces and needs precarity to discipline the workforce. Then, what seems to be new regarding precarity is not its existence "but rather the degree to which it has been generalized: post-Fordism democratizes exploitation" (Brophy and de Peuter 2007, 187). Precarity is the new normal in that populations or workers that used to live relatively stable lives are increasingly finding themselves within unpredictable careers.

In the case of the testers, there are a few remarks to make concerning precarity. First, despite their importance in the development cycle, as a model subject and victim of post-Fordism, testers symbolize an important and equally neglected workforce both in the accounts of the gaming industry (Ramsay 2012) and game studies. Although their skillset is not always highly regarded, their contribution to the production of a high-quality game is noteworthy. Accounts of the industry cover the stories of studio founders, programmers, and designers, but it is the testers that, with the skills they have obtained through play, ensure that a game does not crash and give the studio a good reputation. A good console game without the labor of testers is simply not possible.

Second, while feelings of expendability abound, the desire for alternative modes of production or play does not exist among the testers. Some, if not all, testers prefer to entertain the prospect of temporary employment rather than search for full-time alternatives. Precarity is not just dictated from above (Brophy and de Peuter 2007) through the structural dynamics of the game industry. It is also entrenched due to the productive processes of play, acquisition of symbolic capital, and remnants of hope to attain a more secure position or a new temporary position in the future. Hope matters in the precarious worlds of testers. Cirose called the prospect of further or permanent employment "a cruel joke." This cruelty still involves crumbs of hope. Even though the optimistic attitude toward their job might end up being a cruel joke and hurt the testers in the long run, it does sustain them at least for a brief period. As Miya Tokumitsu (2015, location 960) brilliantly said, "hope is such a powerful tool because, cultivated in specific ways, it facilitates identification with exploitative forces rather than the assertion of one's own interests." The cruelty of this joke is anchored in the degradation of fun and precarity, whereas the symbolic capital of working in a creative industry and the hope of permanent employment signify nodes of the dream job.

Then, in a way, precarity itself is productive. It produces subjects who are keen on the hard work ethos, competitive play, and self-surveillance to secure their temporary position both at present and in the future. When I asked George what he would recommend to people aspiring to set their foot in the gaming industry, he said, "Be proactive, be early, be prepared to hate the game." Unlike Nathan Peters, George was advising prospective testers to act like a start-up and take individual risk in an uncertain work environment. In George's account, pleasure, pain, and care of the self were embodied in the model subject of the video game industry.

Third, the precarity of testers converges with the degradation of fun. Lack of prospects regarding permanent employment is combined with the instrumental logic toward play, which kills the joy at work and during leisure time. It is not that testers do not like their jobs. Rather, the meaning of play is radically transformed. The amount of game play outside work is diminished, or testers engage in it only to keep up with the industry. Fun is further degraded because crunch terminates social life, within which the financial benefits derived from overtime cannot even be enjoyed.

Fourth, the politics of precarity in relation to organization needs to be rethought, as well. The precarity of testers in the video game industry undoubtedly involves more choice than other types of precarity, such as that experienced by an immigrant worker. In this sense, there are "ethical and organizational questions" (Brophy and de Peuter 2007) with respect to the precarity of the testers. When asked what they thought about unionizing to contest precarity, testers never considered organizing as an option. Knowing they were hired as temporary workers, they did not believe in the need for winning workplace benefits and concessions because they "learned a long time ago" that they need to "do what makes you happy," as George said. At times, they spoke the language of capital and told me that their temporary employment "makes sense" from the perspective of the studio. For all the informality and playfulness of the tester pit, market rationalization kept the workplace in order. In short, testers understood or at least experienced precarious employment as an individual problem based on individual choice. Precarity seemed a rational outcome within the market economy where choices were made by individual actors.

This is where the "ideology of creativity" and dynamics of "cool capitalism" (McGuigan 2012) function to make the testers submit to precarity and inhibit unionization. Similar to low-level design workers in Milan who have little space for upward mobility, game testers too subscribe to the ideology of creativity as a set of material practices where "the value of work as well as one's own value as a worker are increasingly conceived in terms of identity and life-style" (Arvidsson, Malossi, and Naro 2010, 306). In this sense, testers decidedly saw themselves as different from blue-collar workers and associated themselves with creative employees for whom the society had higher respect. After all, they had chosen to do what they loved and through these material practices and discourses endured precarity, while purporting high levels of job satisfaction.

To conclude, then, as Rosalind Gill and Andy Pratt (2008, 21) argue, precarity may not always result in transgression and resistance to capital. Rather, precarity might lead to its opposite, subjection to uneven power relations. While it may enable processes of "resisting to capital," it may also pave the way for "binding us to it." When I started my fieldwork, Cirose considered her job "the dream job." Toward the end of her employment, she was "cynically" aware that they were "expendable." "Though we know our work matters, we as individuals don't," she said. In this context, Ricky would recommend this job "to anyone who doesn't have a career path in mind but enjoys video games. 'Cause it's a lot of fun, but I don't know that it necessarily leads anywhere specifically." Cirose agreed, with an even more pessimistic tone: "The longer I have this job, the more time I am wasting on a job with no future. . . . I want to focus on school. Unemployment will be pursued very contently. The reason I was upset and angry wasn't about losing my job, but it was about losing my job to others who I feel I have more experience on. As one of the more experienced testers, I feel like all the work I've put into this department was for nothing, if they hire a new temp in my place or train someone else to my level." While workers like Cirose immensely enjoy doing what they love, they also face persistent precarity. It seems that testers have come to accept precarity as a natural and inevitable feature of their working lives.

PRODUCTION ERROR
Layoffs Hit the Core Creatives

The well-being of Desire's developers and the success of Desire as a workplace structured by the unequal regime of ludopolitics depended on a few immediate factors and some external ones, which earlier chapters have foregrounded. The immediate factors included management's re-organization of the labor process to streamline and better regulate creativity and the construction of a flexible and playful workplace to ensure productivity. Another essential factor was whether a developer was able to draw on the emotional infrastructure of a domestic partner. The level of occupational skills also was crucial to determine a worker's status in the workplace hierarchy. Some of the external factors were related to the scheduling and marketing demands dictated by the parent company, the competitors in the market, the potential birth of a new console generation, and the financial well-being of Desire's parent company. Among these, this last factor—namely, Desire's financially networked relationship with Digital Creatives—had such a determining impact on the developers that when the parent company entered an undesirable financial trajectory, "shit rolled down the hill," as the veteran programmer Matthew emphasized during a conversation on how they were experiencing the parent company's financial downturn.

Precarity is most acutely felt among the testers because they are replaceable, but it is by no means limited to the tester pit. Even senior developers in their spacious open offices experience insecurity due to financialization. Despite their skill sets, star status in the industry press, and relatively secure positions, the lives of core creatives can be precarious even in the flagship studio of a major publisher such as Digital Creatives. I once asked the art director Theodor if he ever worried about the stability of the studio. Without any hesitation and despite his position, he said: "Oh, absolutely, every day." For Theodor, it was not necessarily their studio but a structural problem of the broader industry, as it was "so much more hit driven, either you're a hit or you're not." The lead designer Robert struck me as a confident developer throughout my research. His self-confidence was not unfounded because he had started his position at Desire as an animator and was promoted all the way up in ten years to become a lead designer, who had already produced Desire's most successful franchise. He pointed to the financial crisis in 2008 as a game changer because the economic dynamics of the industry in general had radically shifted since then. He said: "With this hit-driven mentality, we are always worried about the next step, and we need to make as sure as possible that we always make the right step in order to not stumble, as stumbling means potential to fall, which would mean the potential end of the company."

If we juxtapose these statements with the project manager Renata's interview comments, the precarity of the core developers becomes more evident. Renata did not finish college and had been working for almost thirty years. Prior to Desire, she worked at a software company. She had been at Desire for about four years. The deadlines, staffing, and budgets were particularly stressful for her as a project manager. She was aware of the difficulties they faced working in a precarious environment. She said: "When we produce a game, we produce the life of the studio."

It was clear that Desire's relationship with Digital Creatives not only empowered the developers but also put them in a vulnerable situation through a complicated, financialized framework. Desire ultimately survived the financial downturn but not without casualties. The studio's creative game developers now faced the brutal reality of working in a hit-driven industry through layoffs and financial insecurity. These problems emerged not only as a result of the 2008 crash but also Digital Creatives's own market performance. Because Digital Creatives was a publicly traded company, it wasn't able to provide sufficient information to its workers. This lack of communication and Digital Creatives's rush to ship not-quite-finished products created discontent and alienation across Desire's developers, for whom communication was vital.[1]

The narratives of the developers reveal how handling risk in the game industry is extremely individualized (Beck 1992). While Desire's developers do not blame themselves as did the entrepreneurs of the dot-com crash at the end of the 1990s (Neff 2012), the level of indifference toward unionization strikingly confirms how each developer individually deals with precarious employment in a volatile context. Game developers' perception of creative work—that one needs to think outside the box, that creative work is decidedly different from blue-collar work, and that therefore unions would not be helpful—is socially structured. Yet they seem to be indifferent to facing and managing risk in more collective ways.

Titanic Starts Sinking

Digital Creatives was one of the biggest publishers in the 2000s. What were the conditions that led to its bankruptcy? The bankruptcy has to be grasped historically and through the structural dynamics in the broader industry. Industry publications and websites like Kotaku and Gamasutra list plummeting stock prices among the major indicators of the financial downturn of the company. Stock prices reflect how products financially perform in the market and how the public perceives the operations of a company. In that sense, there has been a dramatic loss of Digital Creatives' stock value, which dropped from thirty dollars a share to almost nothing. There was a structural reason behind this, and it was not independent from the very logic of how capitalism works: ceaseless growth and accumulation. With promising stock prices and cash in hand, Digital Creatives desired further growth, pursued studio acquisitions at a global level, and initiated new product developments. Yet this accumulation strategy didn't work out as it was imagined by Digital Creatives.

Developers told me that the fact that their parent company wanted to grow for growth's sake was not a healthy path to take. I discussed the financial context with Vincent. A white man with German and Irish origins, Vincent was an assistant producer in his early thirties. His dad had graduated from community college and was a midlevel police officer. His mom had bumped around job to job, trying to keep herself busy. She had then gone back to school to learn interior design. Vincent thought he had grown up in a safe, community-driven neighborhood in the Midwest. Sports were central to his life. His family was pretty conservative, but Vincent considered himself a lot more liberal than his parents. It wasn't like all "love, hippy liberal," he noted, because they, as a studio, "still wanted to make money."

So I asked Vincent how the conditions for making money got destabilized. He said: "Once they started making money, they started going out and purchasing all these different studios. And . . . they're just like, 'Well, the more games we have out there, the more money we can make,' which wasn't true, because . . . the economy being down didn't help." Industry analysts writing about Digital Creatives would agree with Vincent. Writers in the industry press criticized Digital Creatives for not having a sustainable and carefully devised growth policy, ultimately leading them to recklessly expand in areas in which they were not particularly competitive.

When the reckless growth policy didn't pay off as well as Digital Creatives wished, a "perfect storm," in the words of management, emerged. This perfect storm was a combination of various factors: having to compete with stronger publishers, falling stock prices, and the failure of a major product, which, according to the gaming industry press, proved to be a major revenue loss. Vincent was particularly critical of Digital Creatives when it came to that specific product. For him, it was "the big nail in the coffin" because this product was not even able to interest the developers at the studio, despite the fact that they "got them cheap if we [they] wanted." He continued: "If you can't even interest your own people who are gamers . . . there is something wrong."

Indeed, there was something wrong; earnings in the mid-2000s did not carry into the late 2000s and the early 2010s. Their parent company, according to Vincent, due to the policy of recklessly acquiring studios, had lost "sight of a couple of them [the studios]." Having more studios required careful supervision to create high-quality products. Yet this dream partly failed. The studio-acquisition policy did not evolve in a healthy manner. Consequently, Digital Creatives had to close studios across the globe, as well as killing a franchise, canceling projects, and restructuring business in general.

The upper management at the parent company took responsibility for the direction of the enterprise and took action to slow and stop the financial downturn. As they reached a point where these actions did not work, they had to inform their investors of the company's financial standing, which was beginning to give alarming signals in 2012. More than ever, the parent company was extremely reliant on potential revenues from promising games. The hope was that these games would succeed in a highly competitive and hit-driven market and bring profits. Nobody wanted to think of any scenario other than getting the company back to its past days of growth.

It is important that the upper management at Digital Creatives took responsibility for the direction of the company, but it is vital to remember how layoffs are endemic to the game industry. It was not only Digital Creatives that faced instability. Such industry giants as Blizzard, the owner of *World of Warcraft*, would announce a layoff of around six hundred employees around the same time (Caoili 2012). Similarly, EA laid off what it called a "small number" of employees at its Vancouver branch as part of a restructuring effort "to focus more on its digital content" (Curtis 2012). In fact, an insightful analysis published on the Kotaku website meticulously demonstrates that the industry had been suffering from major instabilities since 2006 and witnessed the closure of ninety-nine studios in that time period (Plunkett 2012).

Although the game industry is very much used to financial ups and downs, the 2008 financial crisis certainly didn't help. For the game developers, there is always hope that new studios will pop up. Entrepreneurialism, libertarianism, and individualism are constitutive of the game industry. If one studio doesn't work out for a developer, he or she can either join another one or found his or her own. Although hoping can be beneficial to one's soul, it doesn't do away with the fact that the gaming industry, especially the console market, is primarily a sink-or-swim business (Whitson 2013). While swimming with the major battleships of a large company might materially be more secure than swimming alone as an independent studio, Desire's developers still felt insecure, since a historically powerful battleship might gradually turn into the *Titanic*. And this transformation took place despite the market success of Desire and its workers. Despite reassurances from their parent company, developers like Harold would constantly insist that they "would rather be on a ship that is not going to sink." While the studio itself did not sink in the end, there were casualties as Digital Creatives was restructured to deal with the financial downturn, laying off core developers for the first time. Developers who had more occupational skills than the testers were not immune to layoffs. Precarity, in a sense, had become relatively democratized in the unequal regime of ludopolitics.

Layoffs Hit the Developers

At Desire, layoffs were largely associated with the QA workers. Apart from individual personnel issues, no layoff had taken place until 2011, which was a matter of pride for management and a source of relief among developers. Moreover, Desire produced the most profitable franchise of Digital Creatives. In that sense, nobody had really thought about layoffs as a serious possibility. That was the common sentiment in 2010 when I first entered the lives of Desire's developers. However, waves of the financial downturn were beginning to hit *Titanic* in 2011 and even those at the "deluxe suit," in the words of Harold, were feeling it.

The layoffs were announced at a time of excitement, as Desire was about to submit its most important game project to Digital Creatives, and I was invited to a studiowide meeting. I was expecting it to feature awards for talented and successful developers. Why else would the studio organize a meeting just a few days before the game shipment party? My expectations proved wrong. I went to a solemn meeting where the main agenda was layoffs.

In these meetings, developers are given the opportunity to question management. Crunch and potential layoffs are usually on the table for discussion. So I was still under the impression that the layoff talk was generic. I couldn't have been more wrong. These weren't studiowide rumors or social media hearsay. The conversation was real. The unfavorable condition of Digital Creatives was now materially affecting developers at Desire: sixteen people had lost their jobs, while those remaining were concerned about their own futures, asking whether there would be more layoffs.

Management was doing its best to reassure the employees but could never completely guarantee there would be no more layoffs. What they were able to say was that there probably would not be more layoffs, but at the same time, who could know the future? The management advised the employees not to believe in anyone who claimed to predict the future. This was a particularly rough process for management, which had seen the studio through the transition from a small independent one to its current stage, where they now had to make tough calls. They made sure to present layoffs not as related to performance but about the allocation of labor power for future projects. They made clear that laid-off developers were encouraged to reapply if there was a new opening.

The anxiety of the developers could be read from the questions they raised: "What can we do to lessen the chance of being laid off?" Management's response was disturbingly ambiguous: "Anyone have a good answer?" Following that, management highlighted how keeping the skills up-to-date and *just being successful* was important. Management especially urged the developers to contextualize their own situation: "You can worry about the security of the situation you're in, or you can step back and look at it and realize that there isn't a company out there that hasn't shut down a studio." That is, studio closure was the norm.

Did anyone have a good answer to how to minimize the risk to be laid off? Not really. The unexpected and troubling impact of the layoffs was felt both in the meeting room and throughout the individual conversations I had with developers. Margaret was one of them. Her dad was a gamer. They had old World War II boardgames at home. They also had early computers, and she grew up playing *Dancing Alphabet* and *Donald Duck Playground*. They had an Atari, where she played *E.T.* She enjoyed *Perils of Rosella*, one of the first adventure games she played. As it had been made by a female game designer, Margaret thought, "Maybe it wasn't strange that I played video games." She had started her career in game development as an audio intern. She then became full time and joined the production team. At the time of our interview, she was an associate producer. The impact of the layoffs was significant. She said: "It took a while, I think, for the team to get back into the swing of things because that was the first time we had layoffs." To lose talent and then "readjust everything was also hard from a work standpoint," she added.

The laid-off personnel would be the hardest hit by the process, though. Vincent was one of them. Despite acknowledging that he was not planning to stay at the studio forever, he underlined how unexpected the layoff had been and how bitter he felt: "Like the mama bird kicking you out of the nest a little bit sooner than you had expected it, we haven't really had that warning this time. With the coming [of the] financial year . . . there's always a little bit of nervousness there, I guess. I didn't think about it 'cause I'm . . . working on the biggest product of the parent company. There's no way. . . . My job is secure."

Unfortunately, Vincent was wrong. Working on the most profitable franchise didn't always make a developer's job safe. As one might guess, the moment of being informed about the layoff was an emotional one. A project manager cried. In the middle of this turmoil, Vincent was even more concerned about his cultural capital and work experience in terms of future employment: "My immediate reaction was, well, what the fuck am I going to do? I don't have a degree, I didn't finish school. . . . I want to go like cry, shout, punch something, but . . . cooler heads prevailed." While educational degrees do matter in the industry, having shipped a game and relevant work experience are indispensable for finding a job. Vincent, at the time, was just about to ship a major project but got laid off, without getting "a project under [his] belt," which troubled him in terms of finding a new job.

There were also cases where even a graduate degree in computer science did not help. I talked to Jose, a game play programmer at the time. Prior to Desire, he had worked at a defense contractor that produced training video games, until he got laid off. With his MS in computer science, he was able to secure two interviews. One was a start-up in Los Angeles, which, at the last minute, decided not to fly him over. His interviews at Desire went well, and he moved to start his job at the studio. During his first year, he worked for a log-in server build to track users and their in-game behavior, which the designers would then interpret and take into consideration for future games. Then he worked as a game play programmer and then at missions and activities for two years until he was laid off.

"I don't think anyone was expecting the layoffs," Jose said. Thinking that he had been invited to a scheduled meeting about a project, he found himself with staff from upper management who explained the rationale for the layoff in budgetary terms. The president "apologized" and detailed the circumstances. The layoff was about finance and the need to restructure labor power for future projects; it was not related to anyone's performance. Upon learning the news, his project manager cried. His lead almost cried. In Jose's somewhat cynical words, it was "probably because he had less people to work with now." Jose emphasized how the downsizing would adversely impact the studio right at a time when they were trying to finish the game. As they had two people left on the game play team, and he was already "double booked," he said: "I don't know how they are gonna get it done."

Among the three laid-off employees I interviewed, James was the most vocal about the layoff—not necessarily the studio—and the broader work dynamics in the industry. It was clear that James desired a healthier relationship between work and life: "I really don't understand that. I mean, people are so terrified of losing their job; it's unhealthy to be that terrified. You should not be afraid of that guy.

'Cause it makes you a slave, a slave." Keen on producing his own IP, James further criticized the regimented IP regime in the digital age quite harshly: "Any creativity, any creative thing is built on sharing, really. . . . We use all these draconian measures to prevent sharing . . . when it's natural and normal . . . If you tell contractors to build a house, it's your house. But I don't think that metaphor really should apply to creativity."

No matter how critical James was of the employment contract and passionate work practices, the pride of not having any layoffs at Desire had gone, and the morale of the team had dropped. They had laid off staff just before the most profitable game project was about to be finished. They now had to accomplish more with even less labor power. Meanwhile, the push for perpetual innovation and new products was on, which would force the developers to produce more downloadable content to retain players and bring in money for the parent company.

The Studio as Machine: Perform Better, Produce Forever

As studio management underlined during the layoffs, Desire's doors were still open to the laid-off developers. Two of the sixteen laid-off developers—one of whom was Vincent—were in fact rehired. This all took place in the middle of a hectic schedule for the release of their game in late 2011. In my conversations with developers and management, they clearly expressed their certainty that the game was going to perform outstandingly in the market. This success was especially vital for Digital Creatives because the studio was in a position to financially help the parent company through this game. As the tech artist Ronaldo put it, "Our future is the future of our parent company."

The financial pressure on Digital Creatives was such that they were at times intervening in game play, which would create a feeling in the studio that the parent company was "acting like QA." The developers were also becoming vocal about the parent company's broader studio-acquisition policy. As if these issues were not enough, the parent company had also changed its bonus plan. Bonuses now became tied to the performance of the parent company rather than the reception of a game produced by the studio and completion of a project. The developers were not happy: while their game might do particularly well, they felt like they were only supporting their parent company in terms of cash flows rather than enjoying the fruits of their own performance. They felt they were being punished because of the poor performance of the sibling studios, despite the fact that the golden child—Desire—was increasing its sales. Ronaldo's analogy was illuminating in terms of how they, as the flagship studio, had no control over Digital

Creatives and the other studios: "If you think of the parent company as a body, you've got one good arm, but you've already amputated a leg, and you've got another arm that needs to be amputated."

Indeed, once it was out in the market, Desire's latest game became the biggest success of the studio, with excellent sales numbers. Yet, not even a month after the game was out, I was at the studio, casually chatting with Harold and Stuart (the community manager) about how they were doing. Although they were thrilled about the performance of their games, they were concerned about stock prices. When I asked what they thought about the stocks, Stuart wittily said that he tried not to think about them. To fix the financial standing of the company, Digital Creatives was constantly thinking about how they could improve stock prices and provide more cash flow. The master plan relied on Desire to produce an expansion game as part of their biggest franchise, sell it at a cheaper price, keep the attention flowing, and hopefully provide cash for the parent company.

Dictated by Digital Creatives, the idea of an expansion game was unexpected. For instance, while he was looking for a break from the franchise, the game's lead designer, Robert, found himself complying with this demand and expanding the franchise. Similarly, Ricardo, an artist who was about to relocate to another studio on the West Coast, would tell how they were not even able to enjoy the moments of joy derived from their market success. Instead, they found themselves not only under the "black cloud" of the stocks but also captured by the mandate to produce downloadable content to financially support Digital Creatives.

This expansion was clearly intended to provide cash for Digital Creatives. Yet it was troubling for the smaller team in charge of the expansion game, who initially thought, "Shit, nobody is gonna buy this." The developers felt like the project was forced upon them, and they "kinda grudgingly said, 'OK, we'll do this.'" Time went by, concepts got into shape, and the team regained confidence in the game as their initial reluctance faded away. But then, when the team began to find its voice and build faith within the project, the new management at Digital Creatives decided to cancel the expansion and make it a full sequel as part of the profitable franchise. That decision "definitely messed up team chemistry," said Robert, adding that they "definitely lost a lot of momentum." These changing decisions would signal the sincere but somewhat futile efforts of Digital Creatives, which couldn't help but create further anxiety, uncertainty, and frustration among the developers.

Despite the overall creative freedom granted by the parent company, its financial structures had created a burden for Desire's developers, because signing a contract not only brings financial freedom but also introduces political bondage based on the promise of delivering profits for the parent company. Failure to bring profits could mean unemployment or precarious employment, implying that developers become indebted to Digital Creatives. They have to produce, produce, and produce and still remain profitable. They produce games that they disown a priori. Being subject to the rules and dynamics of Digital Creatives created problems for communication about the future, which would convince some very talented developers to leave their beloved Desire and explore employment opportunities elsewhere.

Lack of Communication, Plummeting Stocks, and Departure of Talent

Being part of a publicly traded publisher initially brought financial security, but security is never forever, and Desire's was now fundamentally destabilized. Once subjected to the financial markets, the company's performance and the perception of stock prices emerged as an existential concern for the developers. What further complicated matters was that Digital Creatives had to be careful about the amount of information they provided their employees. Given that game developers loved what they did and worked long hours to realize that passion, they hungered for accurate information regarding the status of their parent company. Moreover, when publicly traded companies want to meet specific deadlines to prove growth for the investors and the public, they might force their studios to release games at an earlier time when the developers are not ready or comfortable to do so. In this sense, the requirements dictated by the parent company can be a major source of frustration and lead to periods of crunch for developers.

Among the peculiarities of being a game studio owned by a publicly traded company, the importance of communication and the impact of falling stocks are worth focusing on. There are basically two reasons to do so. First, as illustrated in chapter 4, communication matters to the governance and well-being of game developers, and its lack can and does create dissonance across teams. Second, stocks present an existential source of anxiety because the very interface on the developers' computers—used for internal communication in the studio—displays the stock ticker of the parent company and other major publishers in the game market. That visual presence of the financial performance of Digital Creatives becomes both a warning sign and a disciplinary mechanism. Stocks turn into the sword of Damocles, with the ticker showing the fate of the parent company hanging over every developer's head. Every game developer is aware of it but wants to joke and forget about it since thinking about it simply does not help.

As they became concerned about the health of Digital Creatives, game developers held meetings with the management from the parent company, which were intended to address the questions of the developers, who wanted *any* piece of information that might relieve their anxieties. When I asked the developers how they felt about these explanations from their parent company, some of them would tell me that they did understand the peculiarity of being a publicly traded company but then stated that the parent company was a bit late in informing them about their restructuring plans. As studio management would also underline, the lack of communication so that developers often learned the state of affairs from the media—which did not always provide accurate information—put developers "in limbo, waiting to see what's gonna happen."

In this respect, most of the developers acknowledged that the management at Desire tried to do its best "to be as communicative as possible without being falsely optimistic," as the HR personnel told me on various occasions. However, anxiety did not disappear. Even developers of higher ranks would say, "Last year felt like, day to day . . . [We] came in not even sure . . . OK, are we gonna have a job tomorrow?" Similarly, one of the associate producers said, "There was just a gap of time where there was so much uncertainty because we were not . . . People were betting." Ronaldo, a veteran developer, was particularly concerned and demoralized, saying, "My mood hasn't really changed at all. It already bottomed out."

The diminishing morale was also linked with developers' own investment in Digital Creatives stocks. Some workers were concerned that they wouldn't be able to make any of the money back that they had invested in Digital Creatives stocks. In response to such feelings about stocks values, management asked the developers to focus on making quality games and remember that stocks were about perception. However, among many other factors, it was this very perception that the parent company rigorously wanted to fix by trying to show growth. It was precisely the adverse perception about the company stocks that forced the developers to release games before they were comfortable with them. Again, it was due to the diminishing stock values that the developers had to make new expansion games and downloadable content even before they were completely done celebrating the success of the previous game.

Within this atmosphere, some developers went beyond raising questions and embarked on different strategies to cope with the uncertainties in their professional lives, proactively attempting to subvert their own dismissal from the company. However, none of the developers or testers ever mentioned or even thought about the viability of collective action. During my initial interviews, well before the bankruptcy of Digital Creatives, I was asking the developers what their thoughts on unions were. They either simply responded, "I don't know," or they would state that unions belonged to the era of industrial jobs. In contrast to industrial jobs, their jobs were creative. In this respect, unions and the potential value of unionization seemed far removed from their imaginations.

When unions are not regarded as feasible, trying to find alternative employment venues becomes an option. The disgruntled developers could be divided into two groups in terms of how they searched for alternatives: those who sent CVs elsewhere and those who simply resigned to embark on other adventures. The lead designer Robert didn't want to leave the area but also told me that he was mentally trying to be prepared. And in fact, he has been working at a different studio since 2014. Ronaldo, a longtime technical artist, would for the first time in years update his CV: "The funny thing is, my office mate goes, 'Crap, I gotta start looking for a new job, now.' And I had already started looking. So maybe that's part of it. In May, I had already gotten my résumé together. I was already looking. I was already prepared to leave. I guess I really am. Literally I am."

Others took a step further and went to other studios. For instance, the community manager Stuart told me that he had been asking management about "a path of growth for the last two years" but never got "a solid answer" and decided to leave Desire, where he had worked for four years. While he thought that the studio was relatively safe, he also underlined that "the problem is, most of the people who are leaving are the really talented people. And they are not going to small studios." So it was senior talent that was leaving, and replacing senior talent was a major problem for Desire given its location.

The stories about the departures were quite emotional ones, which mostly did not target the studio. In other words, the breakup was not about Desire but about Digital Creatives. For instance, one developer left despite a big bonus he could have gotten if he had stayed. Another developer, management told me, "couldn't even speak" and "was tearful" as he submitted his resignation letter. While the artist Ricardo's reasons for leaving were mostly about his wife needing a change, he did acknowledge the gloomy atmosphere at the studio: "There is certainly like a funk in the studio, . . . because your parent company is falling apart. People kind of deal with it, . . . just making little jokes, inside comments about our stock situation and whatnot. . . . Really, when our game came out, it was doing fantastic right out of the gate. . . . Everybody should have been on cloud nine." While Ricardo constantly emphasized how he dearly loved the studio, he was also concerned about it being understaffed. He noted the shrinking numbers of artists and the inaction or lack of resources to recruit environment artists, who were crucial to the game genre that the studio produced.

It was not only Ricardo who was concerned about recruitment. Anxiety prevailed throughout the studio. Among 109 employees who participated in my survey, 38 percent agreed and 59 percent strongly agreed with the statement "I am concerned that we are losing senior talent and might not be able to easily replace them." Nevertheless, there was an emotional side to the story, as well. Remaining colleagues were emotionally struck by the departures. The associate producer Margaret vividly described the situation: "I think the biggest impact would be moralewise, seeing friends go, seeing mentors go. . . . You just build a relationship with someone; you look forward to working with them again because you have this good rapport. Knowing that they're going to be gone—that can be hard."

While management did acknowledge that developers were not happy about the exodus and the recruitment problem, their comments particularly revealed the extent to which work and lives were precarious in the broader gaming industry: "In fact one hundred studios have been shut down in the last five years, and everybody's name is on it. . . . All these people that you know, people leaving here to go there. . . . Guess what? That doesn't make you safe. What makes you safe is success. Success in a studio is what makes you safe."

Success surely is defined by market sales, and it does certainly improve team morale. Yet does success really make one safe? Or is there not a tautology in suggesting that success guarantees safety? In the case of Desire, success brought not only money but also more disciplined and regulated work to help Digital Creatives survive. The developers found themselves in a perpetual production machine within which they had to constantly increase sales and respond to the demands of their parent company. Robert described this contradictory situation: "They [the parent company] made a lot of dumb decisions. And they got punished for it. The problem was we got punished with them. . . . Our success was paying for their failures." While it is undeniable that success does increase the relative stability of a studio, it unfortunately may not prevent such undesirable processes as the departure of senior talent or bankruptcy.

"Who's Gonna Buy Us?": Bankruptcy, Auction, and the Bazaar for Intellectual Property

As I was contemplating my exit interviews, which would be conducted in a context where Digital Creatives was not thriving, I was shocked by the news that the company had filed for bankruptcy. I immediately emailed some of the developers to get their initial reactions, which were mixed. On the one hand, there was a feeling of relaxation now that they at least had some information about the future. On the other hand, there was the inevitable uncertainty regarding this new chapter for Desire. The design director Michael, for instance, was feeling "pretty optimistic." In contrast to a year ago, he said there was now "a clear path," which was "well explained." "It feels a lot less uncertain now," he told me. The news of the bankruptcy would confirm once again stratification not only along the lines of labor power but also levels of anxiety and optimism. While the design director would be closer to management in terms of rank, even the longtime, self-confident, and assertive programmer Matthew said of his first reaction to the news, "I will admit I was a little bit nervous." Upon learning the news, the lead designer Robert got "pretty nervous," while the existence of a potential buyer made him more confident. But then again, the emergence of other potential buyers and their visits to the studio threw him "for a loop," so he began to "feel a sense of uncertainty again." He said: "It threw so many ripples on the pond that we can't tell where things are going. I don't know. I prefer stability. . . . I don't take a lot of risks."

Robert's anxiety with respect to the existence of more than one bid at the auction was quite justified, and there are two layers to grasp. Given the geography, it is more difficult for a designer to find immediate employment compared to the programmers, for whom the labor market is more favorable. Second, the level of anxiety depended also on whether one was a tester or a core developer. As the most vulnerable members of the workforce, testers were especially interested in who the owner of the studio would be, because that would reveal whether there would be the need for an internal QA department. It was with these anxieties that the developers went into the auction.

Desire's developers had no information about the auction while it was happening. The waiting was so unnerving that there was a kind of moratorium on work. As Vincent told me, "I think at that point most people were just sort of going through the motions, pretending to work, as awful as that sounds." Matthew confirmed Vincent's assessment: "I don't think people really got a lot of work done that week. Morale was fine. But I find it really interesting that the day of the auction, there was an officially sanctioned party of sorts. We had food, we had drinks, and people just blew off work that afternoon, because it was officially sanctioned." On auction day, they speculated, read rumors online, and made guesses about who was going to buy the studio. "Who's gonna buy us, who's gonna buy us, who's gonna buy us?" was the sentiment, according to Matthew.

While the developers felt relatively confident in terms of the value of their IP, their concerns and anxieties were more about the new buyer, since certain publishers were not regarded as quite desirable to work for. That is to say, the sentiment was "I may have a job, but I don't know that I want to work for those guys," Matthew added. This was a vital issue for the testers but not simply in terms of job security, because they were somewhat used to layoffs and "shrugged it off," and their "jobs have not gotten more volatile than they are on a day to day basis," as the temp tester Andy stated. What concerned the testers was that the new owner could have their own QA personnel. This condition of existential precarity takes us back to the question of unions again. Now, at the time of bankruptcy, were unions now a bit more appealing as it was clear that even being the flagship studio of Digital Creatives did not make one's position safe?

Re-union

Long before bankruptcy and the auction, even as Digital Creatives was not financially troubled, unions were not within the imaginaries of the developers. To understand whether there was any change in their attitude, I asked the same question again after Digital Creatives went bankrupt. What does a union mean to a developer when she or he is in limbo, does not know who the new owner is going to be, and has no control over their means of production? What were developers, as members of the flagship studio, thinking about unions, when their future and well-being were threatened despite their stellar performance?

The developers' perception of unions had not changed even days before the auction. An important distinction the game developers made was specifically related to the "nature" of creative labor versus industrial labor. For the lead designer Robert, "creative industries seem like they're driven more driven by individuals, individual effort, creativity and sort of things that can't be—not cannot be defined, but they're not concrete." For the developers I talked to, unions signified standardized production, laziness, and lack of creativity. They were a thing of the past and related to older forms of labor; they were a "loaded topic" and "a little too adversarial," Matthew said. Especially in their specific case, developers did not think unions made sense because of the lack of other studios in the area. Moreover, developers related the existence of unions in industrial production to issues of mistreatment and exploitation. They believed they were not being taken advantage of, were treated well, and loved what they did. As the associate producer Margaret articulated, "You're not in this industry if you're not a workaholic to some extent." In sum, love of the job, relatively good salaries, and workplace perks negated the possibility of exploitation in the minds of the developers.

A conversation I had with Harold was particularly revealing in terms of evoking the "nomadic nature" of game developers' lives and the generational transition that Richard Sennett (1999) describes in *The Corrosion of Character*. Comparing his situation to that of his family members who were part of unions in the tobacco industry, Harold said, "It's not like you work twenty years in one spot or on a pension and you're done. I'm working in an industry where it's entirely possible that I'll be working in five different places in ten years." He further defined the stereotypical creative worker in the gaming industry as "an individualistic creature" who "continues to evolve," "learns best practices," and refuses to be stagnant. For Vincent, unionization was not viable "because of the nomadic nature of game developers" in that "they move from place to place." The combination of a youthful workforce with doses of libertarian spirit was also a factor, Ronaldo would say: "It's a combination of youth and libertarianism because there is a disproportionate number of libertarians involved in any kind of electronic

technology. It's easy to find those people in a game setting because it's this con-
trolled environment where you can kind of point at things and say this isn't
gonna work. And the industry is full of young people." In the words of one HR
staffer: "People that come into these types of professions aren't the ones with
that kind of mentality of 'I need somebody to represent me as an employee.'"

For the testers, the conditions of temporary employment were already too
pressing for them to consider unionization. The temporary tester George noted:
"We know that we're coming in as temporary workers. We don't have to sit there
and believe we really need to fight for this, this right to have particular days off."
As another temporary tester Andy highlighted, the coolness of being in the gaming
industry also factors in: "Especially because it's game development and it almost
feels like a privilege just to be involved in the industry."

Ultimately, throughout my time at Desire, developers experienced unstable
times, layoffs, and bankruptcy, but unionization never emerged as a natural topic
or option to consider. The game developers saw their labor as completely distinct
from industrial labor, which, in their imagination, was more prone to exploitation and deskilling than creative work. The world of creative production was
based on a culture of constant change and mobility, which would make hard, if
not completely liquefy, efforts toward unionization or other forms of organization. Many of them also highlighted the libertarian and youthful nature of the
workforce as a factor for them not to consider alternative ways of addressing their
problems at work. The discourse concerning "doing what you love" was particularly striking since once somebody was "privileged" to work at a cool job, then
organization seemed to be automatically off the table in a world of precarious
work where finding employment in and outside the creative industries was tough.

Toward a Labor Politics of Love?

The more game developers became integrated into the circuits of capital, the less
control they commanded over the labor process precisely because they were
chained to a financialized perpetual-growth machine. The structural pressures of
capital clearly turned ostensibly secure studio employees into precarious workers. While there was relative autonomy over the labor process, this autonomy was
strictly regulated and dictated by the publicly traded parent company, whose major
concern was growth and investor satisfaction. As shown earlier, the investors' impa-
tience for signs of growth did not always benefit the game studio. On the contrary,
precarity and mechanisms for coping with risk were highly individualized.

The developers did see and enjoy game development as teamwork but at the
same time valued the ways in which their profession supported individual ad-

vancement. Employees refused to stay where they were. Solutions to problems at work were found collectively only when the problem was about work in its literal meaning. Developers discussed problems, complained about them, and shared their concerns with management, but at the end of the day, every developer faced the crisis on his or her own terms. At the same time, risk was very stratified. Certain sections of the workforce, such as testers, were more concerned about the bankruptcy of Digital Creatives than the developers.

In his global mapping and sobering critique of the creative economy, Andrew Ross (2007, 39) writes: "Wherever work has become more feel good and free, it has also become less just. . . . Job gratification, for creatives, has always come at a sacrificial cost—longer hours in pursuit of the satisfying finish, price discounts in return for prestige, and disposability in exchange for mobility and autonomy." Indeed, game developers love their jobs and are passionate about it; they are happy to work long hours, are willing to sacrifice family time during crunch, and are ready to take risks. Nevertheless, as the programmer James underlined in our interview after he was laid off, there are disadvantages to this: "Some people, maybe many people, in the game industry live in order to work. You should work in order to live. . . . That's just a priority you should have."

James's call needs to be taken seriously for the development of a sustainable gaming industry and institution of fair labor practices, because even the prioritization of work over life did not completely make the lives of Desire's developers more stable. While game developers might have enjoyed relative autonomy in the workplace, they lacked control over intellectual property or information about finance. They were strictly subject to the decisions of management with which they had neither an organic relationship nor smooth processes of communication. Moreover, from time to time, they had to comply with the demands of management with respect to not only work schedule but also game play and content. Through financialization, relations of bondage between cognitive capital and game producers were established where the latter considered themselves not as workers but human capital and were strictly tied to the former "at the affective, cognitive and political levels" (Lazzarato 2009, 111).

Desire's developers as a group were not ready to conceptualize collective activity as an alternative to the present conditions of work and were unwilling to engage in political action. Despite emerging struggles, creative industries are still overall "actively disorganized" (Ross 2007, 39). Reasons behind this vary. The number of workers dedicated to the hard and material work of political engagement, personal histories, and geography crucially matter in terms of collectively resisting precarity. The networks of communicative capitalism are influential in not only absorbing resistance but also in reproducing the playful and libertarian spirits of the game developers, who have played the games of empire and now are joyfully—albeit precariously—producing them (Dean 2009). In this sense, it is not quite clear whether the passion for work can automatically turn into what Melissa Gregg (2011, 172) calls a "labor politics of love." Resisting precarious game employment and constructing alternative modes of game work will not depend simply on fluid networks but additionally require collective and material practices of organizing.

CONCLUSION

Reimagining Labor and Love in and beyond Game Production

In this book, I documented the inequalities surrounding video game production as a precarious labor of love. I told Desire's story as it transitioned from being an independent studio to the flagship of Digital Creatives, only to be sold again after the parent company declared bankruptcy. A major lesson Desire's story reveals is that failure and precarity are endemic to game production as innovative and creative work. Dream jobs in the video game industry are surrounded with illusions.

This book illustrates how a decidedly unequal regime of ludopolitics structures game production. At different levels and from varying angles, love anchors many different stories at Desire. When they were independent, it was love, excessive self-exploitation, and the entrepreneurial spirit that pushed Desire's developers to work long hours and succeed, ultimately becoming a desirable enterprise to be acquired by Digital Creatives. Desire's employees were so fond of their creative autonomy that the initial stages of their integration into Digital Creatives produced frictions at work.

Upon acquisition, Desire needed a new playground. Hence, the spatialization process through which the studio relocated and transformed the city along neo-liberal lines that are likely to reproduce urban inequalities. Desire's developers moved into their new corporate plaza, but management's question of how to boost the productivity of its labor force was not resolved. Therefore, management allowed Desire's developers to "playbor" (Kücklich 2009) flexibly in their new play-ground, since communication and socialization were vital to their well-being. They thoroughly enjoyed such perks as alcohol consumption or Nerf gun fights at work, but their playful and passionate labor practice had a cost, paid by their partners, whose unpaid labor, legitimized through the discourse and practice of love, enabled Desire's success.

Love again was what energized Desire's testers as they endured repetitive tasks without much tangible hope of permanent employment. Their love for video games empowered them but also intensified their precarization. Finally, when Digital Creatives declared bankruptcy, Desire's developers were unable to celebrate the fruits of their love since the moment their franchise secured a relatively solid place in the market, they were sold to another company. Success, in other words, was not enough.

In this new context, the future was uncertain, and some developers left their beloved Desire. Through email, I approached one of these artists and asked if he wanted to give an interview. He responded: "I am sorry but I feel I am a bit too emotional to talk about it in details. It is a very complicated issue for me that doesn't break down into a simple explanation. I'll let you know how I feel next week as I might have settled down a bit, emotionally."

How do we make sense of this emotional statement? How do we understand the fact that another developer, despite being laid off, still wanted to stay at the studio so that she could help her colleagues by crafting code for the game? How can we critically grasp that another developer had drawn a heart symbol next to the studio's name on the visitors' sign-up sheet where I put my name every time I visited Desire? What kind of love is at work in game development, and what do we do with it?

Down with Love in Game Development?

As I emphasized earlier in the book, doing what one loves is probably one of the best things that can happen to anybody because jobs currently are not only scarce but also increasingly standardized, meaningless, and administrative. Yet, at the same time, doing what one loves can be a mixed blessing; joyful as it is, love can be precarious and alienating. In fact, leading to illusions, love does hurt in the game industry. A critique of love, then, is in order. Why now this discourse of love? Why now the global transformation of workplaces into playgrounds? What do these mean as far as class politics is concerned?

An examination of how game development is imagined and talked about by its practitioners could be useful here. The founding president and CEO at the Entertainment Media Council, Morgan Ramsay (2012), interviewed industry professionals, including legends like Electronic Arts founder Trip Hawkins and Nolan Bushnell from Atari. Even though not all the interviewees carry such legendary status, the connecting thread between them is that all seventeen are either founders or cofounders of a game company.

Aside from narrating valuable oral histories of the industry, contributors to *Gamers at Work* (Ramsay 2012) unsurprisingly and almost religiously underline one aspect of how they imagine game development: love and passion. Trip Hawkins of EA, for instance, talks about making sure that they "were hiring true believers who were passionate" (7). Chris Ulm, cofounder of Appy Entertainment, concludes his interview by advising, "Do what you love" (260). Jason Rubin, cofounder of Naughty Dog, speaks almost in a theological manner: "I think you have to have a certain amount of blind, naïve faith in yourself to be an entrepreneur. I truly believed that it was inevitable that I would be successful. If I hadn't had such an unfounded certainty in myself, I would have taken a safer route through life."

There is much to unpack here. On the one hand, all the interviewees in this book, except for one, are men. That is, a gendered politics of editorial inclusion is at work. On the other hand, an important criterion to be included in a volume on game production seems to largely depend on one's visibility, seniority, and name in the industry (Tokumitsu 2015). In other words, class matters. These terms of inclusion and exclusion with respect to the historiography of game production are undoubtedly rooted in the unequal regime of ludopolitics. An almost religious vocabulary of love and risk taking sets the boundaries of who can speak and narrate what it means to be a game developer. In doing so, these hegemonic narratives in the video game industry mythologize success, individualize creative work, and therefore render both workplace inequalities and collaborative creativity invisible.

The success of anybody and any institution depends on the hard work of other laboring bodies, institutions, and infrastructures. Behind every developer who puts enormous hours in making a terrific video game publicized at the Electronic Entertainment Expo summits, there is considerable invisible work performed by their significant others. Similarly, precarious testers and hardware workers performing repetitive and dangerous tasks make major contributions to the production of games, although without proper acknowledgment.

Second, the advice to do what one loves is discriminatory in terms of class, gender, race, sexuality, and disability. The discourse is classist as it glamorizes certain professions and makes others less valuable. What if one cannot intern for a profession that one loves due to lack of parental support or the financial pressures of college debt? Who are the proper subjects that can embrace risk and uncertainty? What is the politics of visibility in relation to labor of love in the video game industry? It seems that in the video game industry, only *some* bodies are visible. Only *some* bodies seem to be able to practice a labor of love and take risks, revealing once again how high-tech industries have a lot to accomplish in terms of becoming democratic and inclusive workplaces.

A third problem with imagining game development as a labor of love is that it negates the possibilities for individual and social critique. Liberal conceptions of work in the creative industries frame employment as a matter of pleasure and choice. Surely, working in the game industry as a programmer guarantees a lot more choice compared to low-wage service jobs. Yet framing employment through pleasure and choice is dangerous because the precarious pain derived from creative work becomes negligible. As a matter of fact, others might frown on those who complain about exploitative labor practices in a profession where shooting Nerf guns in the workplace is allowed.

So, might the "do what you love" mantra imply something more nebulous than what it preaches? With its assumption of the liberal individual free to make employment choices, the "do what you love" discourse perhaps fosters a "take it or leave it" approach. Although it seemingly preaches thinking outside the box, it enacts an authoritarian labor regime that commands us how to approach work: love it. Anything other than love toward work becomes unacceptable.

Finally, the association of labor with love trivializes the mental and bodily dimension of passion. Creativity and love in fact can be very destructive even when one finds love at work. As Desire's story reveals, love is demanding and exploitative. It is exhausting, both physically and mentally. There is a biological cost to constantly solving problems, communicating, and being attentive to details in a labor process comprised of almost two hundred people. After all, developers' bodies have physical limits no matter how much they love their job. Fortunately, the game industry has for some time been discussing the extent to which things could be different. In fact, workers are starting to organize to resist the instrumentalization of love and passion. Silicon Valley is discussing whether universal basic income might be an option. And the broader question remains of what is to be done in an industry that is structurally insecure.

Work-Life Balance in the Game Industry?

As Digital Creatives went bankrupt and sold Desire to its new owner, there was news of layoffs across the industry (Ligman 2013; Rose 2013). I was discussing these layoffs with Robert, a highly experienced designer who had a couple of successful titles under his belt. In contrast to his very confident days when I had first interviewed him, he now looked a bit anxious. His remarks confirmed the precarious and unsustainable nature of the console business, where failure is not an option: "We are below those triple-A titles that sell fifteen, twenty, twenty-five million units. And those are the ones that are bankable. Those are always gonna be successful, whereas us—we have a couple of failures, we are dead."

Robert's remarks as an experienced designer provide an entry point for thinking about stability, quality of life, and work-life balance in the game industry. If failure means death and if failure is in fact common, is the video game industry a fleet of *Titanics*? Mainstream discourses regarding the game industry largely ignore structural failures and destruction and foreground attainable goals to sustain creativity. A good work-life balance is one of these goals. Game developers are often told that they can learn to maintain a good work-life balance, but is that really easy?

Game Developer magazine's findings over the years on salary satisfaction and job security have been ambivalent, if not discouraging, about this question. The magazine's eleventh annual salary survey suggested an atmosphere of "cautious optimism" in that while there had been an increase of salaries, game developers were critical of layoffs and the hit-driven mentality of the industry. According to some of the participants, the hit-driven mentality hurt innovation and creativity. A participant found the industry's "attitude toward work life balance absolutely terrible" (Miller 2012, 13). The twelfth annual survey also reported a salary increase but still foregrounded concerns about industry stability. A forty-one-year-old participant expressed how she was distressed about the failure of more studios, including "some spectacular" ones, and worried about "long term sustainability" for her career (Miller 2013). Long-term sustainability was a concern for Desire's experienced programmer Matthew, too. We were once talking about Desire's future after they were sold. Just like Robert, Matthew had contributed to some major titles, but the weather was changing slightly: "I am a little bit nervous to think what's gonna happen if we come up with a title that is not very profitable. I am actually a little bit concerned for our next game. It is not as strong of a title as our previous game."

A survey I conducted in mid-2012 at Desire confirmed Matthew's anxieties. Out of 186 full-time employees, 109 participated in this survey. Among the participants, 65 percent had concerns regarding job security, while 63 percent expressed distress with respect to studio stability. Also, 96 percent of the participants were troubled by losing senior talent and felt uneasy about the difficulty in replacing it. Desire's developers were also critical of producing sequels and desired the creative freedom to work on different titles. Slightly more than half of the developers found the gaming industry to be unstable in general. Finally, 88 percent of them wished to see more studios in the area, implying that they were eager to expand their employment and networking opportunities.

In this insecure context, game developers' first individual response to uncertainties in their everyday lives is to quit. If dissatisfied with working conditions, game developers can move to another studio, start their own business, or quit the industry for good. In that regard, love for the job faces an extremely individualized "take it or leave it" approach from the industry, where developers are more inclined to find employment elsewhere rather than confronting the studios (Legault and Weststar 2013). This option works especially in geographies with a large ecosystem of game studios. Another alternative is sabotage. If not in the form of leaking information, sabotage can include acts of taking office materials, vandalizing equipment, or dropping a so-called Easter egg—a hidden video game feature—in a particular section of the game to draw attention to intellectual property issues (Legault and Weststar 2013).

Developers' dissent has found a somewhat institutional base, too. As an organized body, the International Game Developers Association (IGDA) in the past encouraged some studios to stop undesirable workplace policies. However, these actions have limits because of IGDA's voluntary basis of participation. It can invite studios to improve working conditions but cannot enforce legal action.

Aside from direct communication with game studios, IGDA has also been addressing what is commonly called the "quality of life" in the industry. It has produced quite a few white papers, including *Developers Satisfaction Survey 2014: Employment Report* (Weststar and Legault 2014). This report covers such diverse issues as autonomy, working time, compensation, confidence in management, and job satisfaction. Especially notable is that compared to IGDA's 2009 white paper on quality of life, the 2014 document does not report much progress on work-life balance. As mentioned in the report, "almost half of the sample felt constantly behind at home and at work and emotionally drained by the effort to keep up" (Weststar and Legault 2014, 51). In addition, compared to 36 percent in 2009, 41 percent of the sample felt that their "work interferes with my ability to spend time with my family" (Weststar and Legault 2014, 52). And more game developers "worry that time spent away from work diminishes their chance of promotion or advancement" (Weststar and Legault 2014, 52). Finally, "39 percent said they left for a better quality of life" and as concluded in the report, "quality of life remains the most important concern among people who leave the industry" (Weststar and Legault 2014, 74).

Since the EA Spouse controversy and the ensuing legal actions, studios have been attempting to improve work-life balance, and Desire has done its share by introducing a flexible work environment policy. Implementing an open-door policy, Desire's management has been organizing various activities for the developers' spouses. Yet, since it is precisely the transformation of the workplace into a playground and mutation of leisure and social life into work without spatiotemporal boundaries, we should question the very discourse of work-life balance. Given the accounts of Desire's developers, game development has a contested status in that it swings between play and work. Its practitioners do not strictly regard it as a job since it's defined by love. Rather, it is "something we [game developers] are as opposed to something we [they] merely do" (Fleming 2015, location 427).

How feasible, then, is it to achieve a work-life balance in this industry? The centrality of passion to work, the fusion of work and play, the ludic structure of the workplace, the perpetual innovation dynamics of the industry (Schreier 2017), and financialization seem to make the idea of a work-life balance untenable (Fincham 2008; Land and Taylor 2010; Lewis 2003). Desire's developers' feelings, subjectivity, and interpersonal relationships are monetized as the spatial and temporal boundaries of the workplace collapse. Drinks, partying, and Nerf guns render work pleasurable, which is further intensified through the convenience of the flexible work environment policy and mobile devices.

The disruption of a healthy work-life balance is most visible at home as both Desire and the industry rely heavily on domestic labor: no relief at work, no relief at home. In sum, although commendable, the search for a work-life balance *without a political vision* is questionable given the various forms of stress, bodily pain, and anxiety related to precarization. In fact, with these existing work dynamics, the industry may well be shooting its own feet because these intense work rhythms threaten creative production. Creativity requires deep reflexivity, for which there is not enough space in the accelerated rhythms of the industry. The desires of a demanding audience, the industry's own push for quality games, and the unending production cycles of downloadable content leave little room for sitting back and reflecting on how game production could be devised differently while simultaneously satisfying the creative desires and well-being of its workforce.

Resisting Precarity and Emotional Toxicity at Work: Unions and Universal Basic Income

If Desire's workers are largely indifferent to or against unions, does this mean that game workers are being duped? Are their creative desires co-opted by the game industry? Casey O'Donnell (2014, 161) rightly suggests that thinking of game developers as the "dupes of a post-industrial system that exploits them" would be an easy answer. He acknowledges that game studios are corporations but then highlights how professionals in the industry are driven by the "intellectual, visual, collaborative aspects" (161) of their work. Game developers work hard, O'Donnell argues, because, just like hackers, they are curious about the systems they work with. They desire to explore these systems. This desire simultaneously pushes them to work harder and enables them to subvert the hegemonic systems within which they operate.

Game developers do love experimenting with advanced technological systems. They regard the development kits as toys to mess and play with. But an intellectual guard against developers' being duped makes sense if we also remember that there is a political and emotional economy structuring developers' hacker-like work ethic. An overemphasis on this hacker practice might obstruct our vision to sufficiently see the political-economic dimensions of the "do what you love" mantra especially because it is the game industry's rigid IP regime that produces "cultures of secrecy" and prevents a sharing-based work culture (O'Donnell 2014). Then the question is, if developers at Desire and in the industry have concerns regarding overwork, how interested are they in extending the boundaries of their autonomy toward sharing-based frameworks of creative production as well as institutionally establishing more humane working conditions?

Until very recently, the response to this question would be "not very much." One reason behind game developers' indifference to collective action could be related to the governmental logic of precarization in the industry. As I argued earlier, Desire's acquisition by Digital Creatives only changed the dimensions of insecurity associated with being an independent studio rather than terminating it. The unfortunate outcome of this precarization is that those who perform immaterial labor at work may not always be open to political resistance (Gill and Pratt 2008, 21). Matthew, for instance, believes that forming a union is "a little bit like biting the hand that feeds you." Under precarious conditions, developers can opt for certainty rather than signing up for the hard political work of organizing or imagining alternative ways of working. As the lead designer Robert also agreed, sometimes people just want to know who they will be working for and not worry about what the next stage of their lives will be like. While the prospect of working on different projects is exciting, Desire's workers yearn for a safe harbor that provides a place-bounded identity in the hectic conditions of precarious creative production.

Another reason for the lack of interest in collective action lies in the class politics surrounding the industry. Glorifying the "do what you love" mantra, video game production is yet another creative industry where employment is competitive and individualistic. I was once invited to a promotional game launch party. It was dark inside, and I approached two very happy programmers, who were sipping their drinks. We were almost shouting at each other since the party was very loud. Chris would tell me that during his job interview at Desire, he had turned Matthew and said, "I want your job." This overt statement and its competitive tone should be interpreted vis-à-vis the industry's competitive, techno-utopian, and libertarian politics. The reluctance to engage in collective action stems from the developers' consideration of game production as a neutral, meritocracy-based creative profession rather than concrete work defined by politics. In other words, while Desire's workers do enjoy game development as a fulfilling cocreative activity, they are in competition with each other.

A third structural reason as to why game developers are indifferent or opposed to the idea of unions is because their imagination, like many of us in the neoliberal moment, is strictly anchored in "the fantasy of work society" (Chamberlain 2018). This fantasy is so powerful that relations outside money and wage work are unimaginable.

However, despite the ideology of individualism, meritocracy, and the prevalent attitude toward work itself, antagonisms have recently become more visible in the industry. One of these instances concerns Rockstar, the studio behind such hits as *Grand Theft Auto* and *Read Dead Redemption*. In an interview with *Vulture*, Rockstar cofounder Dan Houser declared how they "were working 100-hour-weeks" several times in 2018 for *Red Dead Redemption 2*, which included "300,000 animations, 500,000 lines of dialogue and many more lines of code" (Klepek 2018). Houser later clarified that it was him and a few other senior writers rather than the whole studio that put in these insane hours.

The debates didn't wind down, and Rockstar lifted a social media ban in place for its employees that prevented them from commenting on the studio's work culture. Those who then went on to comment on social media emphasized that they were not mistreated or forced to work one hundred hours. At the same time, they did acknowledge that there was crunch. For instance, while Rockstar North's Tom Fautley expressed how he enjoyed being at Rockstar, he underlined that crunch was not always great especially because he had "health issues linked to stress and anxiety." Similarly, the tools programmer Vivianne Langdon said although she didn't feel "overworked or mistreated," she highlighted how she didn't want this "to diminish any others' stories should they arise" (Kerr 2018).

Rockstar's oppressive work practices in the production of *L.A. Noire* had also previously been brought under media attention. And aside from this, they are generally secretive about work practices. Therefore, allowing their workers to express opinions on social media is important since it demonstrates that game studios do not want to be associated with the mistreatment of workers. At the same time, although these social media posts are important, relying too much on them as evidence may be tricky. First, those who had to leave Rockstar because of working conditions would likely have had different experiences, and their opinions are not easily found in the conversation, as they are no longer employees. One needs to search deeply for such comments. For instance, the deleted tweet of a former QA worker read: "I worked 80-hour weeks at Rockstar until I had a breakdown. If I hadn't, my contract would have been terminated. There are plenty of ways to force a person" (MacDonald 2018). Keza MacDonald's (2018) story for *The Guardian* gives voice to another former Rockstar worker, this time working for PR and social media: "It's been nearly a decade since I parted from Rockstar, but I can assure you that during the *GTA IV* era, it was like working with a gun to your head seven days a week. Be here Saturday & Sunday too, just in case Sam or Dan come in, they want to see everyone working as hard as them."

Second, in addition to the relative exclusion of former employees' voices, not everyone feels comfortable, powerful, and secure enough to speak online (O'Connor 2018). There are differential power relations and inequalities across various workers and disciplines, as the remarks of an anonymous employee who wrote to the video game blog VG247 illustrate: "Hey, just going to add my piece as a Rockstar employee. Not every studio gets paid overtime. We certainly don't. Other departments may not feel forced, but I doubt you'll see many tweets from Design or QA. The average from all departments makes overtime not look too bad, but I've done 50+ hour weeks as standard since I started. Even if there is no work, we are told to come in every weekend anyway. I believe the people are being honest when they tweet, but they can only speak for themselves. Just needed that off my chest" (Kerr 2018). In that regard, who can or cannot express dissent is embedded in inequalities and therefore may not always visible.

Third, although Dan Houser tried to clarify his comments and emphasized that the "additional effort is a choice" and "they don't ask or expect anyone to work anything like this," the word "choice" is not innocent. It enforces "passion" upon all other workers, leading to the production of what I call emotional toxicity, which softly dictates the performance of emotional labor by everyone else (Cross 2018). This emotional toxicity frames passion as a choice-based practice that comes from one's heart although it is rooted in political economy. Those that question its politics are outcast as failures or killjoys.

Rockstar has not been alone in creating industrial controversies and workplace antagonisms. Activision Blizzard hit the news due to its massive downsizing in 2019. After announcing record revenues for 2018, the company laid off 800 employees, which is 8 percent of its workforce. The massive layoff immediately raised eyebrows. On the one hand, the company witnessed a "record fiscal 2018 revenues of $7.5 billion, up 7.1 percent year-over-year" (Perez 2019). On the other hand, in order to focus on certain games such as *Call of Duty*, *Overwatch*, *Hearthstone*, *Diablo*, and *Candy Crush*, they had decided to "restructure" by cutting "disappointing initiatives and employees layoffs" (Perez 2019). It is at this point that controversies exploded because the restructuring logic was selective, targeting employees from "nondevelopment and administrative-related parts of the business" (Perez 2019). Those occupying much higher positions were not affected.

To make things worse, Activision Blizzard granted a $15 million bonus, on top of his $900,000 salary, to its new CFO in early 2019.

These recent Rockstar and Activision Blizzard debates have been only the latest additions to the brief history of antagonisms in the industry, including EA Spouse, Rockstar Spouse, and the 38 Studios case (Vanderhoef and Curtin 2016).[1] Fortunately, game workers are speaking up to change how business is done. They have recognized that a collective struggle, rather than individual reactions and resolutions, might be a more powerful strategy to ameliorate the working conditions in the industry. Currently, game developers are unionized in France (STJV: Syndicat des Travailleurs du Jeu Video) and in the UK (Game Workers Unite UK). While STJV is the first video game industry union, Game Workers Unite UK is a branch of Independent Workers Union of Great Britain (IWGB). As an umbrella union, IWGB represents precarious workers such as migrant workers, security guards, and workers of the gig economy, including Deliveroo riders and Uber drivers. Connecting different groups of precarious workers across seemingly unrelated industries, IWGB is a source of inspiration for game industry unionization attempts and experimentations elsewhere.

The steps in forming a game workers' union accelerated prior to and during the Game Developers Conference (GDC) in March 2018. Before this gathering in San Francisco, the IGDA's director Jen MacLean gave an interview to the website USGamer. Commenting on how small studios deal with adverse financial conditions, MacLean said: "For example, if you are a relatively small studio that has laid off a team, odds are you laid them off because you can't afford them anymore. . . . A union's not going to change that; access to capital is going to change that" (Kim 2018). These remarks created controversy and were labeled antiunion rhetoric. And during the GDC, MacLean organized a roundtable entitled Unions Now? Pros, Cons, and Consequences of Unionization for Game Devs. The fate of this roundtable changed with the organized participation of the grassroots organization Game Workers Unite (GWU).

GWU initially started as a private Facebook group. They soon expanded their discontent to a Discord server, where their membership went beyond one hundred people. This then grew into a website and became a transnational movement with a concrete goal to unionize in the game industry. GWU members from the United States, Canada, Australia, France, and Finland shared handouts and buttons with participants during the GDC and finally attended MacLean's roundtable. There was no space to sit in the room. Game developers, academics, and union representatives from the French STJV and SAG-AFTRA (Screen Actors Guild–American Federation of Television and Radio Artists) who had supported a voice actors' strike in 2017 were all present to share their thoughts and experience. The discussions were intense, leading to criticism of MacLean's earlier remarks not only about capital's contributions to sustaining the industry but also unions' benefits in protecting those with mental challenges (Frank 2018a, 2018b; Williams 2018).

Emma Kinema (pseudonym) is a developer based in Los Angeles and, together with Liz Ryerson, she is one of the cofounders of GWU. For Kinema, the industry has various problems, including "rampant crunch due to bad management, lack of studio stability, large-scale contract employment, unpaid overtime, lack of comprehensive health care, and poor crediting practices" (Arndt 2018). The goal behind their powerful presence at the GDC stemmed from their frustration about how the roundtable would mostly involve talk without much action.

With the momentum it gained, GWU aims to build community and empower workers through sharing resources, bringing direct action, and instilling hope in workers. They have three strategies: cultivating solidarity locally, carrying out educational campaigns about unions and workers' legal rights and status if unionized, and collaborating with and learning from SAG-AFTRA and the Writers' Guild of America. Small but important steps like establishing whistle-blowing sites and legal defense funds are also part of their resistance reper-toire (Wilde 2018).

Kinema is aware of the difficulties GWU faces, such as conservative and liber-tarian leadership structures, greedy studios, and the personal investment of work-ers in their work. At the same time, she highlights how there are some workers who are both passionate about work but also interested in unionization. She is especially critical of the accepting mentality about crunch and industry practices and emphasizes how the discourse of passion normalizes overwork and self-exploitation (Arndt 2018). Similarly, Liz Ryerson believes that a union needs to replace the IGDA since this union would "do what IGDA claims to do, but actu-ally does it" (Williams 2018).

The work ethic and the highly masculine "nerd bravado" (Wright 2018) in the industry has long been an issue, but GDC 2018 was a turning point in shap-ing the industry's pro-union undercurrent. Workers' unionization efforts and sentiments should not be situated as a coincidental eruption, though. Rather, IWGB and the broader GWU movement is more like the culmination of unionization struggles in the French video game industry, the game industry's long-term internal problems related to institutional sexism (Consalvo 2008), emerging forms of resistance across digital media industries (Cohen and de Peuter 2018), the #MeToo movement and GamerGate (Braithwaite 2016; deWinter and Kocurek 2017).

Although Desire's own workers were indifferent to the idea of unionization, the developments since GDC 2018 are heartening because they make workplace discontent visible in an industry where unions were nothing but a utopian idea until recently. It will undoubtedly be the workers that will shape how the union of a fragmented and globalized workforce will look. GWU as a global movement can revitalize older traditions of collective action, or they can also invent new hybrid models that speak to the experiences of video game workers through new forms of care and compassion (Bain and McLean 2012; Cohen 2016; McRobbie 2016). Regardless, GWU members and its leadership are clearly alert to the difficulties, which seem to be outweighed by the joy of organizing. They are open to learning from other creative industry unions and are aware of the distinct union organizing they may have to perform given the workers' libertarian ethos and their emotional investment in production (Umney and Coderre-LaPalme 2017).

Although not yet brought up in relation to the exciting developments regarding unionization, the introduction of universal basic income (UBI) could be another useful strategy in resisting precarity. UBI is "the payment of a regular sum by a government to each individual (citizen) over an adult lifetime, with no conditions attached" (Pateman 2004, 89). UBI has for some time been on the agenda of libertarians, liberals, and the Left.[2] Completely against stipulations, such as means tests and prior contributions to gain income, it is meant to increase employment, reduce poverty, improve workers' employability, potentially reduce working hours, and ensure distributive justice under the flexible regime of neoliberalism (Van Parijs 1995).

At a practical level, UBI could have some positive impact on the game industry. It could secure a consistent income for all workers, which would be especially important to the more precarious ones, who would enjoy "the freedom not to be employed" (Pateman 2004, 93). UBI would significantly help those making and recycling game hardware and empower them to say no to despotic labor regimes. When their liberties are threatened, Asian manufacturing workers would be able to leave demeaning working conditions as they would have bargaining power. Desire's testers would similarly be empowered to resist the seductive and symbolic economy of play and its supposedly meritocratic rules. UBI would enable testers to enjoy what they call "funemployment" and pursue opportunities to improve their skills, invest in education, and still play video games. Destabilizing the regime of meritocracy, UBI would restore unemployed game workers' self-confidence and dignity. Game workers who are disillusioned by the "one-dimensional creativity" (Bulut 2018) in the triple-A sector would be able to take a break from blockbuster production and renew themselves by, for instance, experimenting in the indie scene. Marginalized game makers would be able to form co-operatives and thrive outside discriminatory regimes of production.

Therefore, it would be more possible to establish a proud and equal culture of citizenship in the game industry. UBI would be not an ultimate panacea but a meaningful step in challenging the unequal production logic in the game industry, reducing the advantages derived from one's privileges (middle class, white, male) and getting us closer to egalitarian practices of creativity.

Through UBI, industry professionals could also seek out spaces, like unions, for instance, to engage in political work and challenge the unequal regime of ludopolitics. This is where the leftist endorsement of UBI comes in. For the Left, UBI is not just extra money given to someone for simply being a citizen. It stands in for a more radical demand to interrogate the wage system and work ethic and raise awareness to abolish paid work by challenging work society itself (Chamberlain 2018; Frayne 2015; Pateman 2004; Weeks 2011). A more radical interpretation of UBI then would be invested in democratic citizenship, individual autonomy, new spaces of care, and collective struggle and ultimately open the political space for workers to rethink employment as a problem of democracy rather than simply individual freedom. In sum, although there are objections that UBI would yield to laziness and free riders,[3] from the very moment UBI becomes a possible intervention, it expands our political imagination about work.

Exodus from the Work/Play Society?

Work in the game industry is glamorous but also precarious. It is fun, but it doesn't seem to have an end. Then, for an industry that boasts a lot about thinking outside the box, it is perhaps time to start thinking about changing the game dynamics. That is, if the game industry itself is a game, how can the workers rewrite its rules? How can they redesign the game so that playing it becomes more rewarding and collective rather than illusionary? Being a player in the industry as a worker is a very emotional mode of existence. When game developers lose their jobs due to reasons completely unrelated to their performance or prefer to quit before somebody fires them and express their feelings with their tears, this says a lot about the articulation of love with work. In that regard, rewriting the rules of employment in the industry should involve also strategies that channel game workers' emotions into alternative forms of politics and imagination of life.

Therefore, in addition to unions and UBI, game workers might start imagining a postwork society, engage in refusal of work, and demand shorter work hours. These all sound utopian, but there is no reason to apologize for making these demands, because as Kathi Weeks (2011) argues, rather than apologizing for thinking in utopian terms, it is time to discuss what utopias can achieve and realize. Utopias are not simply manifestos about society. They refer to "a variety of partial glimpses of and incitements towards the imagination and construction of alternatives" (176), which GWU has already sparked. GWU's organizing work and the broader discussions of UBI imply not "a narrowly pragmatic reform but a more substantial transformation of the present configuration of social relations" (176). Drawing on Ernst Bloch, Kathi Weeks lists the political uses of daydreaming where the dreamers can distort reality and make choices. Desires are free in daydreaming, which involves "world-improving exercises" (192). True, daydreaming can lead to escapism, but its other part has "hoping at its core" and is "teachable."

It's ironic that, although video games are mostly marketed as digital venues where players' dreams and utopias are realized through interactive technology, the industry becomes suddenly serious when workers start daydreaming. The neoliberal society is such that it promises the universe, but workers are not even allowed to dream. That is where GWU is putting its fingers on a sector where unionization was nothing but a utopia until recently. In such a precarious and troubling historical context regarding labor, gender, and human rights, it is time to hope and teach each other how to hope. It is through hope and praxis that game developers, and workers globally, can provide partial answers to how we can disautomatize ourselves, denaturalize our commitment to work, liberate play from its instrumentalized forms, and reconstruct work as collaborative and creative activity outside relations of domination.

If the only future that we are allowed to dream promises us nothing other than corporatized, precarious, and exploitative forms of love and joy, let's be killjoys and resist the emotional toxicity in the game industry and workplaces at large. Let's be against this future, because that supposedly one and only future will still be shaped by the unequal regime of ludopolitics, producing nothing but massive inequalities. And game workers, players, and we, as citizens, deserve better.

Notes

INTRODUCTION

1. All quotations from Desire personnel are from my field notes, transcriptions of recorded conversations, and other forms of communication. I use pseudonyms for my research participants. Unless a quote is referred to by a pseudonym, I am drawing on field notes. To protect my research participants' anonymity, I am at various points unable to provide links to news articles.

2. Triple-A (or AAA) refers to digital games developed by large studios with massive budgets for both development and marketing. They are the blockbusters of the game industry.

3. I provide detailed information about the industry below, but for a critical political economic analysis of the industry, Randy Nichols's (2014) *The Video Game Business* is useful. For a global analysis, including India, Brazil, Turkey, Czechoslovakia, and Japan, Nina Huntemann and Ben Aslinger's (2013) edited volume is priceless.

4. Desire was founded as an independent studio in the mid-1990s and was acquired by the publicly traded Digital Creatives in the 2000s. Digital Creatives went bankrupt in the 2010s, and Desire was sold to a private company. To protect the anonymity of Desire's employees, I cannot give precise dates.

5. When I refer to precarity in the case of Desire, I do acknowledge the racialized production logics within the game industry (Srauy 2017), as well as the racialized and gendered history of creative technology production within and beyond the Global North (Abbate 2012; Amrute 2016; Crain, Poster, and Cherry 2016; Ensmenger 2010; Hicks 2017; Nakamura 2014; Qiu 2016). I elaborate more on racialized and gendered production logics in chapter 1.

6. Most of these discussions claim to be purely rational and economic, missing how politics informs economic imagination and action. Although the public is mostly geared toward an apocalyptic version of a robot invasion, the political nature of automation is ignored. Crucial questions are not posed, since even the discourse of "future of work" is not independent from power relations involving race, gender, and class. Who can think about the future and mobilize the resources to shape it? The future of work perhaps lies not in the future or in some technological developments that await us but in the past and the future outcome of ongoing social struggles and discourses around work or a specific technology.

7. My concept of "ludic contract" is a political modification to the social contract. The social contract as suggested by Hobbes, Locke, and Rousseau is about how a society becomes possible based on the rights and obligations of citizens. Yet, the universal subject in all these accounts is a man. Just like the social contract, the ludic contract is also exclusionary but operates even more insidiously to undermine equality. While the social contract is between men and other men, the ludic contract is primarily a contract between game corporations and governments or game corporations and other game corporations. Drawing on Carole Pateman's (1988) critique of the social contract, but also on the insightful technological critique of media and cultural studies scholars (Carey 2009; Mosco 2004; Nakamura 2008; Slack and Wise 2015), the notion of the ludic contract expands the critique of the social contract to grasp the gamification of social life. The ludification of the social contract redefines citizenship and leaves two major marks on how we work and

play. As far as work is concerned, the ludic contract rearranges the work ethic by making it more gamelike. Work is no more about toil or abstinence. It involves participation, excess, joy, and even addiction in that one cannot stop working that easily anymore (Weeks 2011). The ludic contract also transforms how we play by instrumentalizing it for economic means (Bulut 2018; Grimes and Feenberg 2009).

8. I define *immaterial labor* as "the labor that produces the informational and cultural content of the commodity" (Lazzarato 1996, 132). In the next chapter, I expand on how I both use and critique the term.

9. This organizational capacity does not imply that the industry works like a flawless conspiracy. On the contrary, it consists of overlapping networks of interaction, and success is never guaranteed. Crises, failures, and antagonisms are endemic to the industry.

10. *Crunch* is a common term used by game developers, and it refers to the long hours of work extended over a long period where the primary goal is to either complete a project or possibly meet a crucial milestone. It might take place due to poor planning or budgetary issues, among other reasons, but it is a topic often discussed among game developers and labor-oriented scholars of game studies.

11. Miranda Banks's (2009) research on how the work of costume designers is immediately coded as women's work deserves mentioning. Vicki Mayer (2008) discusses how soft-core reality laborers deploy masculine discourses of professionalism, relying on ideals of meritocratic success, as well as narratives of self-making through professional performativity. Quite interestingly, her research interlocutors also use phrases like "battleground," "hit and miss," and "hunting." John Caldwell's (2008) classic study examines the gendered practices in television and film production that become visible in workers' descriptions of themselves as wartime heroes, who, thanks to their mastery of technical equipment, can survive intense labor regimes.

12. GamerGate is the name given to an online harassment campaign by self-described real gamers who felt "threatened" by progressive changes in game culture. Supporters of GamerGate wanted to protect their "authenticity" from an "invasion" of feminists. It started in 2014 when a man sought to harass and torment his ex-girlfriend, the game developer Zoe Quinn; it soon became a widespread campaign, targeting many progressive figures both in the industry and game studies scholarship. Death and rape threats were circulated against the game developer Brianna Wu and the prominent technology writer Leigh Alexander. GamerGate's political relevance extends beyond the industry; Steve Bannon, the former executive chair of Breitbart News, was influential in bringing into the limelight Milo Yiannopoulos, a prominent cheerleader of GamerGate. Breitbart owes its success partly to its ability to capitalize on the GamerGate audience, who claimed to be waging a war against "social justice warriors" on behalf of "ordinary men." There are strong cultural links between the GamerGate audience and Trump supporters, as Steve Bannon was the former chief executive of Trump's presidential campaign (Lees 2016).

1. THE UNEQUAL LUDOPOLITICAL REGIME OF GAME PRODUCTION

1. Formerly constrained to the private sphere, love is now at the very core of public life (Weeks 2017). It is at the heart of the buzz around the contemporary economy, whose energy is derived from gigs, algorithms, robots, smart technologies, and human creativity. Love as extramonetary energy fuels technology companies, including Google, Facebook, and the game publisher Electronic Arts. Such companies do not even look like workplaces. They are playful campuses, offering their employees flexible work environments, free massage, swimming pools, and a soccer field, among other things. These are not perks. They are the essence of these campuses that employees live in. And employees love their work. My use of the term *love* draws on feminist scholarship and social reproduction theory (Bhattacharya 2017; Jarrett 2016; Weeks 2017), especially because labor

power itself is no longer enough for capital within the context of the information economy. In this new context, capital also needs our "love power" (Jónasdóttir 1994), which is "the basic human capacity by means of which we empower each other as persons" (Gunnarsson 2014, 104). It is in this sense as a form of working and value-generating capacity that I define love. I am especially inspired by Kathi Weeks (2017, 48), for whom the mandate to do what one loves is "a biopolitical project rather than a traditionally ideological one." Indeed, as the school visits and ordinary play practices reveal, love is not simply a top-down project. Subjects practice it, talk about it, and live it in various places with different objects.

2. Alternative concepts, such as creative labor (Hesmondhalgh and Baker 2011) and cultural work (Banks 2007), also offer useful insights for attending to the subjective aspects of the labor process. However, approaches to creative work through the lens of justice rather than politics may be misguided. Even when one possesses all the features of good work, there might still be alienation simply because there is no security or clarity concerning one's employment future. If we look for justice in the media workplace and prefer terms like *good work* to alienation, we might ignore the political nature of employment. A game studio, at the end of the day, is a political community "if we call political any situation in which there is a composition of powers of acting" (Lordon 2014, 127). We need to politicize the discussion of good and bad work when it is precisely the soul of the worker that game companies want. At the same time, I am not uncritical of the term "immaterial labor." Therefore, I take an intermediate position. I do acknowledge both the criticisms about the concept (Schumacher 2006) and disagreements regarding the work of the autonomist Marxists, specifically Michael Hardt and Antonio Negri (Fortunati 2007; Passavant and Dean 2004). I address the criticisms against Hardt and Negri's neglect of domestic labor through what I call the regime of ludopolitics (see also chapter 5). Still, I do think that their emphasis on the qualitative shift with respect to the hegemony of immaterial labor is purposefully sidelined. These authors talk more about a tendency than absoluteness. Bifo Berardi's (2007, 76) remarks with respect to how the mind has always been central to human production are noteworthy because, as he writes, "in the sphere of industrial labor, the mind was put to work as a repetitive automatism, as the physiological support of muscular movement. Today the mind is at work as innovation, as language and as communicative relation." Therefore, despite problems, I deploy this concept for two main reasons. First, it takes seriously the dialectical struggle between capital and labor in that the former's existence depends on the exploitation and control of the latter through automation, lengthening the workday, introducing flexible work environments, or turning workplaces into rebellious playgrounds. Second, this concept approaches intellectual property as the material embodiment of alienation where game developers are disassociated from their own products and labor.

3. Their disassociation from their products became particularly evident when Digital Creatives declared bankruptcy and had to sell Desire (see chapter 7).

4. As I was finishing this present work, I recognized that Liam Mitchell's *Ludopolitics: Videogames Against Control* (2018) came out. Mitchell's study is invested in software studies, political theory, and cybernetic theory and examines the relationship between code in video games and politics in everyday life. Theoretically and methodologically, my use of the terms "ludopolitics" and "ludopolitical" differs from Mitchell in terms of my focused interest in labor and political economic inequalities through an ethnographic lens.

2. THE END OF THE GARAGE STUDIO AS A TECHNOMASCULINE SPACE

1. Other critical scholars of media production also pointed to the continuities of the capitalist mode of production regarding the organization of the labor process. Uniting themes in such criticism have been the materiality of production in the new economy and

continuities with respect to the historical role of knowledge in capitalist production (Downey 2002; Huws 2003; McKercher and Mosco 2007), the persistence of degradation of labor in the new economy (Brophy 2008; Head 2003), flexibility and exploitation in traditional and new media workplaces (Cohen 2012; Deuze 2007; Neff 2012; Rodino-Colocino 2007; Ross 2003), and the continuation of a labor hierarchy and a star system in the new TV economy (Mayer 2011).

2. For the vibrant and almost chaotic history of game studios, their adventures, and business connections, see http://gamesareevil.com/wp-content/uploads/2010/03/History-of-Video-Game-Development-Studios-Flow-Chart-2.jpg.

3. The remarks of the developers suggest a glorification of the garage days and nostalgia. In one sense, it is understandable for these longtime employees to make such statements because they want to underline how much they worked. At the same time, this language of dedication is gendered.

4. These undoubtedly remind one of game workers' habitus, which Robin Johnson (2018) deploys in his work on gendered work cultures in the industry. Johnson investigates game production as a field where gendered professional ideologies and organizational cultures become invisible to its practitioners. The shared habitus of game developers at Desire also functions to invisibly make them believe that their material practices, assumptions, and beliefs about work are just natural and reasonable since habitus is a "universalizing mediation" (Bourdieu 1977, 79). It is the same habitus shaped by white technomasculinity that informs what I called ludic religiosity in the previous chapter.

5. A relatively recent study reveals the differences between how male and female workers perceive the lack of diversity in the industry. Male developers believe that there are not enough applications by female workers. For them, the applications from female candidates are low because of the negative representations of the game industry. Female workers, on the other hand, consider the industry to be still an old boys' club. They underline such issues as how some male workers are not even aware of the fact that flirting with female colleagues is a problem (O'Meara et al. 2017). In addition, although female workers have recently become more visible, the inclusion of more women is a complicated issue that needs to be considered beyond numbers. Rather, the question of female worker participation has to be examined in relation to the politics and nature of the kind of labor expected in the industry. That is, the expectation toward the performance of affective labor at work complicates issues even more at workplaces run by women. These expectations of performing extra affective labor even within production scenes populated by women perpetuate exclusionary practices, as well as reproduce narrowly defined, masculine notions of professionalism and technical capacities in these environments (Harvey and Shepherd 2017).

6. When developers work hard and push each other and enact a discourse of passion, what I call emotional toxicity emerges. This is a masculine culture of overwork within game development, a field structured by extreme practices of competitive work, meritocracy, and a discourse of love, where resistance to or reflexivity about sacrificial labor renders one's work ethic questionable.

7. This tough and ludic entrepreneurial archetype at Desire has precedents, such as the self-made man of personal capitalism and the organization man of managerial capitalism. What is relatively new here is the mediation of entrepreneurialism through digital utopianism. The archetype at Desire meshes digital utopianism with the earlier archetypes. There is a hybrid endorsement of both traditional and alternative masculinities at Desire through a form of geek culture.

3. GAMING THE CITY

1. *Micro-urban(ism)* refers to the concept used by local actors to brand and market Game City, the pseudonym of the city under consideration in this chapter. It is a concept that might be relevant for small or medium-sized cities, which do not necessarily constitute a significant node in the global economy but still do have a major impact and are seen as desirable by some members of the creative class. Micro-urban spaces are defined as urban centers with a population of up to 250,000 people. They possess some of the cultural markers that many internationally recognized cities have, such as arts, nightlife, strong technological infrastructure, and an awareness of environmental issues.

2. This was a different story from the perspectives of their partners as I elaborate in chapter 5.

3. The first TIF district in Game City was adopted in 1981. While these TIFs were set to expire in 2005, they have been extended to 2021. As of 2006, $14 million in funds for the redevelopment of downtown had been collected. As a concept, TIF set the ground for the Downtown Plan and is important in terms of assessing its impact as a finance tool to enable redevelopment through increases in property taxes above the base year and initiate improvements in the downtown area.

4. In order to preserve anonymity, I am not able to provide full citations for these remarks from local residents.

6. GAME TESTERS AS PRECARIOUS SECOND-CLASS CITIZENS

1. A previous version of this chapter was published earlier in *Television and New Media* (Bulut 2015).

2. "Skills" in the industry generally refer to the core creative team, and the industry perpetuates a perception that anyone can be a tester. However, this is a contested claim in that testers' off-the-clock play activities do constitute a crucial skill set.

7. PRODUCTION ERROR

1. In documenting Digital Creatives's market failure, I can only paraphrase industry publications in order to protect the anonymity of Desire's employees.

CONCLUSION

1. Most of these incidents, especially EA Spouse and Rockstar Spouse, are rooted in the domestic space, demonstrating once again that we should rethink game production not just as a workplace or industry issue but as a question of social reproduction rooted in politics. It is also telling that the cofounders of Game Workers Unite are also female. Perhaps these are the signs of our contemporary moment, where social movements against the rise of right-wing populism will likely be women's movements.

2. For a discussion on historical precedents to and various political positions on UBI, a useful list of works includes Birnbaum 2016, Chamberlain 2018, and Pateman 2004.

3. Carole Pateman (2004) makes an excellent point about the gendered construction of "idleness." When we think about idleness, we are still stuck to the figure of the male breadwinner, who is hegemonically imagined to be the historical breadwinner in the first place.

References

Abbate, Janet. 2012. *Recoding Gender: Women's Changing Participation in Computing.* History of Computing. Cambridge, MA: MIT Press.

Adkins, Lisa, and Maryanne Dever, eds. 2016. *The Post-Fordist Sexual Contract: Working and Living in Contingency.* Basingstoke: Palgrave Macmillan.

Adkins, Lisa, and Eeva Jokinen. 2008. "Introduction: Gender, Living and Labour in the Fourth Shift." *NORA—Nordic Journal of Feminist and Gender Research* 16 (3): 138–49.

Adorno, Theodore, and Max Horkheimer. 1944/2010. "The Culture Industry: Enlightenment as Mass Deception." In *Cultural Theory: An Anthology*, edited by Imre Szeman and Timothy Kaposy, 40–53. Chichester: Wiley-Blackwell.

Ahmed, Sara. 2004. *The Cultural Politics of Emotion.* New York: Routledge.

——. 2006. "Doing Diversity Work in Higher Education in Australia." *Educational Philosophy and Theory* 38 (6): 745–68.

Albom, Mitch. 2013. "Live in Your Office? You Might at Google." *Detroit Free Press*, March 17, 2013.

Alexander, Leigh. 2013. "Playing Outside." *New Inquiry*, June 17, 2013. https://thenew inquiry.com/playing-outside/.

Alloway, Nola, and Pam Gilbert. 1998. "Video Game Culture: Playing with Masculinity, Violence, and Pleasure." In *Wired Up: Young People and the Electronic Media*, edited by Sue Howard, 95–114. London: Routledge.

Amrute, Sareeta Bipin. 2016. *Encoding Race, Encoding Class: Indian IT Workers in Berlin.* Durham, NC: Duke University Press.

Andrejevic, Mark. 2013. "Estranged Free Labor." In *Digital Labor: The Internet as Playground and Factory*, edited by Trebor Scholz, 149–65. New York: Routledge.

Anthropy, Anna. 2012. *Rise of the Videogame Zinesters.* New York: Seven Stories.

Arndt, Dan. 2018. "Nerf Bosses: An Interview with Game Workers Unite." The Fandomentals. September 10, 2018. https://www.thefandomentals.com/nerf-bosses-an-interview -with-game-workers-unite/.

Arvidsson, Adam, Giannino Malossi, and Serpica Naro. 2010. "Passionate Work? Labour Conditions in the Milan Fashion Industry." *Journal for Cultural Research* 14 (3): 295–309.

Ash, James. 2015. *The Interface Envelope: Gaming, Technology, Power.* London: Bloomsbury.

Bain, Alison, and Heather McLean. 2012. "The Artistic Precariat." *Cambridge Journal of Regions, Economy and Society* 6 (1): 93–111.

Banks, John, and Jason Potts. 2010. "Co-creating Games: A Co-evolutionary Analysis." *New Media and Society* 12 (2): 253–70.

Banks, Mark. 2007. *The Politics of Cultural Work.* Basingstoke: Palgrave Macmillan.

Banks, Miranda. 2009. "Gender Below-the-Line: Defining Feminist Production Studies." In *Production Studies: Cultural Studies of Media Industries*, edited by Vicki Mayer, Miranda Banks, and John Thornton Caldwell, 87–99. New York: Routledge.

Barbrook, Richard, and Andy Cameron. 1996. "The Californian Ideology." *Science as Culture* 6 (1): 44–72.

Beck, Ulrich. 1992. *Risk Society: Towards a New Modernity.* London: Sage.

Bennett, Jane. 2004. "The Force of Things: Steps toward an Ecology of Matter." *Political Theory* 32 (3): 347–72.

Berardi, Franco. 2007. "Schizo-Economy." *SubStance* 36 (1): 76–85.

Berlant, Lauren. 2011. *Cruel Optimism*. Durham, NC: Duke University Press.

Bhattacharya, Tithi, ed. 2017. *Social Reproduction Theory: Remapping Class, Recentering Oppression*. London: Pluto.

Birnbaum, Simon. 2016. "Basic Income." *Oxford Research Encyclopedia of Politics*. https://doi.org/10.1093/acrefore/9780190228637.013.116.

Boellstorff, Tom. 2009. *Coming of Age in Second Life: An Anthropologist Explores the Virtually Human*. Princeton, NJ: Princeton University Press.

Bogost, Ian. 2011. *How to Do Things with Videogames*. Minneapolis: University of Minnesota Press.

Boltanski, Luc, and Eve Chiapello. 2005. *The New Spirit of Capitalism*. London: Verso.

Bonilla-Silva, Eduardo. 2014. *Racism without Racists: Color-Blind Racism and the Persistence of Racial Inequality in America*. 4th ed. Boulder, CO: Rowman & Littlefield.

Bourdieu, Pierre. 1977. *Outline of a Theory of Practice*. Cambridge: Cambridge University Press.

Braithwaite, Andrea. 2016. "It's about Ethics in Games Journalism? Gamergaters and Geek Masculinity." *Social Media + Society* 2 (4): 1–10.

Braverman, Harry. 1974. *Labor and Monopoly Capital: The Degradation of Work in the Twentieth Century*. New York: Monthly Review.

Briziarelli, Marco. 2016. "Invisible Play and Invisible Game: Video Game Testers; or, The Unsung Heroes of Knowledge Working." *TripleC: Communication, Capitalism and Critique* 14 (1): 249–59.

Brophy, Enda. 2008. "The Organization of Immaterial Labour: Knowledge Worker Resistance in Post-Fordism." PhD diss., Queen's University.

Brophy, Enda, Nicole Cohen, and Greig de Peuter. 2015. "Labour Messaging: Practices of Autonomous Communication." In *The Routledge Companion to Labor and Media*, edited by Richard Maxwell, 315–26. New York: Routledge.

Brophy, Enda, and Greig de Peuter. 2007. "Immaterial Labor, Precarity, and Recomposition." In *Knowledge Workers in the Information Society*, edited by Catherine McKercher and Vincent Mosco, 177–91. Lanham, MD: Lexington.

Bulut, Ergin. 2015. "Playboring in the Tester Pit: The Convergence of Precarity and the Degradation of Fun in Video Game Testing." *Television and New Media* 16 (3): 240–58.

——. 2016. "Dramın Ardındaki Emek: Dizi Sektöründe Reyting Sistemi, Çalışma Koşulları ve Sendikalaşma Faaliyetleri." *İLETİ-Ş-İM* (24): 79–100.

——. 2018. "One-Dimensional Creativity: A Marcusean Critique of Work and Play in the Video Game Industry." *TripleC: Communication, Capitalism and Critique* 16 (2): 757–71.

Burawoy, Michael, ed. 2000. *Global Ethnography: Forces, Connections, and Imaginations in a Postmodern World*. Berkeley: University of California Press.

Burston, Jonathan, Nick Dyer-Witheford, and Alison Hearn. 2010. "Digital Labour: Workers, Authors, Citizens." *Ephemera* 10 (3/4): 214–537.

Caffentzis, George. 2011. "A Critique of 'Cognitive Capitalism.'" In *Cognitive Capitalism, Education and Digital Labor*, edited by Michael Peters and Ergin Bulut, 23–57. New York: Peter Lang.

Caldwell, John Thornton. 2008. *Production Culture: Industrial Reflexivity and Critical Practice in Film and Television*. Durham, NC: Duke University Press.

Calo, Ryan, and Alex Rosenblat. 2017. "The Taking Economy: Uber, Information, and Power." *Columbia Law Review* 117:1623–90.

Caoili, Eric. 2012. "Blizzard Cuts 600 Employees in Organizational Shift." Gamasutra, February 29, 2012. http://www.gamasutra.com/view/news/163398/Blizzard_cuts_600 _employees_in_organizational_shift.php.

Carey, James W. 2009. *Communication as Culture: Essays on Media and Society.* Rev. ed. New York: Routledge.

Castranova, Edward. 2005. *Synthetic Worlds: The Business and Culture of Online Games.* Chicago: University of Chicago Press.

Chakravartty, Paula, and Denise Ferreira da Silva. 2012. "Accumulation, Dispossession, and Debt: The Racial Logic of Global Capitalism." *American Quarterly* 64 (3): 361–85.

Chamberlain, James. 2018. *Undoing Work, Rethinking Community: A Critique of the Social Function of Work.* Ithaca, NY: Cornell University Press.

Charrieras, Damien, and Myrtille Roy-Valex. 2008. "Video Game Culture as Popular Culture? The Productive Leisure of Video Game Workers of Montreal." Presented at the Annual Conference of International Communication Association, Montreal, Quebec, Canada, May 21, 2008. Quebec: Canada.

Cherry, Miriam. 2012. "The Gamification of Work." *Hofstra Law Review* 40 (4): 851–58.

Chess, Shira. 2015. "Youthful White Male Industry Seeks 'Fun'-Loving Middle-Aged Women for Video Games—No Strings Attached." In *The Routledge Companion to Media and Gender,* edited by Cynthia Carter, Linda Steiner, and Lisa McLaughlin, 168–79. New York: Routledge.

Cohen, Nicole S. 2012. "Cultural Work as a Site of Struggle: Freelancers and Exploitation." In "Marx Is Back," edited by Christian Fuchs and Vincent Mosco, special issue, *TripleC: Communication, Capitalism and Critique* 10 (2): 141–55.

———. 2016. *Writers' Rights: Freelance Journalism in a Digital Age.* Montreal: McGill-Queen's University Press.

Cohen, Nicole S., and Greig de Peuter. 2018. "'I Work at VICE and I Need a Union': Organizing Digital Media." In *Labour Under Attack: Anti-Unionism in Canada,* edited by Stephanie Ross and Larry Savage, 114–28. Halifax, Canada: Fernwood.

Coleman, Sarah, and Nick Dyer-Witheford. 2007. "Playing on the Digital Commons: Collectivities, Capital and Contestation in Videogame Culture." *Media, Culture and Society* 29 (6): 934–53.

Consalvo, Mia. 2008. "Crunched by Passion: Women Game Developers and Workplace Challenges." In *Beyond Barbie and Mortal Kombat: New Perspectives on Gender and Gaming,* edited by Yasmin Kafai, Carrie Heeter, Jill Denner, and Jennifer Y. Sun, 177–92. Cambridge, MA: MIT Press.

Cooper, Marianne. 2000. "Being the 'Go-To Guy': Fatherhood, Masculinity, and the Organization of Work in Silicon Valley." *Qualitative Sociology* 23 (4): 379–405.

Cote, Mark, and Jennifer Pybus. 2011. "Learning to Immaterial Labour 2.0: Facebook and Social Networks." In *Cognitive Capitalism, Education and Digital Labor,* edited by Michael Peters and Ergin Bulut, 169–95. New York: Peter Lang.

Crain, Marion G., Winifred Poster, and Miriam A. Cherry. 2016. *Invisible Labor: Hidden Work in the Contemporary World.* Oakland: University of California Press.

Cross, Katherine. 2018. "What Will Be Left of the People Who Make Our Games?" Polygon, October 17, 2018. https://www.polygon.com/2018/10/17/17986562/game -development-crunch-red-dead-redemption-2-rockstar.

Curtin, Michael, and Kevin Sanson. 2016. "Precarious Creativity: Global Media, Local Labor." In *Precarious Creativity: Global Media, Local Labor,* edited by Michael Curtin and Kevin Sanson, 1–19. Oakland: University of California Press.

Curtis, Tom. 2012. "Report: Layoffs Hit EA's Vancouver Branch as Company Makes Digital Shift." Gamasutra, February 3, 2012. http://www.gamasutra.com/view/news

/40099/Report_Layoffs_hit_EAs_Vancouver_branch_as_company_makes_digital _shift.php.

Dalla Costa, Mariarosa, and Selma James. 1975. *The Power of Women and the Subversion of Community.* 3rd ed. London: Falling Wall.

D'Anastasio, Cecilia. 2018. "Inside the Culture of Sexism at Riot Games." Kotaku, August 7, 2018. https://kotaku.com/inside-the-culture-of-sexism-at-riot-games-1828165483.

Daviault, Christine, and Gareth Schott. 2015. "Looking beyond Representation: Situating the Significance of Gender Portrayal within Gameplay." In *The Routledge Companion to Media and Gender*, edited by Cynthia Carter, Linda Steiner, and Lisa McLaughlin, 440–50. New York: Routledge.

Dean, Jodi. 2009. *Democracy and Other Neoliberal Fantasies: Communicative Capitalism and Left Politics.* Durham, NC: Duke University Press.

Deuze, Mark. 2007. *Media Work.* Cambridge: Polity.

deWinter, Jennifer, and Carly A. Kocurek. 2017. "'Aw Fuck, I Got a Bitch on My Team': Women and the Exclusionary Cultures of the Computer Game Complex." In *Gaming Representation: Race, Gender, and Sexuality in Video Games*, edited by Jennifer Malkowski and TreaAndrea M. Russworm, 57–74. Bloomington: Indiana University Press.

de Peuter, Greig. 2010. "The Contested Convergence of Precarity and Immaterial Labour." PhD diss., Simon Fraser University.

——. 2011. "Creative Economy and Labor Precarity: A Contested Convergence." *Journal of Communication Inquiry* 35 (4): 417–25.

——. 2012. "Level Up: Video Game Production in Canada." In *Cultural Industries.ca: Making Sense of Canadian Media in the Digital Age*, edited by Ira Wagman and Peter Urquhart, 78–94. Toronto: Lorimer.

Dinerstein, Joel. 2006. "Technology and Its Discontents: On the Verge of the Posthuman." *American Quarterly* 58 (3): 569–95.

D'Onfro, Jillian. 2018. "Techsploitation Protests in San Francisco." CNBC.com, May 31, 2018. https://www.cnbc.com/2018/05/31/techsploitation-protests-in-san-francisco .html.

Dovey, Jon, and Hellen W. Kennedy. 2006. *Game Cultures: Computer Games as New Media.* Berkshire, UK: Open University Press.

Dowling, Emma. 2007. "Producing the Dining Experience: Measure, Subjectivity and the Affective Worker." *Ephemera* 7 (1): 117–32.

Downey, Gregory J. 2002. *Telegraph Messenger Boys: Labor, Technology and Geography, 1850–1950.* New York: Routledge.

Downs, Edward, and Stacy L. Smith. 2010. "Keeping abreast of Hypersexuality: A Video Game Character Content Analysis." *Sex Roles* 62 (11–12): 721–33.

Duffy, Brooke Erin. 2017. *(Not) Getting Paid to Do What You Love: Gender, Social Media, and Aspirational Work.* New Haven, CT: Yale University Press.

Dyer, Richard. 1997. *White: Essays on Race and Culture.* London: Routledge.

Dyer-Witheford, Nick. 1999. *Cyber-Marx: Cycles and Circuits of Struggle in High-Technology Capitalism.* Urbana: University of Illinois Press.

Dyer-Witheford, Nick, and Greig de Peuter. 2006. "'EA Spouse' and the Crisis of Video Game Labour: Enjoyment, Exclusion, Exploitation, Exodus." *Canadian Journal of Communication* 31 (3). https://www.cjc-online.ca/index.php/journal/article/view /1771/1893.

——. 2009. *Games of Empire: Global Capitalism and Video Games.* Minneapolis: University of Minnesota Press.

Edensor, Tim, Deborah Leslie, Steve Millington, and Norma Rantisi. 2010. "Rethinking Creativity: Critiquing the Creative Class Thesis." In *Spaces of Vernacular Creativity:*

Rethinking the Cultural Economy, edited by Tim Edensor, Deborah Leslie, Steve Millington, and Norma Rantisi, 1–16. New York: Routledge.

English-Lueck, J. A. 2002. *Cultures@Silicon Valley*. Stanford, CA: Stanford University Press.

Ensmenger, Nathan. 2010. *The Computer Boys Take Over: Computers, Programmers, and the Politics of Technical Expertise*. History of Computing. Cambridge, MA: MIT Press.

Ernkvist, Mirko. 2006. "Down Many Times, but Still Playing the Game: Creative Destruction and Industry Crashes in the Early Video Game Industry, 1971–1986." Paper presented at XIV International Economic History Congress, Helsinki, Finland. Helsinki. https://www.researchgate.net/publication/237434904_.

Fairclough, Norman. 2006. *Language and Globalization*. London: Routledge.

Federici, Silvia. 1975. "Wages against Housework." In *The Politics of Housework*, edited by Ellen Malos, 187–94. Cheltenham, UK: New Clarion.

——. 2012. *Revolution at Point Zero: Housework, Reproduction, and Feminist Struggle*. New York: PM Press/Common Notions/Autonomedia.

——. 2014. "The Reproduction of Labour Power in the Global Economy and the Unfinished Feminist Revolution." In *Workers and Labour in Globalised Capitalism: Contemporary Themes and Theoretical Issues*, edited by Maurizio Atzeni, 85–111. New York: Palgrave Macmillan.

Fincham, Ben. 2008. "Balance Is Everything: Bicycle Messengers, Work and Leisure." *Sociology* 42 (4): 618–34.

Fineman, Stephen, ed. 1993. *Emotion in Organizations*. London: Sage.

Firestone, Shulamith. 1970. *The Dialectic of Sex: The Case for Feminist Revolution*. New York: Farrar, Straus and Giroux.

Fleming, Peter. 2014. *Resisting Work: The Corporatization of Life and Its Discontents*. Philadelphia: Temple University Press.

——. 2015. *The Mythology of Work: How Capitalism Persists despite Itself*. London: Pluto. Kindle.

Fortunati, Leopoldina. 2007. "Immaterial Labor and Its Machinization." *Ephemera* 7 (1): 139–57.

Foucault, Michel. 2008. *The Birth of Biopolitics: Lectures at the Collège de France, 1978–79*. Basingstoke, UK: Palgrave Macmillan.

Frank, Allegra. 2018a. "Pro-Union Voices Speak Out at Heated GDC Roundtable." Polygon, March 22, 2018. https://www.polygon.com/2018/3/22/17149822/gdc-2018 -igda-roundtable-game-industry-union.

——. 2018b. "This Is the Group Using GDC to Bolster Game Studio Unionization Efforts." Polygon, March 21, 2018. https://www.polygon.com/2018/3/21/17145242/game -workers-unite-video-game-industry-union.

Frase, Peter. 2016. *Four Futures: Visions of the World after Capitalism*. London: Verso.

Frayne, David. 2015. *The Refusal of Work: The Theory and Practice of Resistance for Work*. London: Zed.

Fuchs, Christian. 2014. *Digital Labour and Karl Marx*. New York: Routledge.

Fuller, Glen. 2015. "In the Garage." *Angelaki* 20 (1): 125–36.

Fuller, Matthew. 2005. *Media Ecologies: Materialist Energies in Art and Technoculture*. Cambridge, MA: MIT Press.

Fumagelli, Andrea, and Cristina Morini. n.d. "The Precarity-Trap and Basic Income: The Labour Market in Cognitive Bio-capitalism; the Italian Case." https://basicincome .org/bien/pdf/munich2012/fumagalli.pdf.

Fung, Anthony Y. H. 2016. "Comparative Cultural Economy and Game Industries in Asia." *Media International Australia* 159 (1): 43–52.

Galloway, Alexander. 2006. *Gaming: Essays on Algorithmic Culture*. Minneapolis: University of Minnesota Press.

Gamasutra. 2012. "'38 Studios Spouse' Speaks Out." Gamasutra, June 13, 2012. http://www
    .gamasutra.com/view/news/172303/38_Studios_Spouse_speaks_out.php.
Gandini, Alessandro. 2019. "Labour Process Theory and the Gig Economy." Human Rela-
    tions, 72 (6), 1039–1056.
Geertz, Clifford. 1973. The Interpretation of Cultures: Selected Essays. New York: Basic.
Gill, Rebecca. 2013. "The Evolution of Organizational Archetypes: From the American to
    the Entrepreneurial Dream." Communication Monographs 80 (3): 331–53.
Gill, Rosalind. 2007. Technobohemians or the New Cybertariat? New Media Work in Am-
    sterdam a Decade after the Web. Amsterdam: Institute of Network Cultures.
Gill, Rosalind, and Andy Pratt. 2008. "In the Social Factory? Immaterial Labour, Precari-
    ousness and Cultural Work." Theory, Culture and Society 25 (7–8): 1–30.
Gray, Kishonna. 2014. Race, Gender, and Deviance in XBox Live. Oxford: Anderson /
    Elsevier.
Gregg, Melissa. 2011. Work's Intimacy. Cambridge: Polity.
Grimes, Sara M., and Andrew Feenberg. 2009. "Rationalizing Play: A Critical Theory of
    Digital Gaming." The Information Society 25 (2): 105–18.
Gunnarsson, Lena. 2014. "Loving Him for Who He Is: The Microsociology of Power." In
    Love: A Question for Feminism in the Twenty-First Century, edited by Anna Jónas-
    dóttir and Ann Ferguson, 97–110. London: Routledge.
Hage, Ghassan. 2003. Against Paranoid Nationalism: Searching for Hope in a Shrinking So-
    ciety. Annandale, Australia: Pluto.
Hall, Stuart. 1995. "The Whites of Their Eyes: Racist Ideologies and the Media." In Gen-
    der, Race and Class in the Media, edited by Gail Dines and Jean M. Humez, 18–22.
    London: Sage.
——, ed. 1997. Representation: Cultural Representations and Signifying Practices. London:
    Sage.
Hardt, Michael, and Antonio Negri. 2000. Empire. Cambridge, MA: Harvard University
    Press.
Harrer, Sabine. 2018. "Casual Empire: Video Games as Neocolonial Praxis." Open Library
    of Humanities 4 (1): 1–28.
Harvey, Alison, and Stephanie Fisher. 2013. "Making a Name in Games." Information, Com-
    munication and Society 16 (3): 362–80.
Harvey, Alison, and Tamara Shepherd. 2017. "When Passion Isn't Enough: Gender, Affect
    and Credibility in Digital Games Design." International Journal of Cultural Studies
    20 (5): 492–508.
Harvey, David. 1990. The Condition of Postmodernity. Oxford: Blackwell.
——. 2010. A Companion to Marx's Capital. London: Verso.
Hay, James. 2011. "The Birth of the 'Neoliberal' City and Its Media." In Communication
    Matters: Materialist Approaches to Media, Mobility and Networks, edited by Jeremy
    Packer and Stephen Wiley, 121–41. London: Routledge.
Hayns, Joe. 2016. "A Sharing Economy Strike." Jacobin, August 16, 2016. http://jacobinmag
    .com/2016/08/deliveroo-strike-sharing-economy-living-wage/.
Head, Simon. 2003. The New Ruthless Economy: Work and Power in the Digital Age. Ox-
    ford: Oxford University Press.
Hearn, Alison. 2010. "Reality Television, the Hills, and the Limits of the Immaterial Labour
    Thesis." TripleC: Communication, Capitalism and Critique 8 (1): 60–76.
Henwood, Doug. 2003. After the New Economy. New York: New Press.
Herod, Andrew. 2012. "Placing Labor." In Labor Rising: The Past and Future of Working
    People in America, 83–99. New York: New Press.
Hesmondhalgh, David, and Sarah Baker. 2011. Creative Labour: Media Work in Three
    Cultural Industries. London: Routledge.

Heynen, Hilde. 2012. "Genius, Gender and Architecture: The Star System as Exemplified in the Pritzker Prize." *Architectural Theory Review* 17 (2–3): 331–45.

Hicks, Marie. 2017. *Programmed Inequality: How Britain Discarded Women Technologists and Lost Its Edge in Computing*. Cambridge, MA: MIT Press.

Hochschild, Arlie Russell. 1989. *The Second Shift: Working Parents and the Revolution at Home*. New York: Viking Penguin.

Howard, Philip. 2002. "Network Ethnography and the Hypermedia Organization: New Media, New Organizations, New Methods." *New Media and Society* 4 (4): 550–74.

Huntemann, Nina. 2013. "Women in Video Games: The Case of Hardware Production and Promotion." In *Gaming Globally: Production, Play, and Place*, edited by Nina Huntemann and Ben Aslinger, 41–59. New York: Palgrave Macmillan.

Huntemann, Nina, and Ben Aslinger, eds. 2013. *Gaming Globally: Production, Play, and Place*. New York: Palgrave Macmillan.

Huws, Ursula. 2003. *The Making of a Cybertariat: Virtual Work in a Real World*. New York: Monthly Review Press.

———. 2014. *Labor in the Global Digital Economy: The Cybertariat Comes of Age*. New York: Monthly Review Press.

———. 2016. "Logged Labour: A New Paradigm of Work Organisation?" *Work Organisation, Labour and Globalisation* 10 (1): 7–26.

Illouz, Eva. 2007. *Cold Intimacies: The Making of Emotional Capitalism*. Cambridge: Polity.

Irani, Lilly. 2015. "Justice for 'Data Janitors.'" *Public Books*, January 15, 2015. https://www.publicbooks.org/justice-for-data-janitors/.

Jackson, Stevi. 2001. "Love and Romance as Objects of Feminist Knowledge." In *Women and Romance: A Reader*, edited by Ostrov Susan Weisser, 254–267. New York: NYU Press.

Jarrett, Kylie. 2016. *Feminism, Labour and Digital Media: The Digital Housewife*. New York: Routledge.

Jin, Dal Yong. 2010. *Korea's Online Gaming Empire*. Cambridge, MA: MIT Press.

Johnson, Robin. 2018. "Technomasculinity and Its Influence in Video Game Production." In *Masculinities in Play*, edited by Nicholas Taylor and Gerald Voorhees, 249–62. New York: Palgrave Macmillan.

Jónasdóttir, Anna. 1994. *Why Women Are Oppressed*. Philadelphia: Temple University Press.

Kalleberg, Arne L. 2011. *Good Jobs, Bad Jobs: The Rise of Polarized and Precarious Employment Systems in the United States, 1970s to 2000s*. New York: Russell Sage Foundation.

Kennedy, Elizabeth J. 2017. "Employed by an Algorithm: Labor Rights in the On-Demand Economy." *Seattle University Law Review* 40 (3): 987–1048.

Keogh, Brendan. 2015. "Between Triple-A, Indie, Casual, and DIY: Sites of Tension in the Videogames Cultural Industries." In *Routledge Companion to the Cultural Industries*, edited by Justin O'Connor and Kate Oakley, 152–62. New York: Routledge.

Kerr, Aphra. 2013. "Space Wars: The Politics of Games Production in Europe." In *Gaming Globally: Production, Play, and Place*, edited by Nina Huntemann and Ben Aslinger, 215–33. New York: Palgrave Macmillan.

———. 2017. *Global Games: Production, Circulation and Policy in the Networked Era*. New York: Routledge.

Kerr, Chris. 2018. "Rockstar Devs Comment on Work Culture after 100-Hours Backlash." Gamasutra, October 18, 2018. https://www.gamasutra.com/view/news/328940/Rockstar_devs_comment_on_work_culture_after_100hours_backlash.php.

Kim, Matt. 2018. "IGDA Director Says Capital, Not Unions, Will Keep Game Development Jobs Secure." USGamer, March 19, 2018. https://www.usgamer.net/articles/igda-director-union-crunch-interview.

Klepek, Patrick. 2018. "The Industry Won't Change if Reporters Let the Powerful off the Hook." Vice.com, October 22, 2018. https://www.vice.com/en_in/article/bj4ajw/the-industry-wont-change-if-reporters-let-the-powerful-off-the-hook.

Kocieniewski, David. 2011. "Rich Tax Breaks Bolster Video Game Makers." *New York Times*, September 10, 2011, sec. Technology. http://www.nytimes.com/2011/09/11/technology/rich-tax-breaks-bolster-video-game-makers.html.

Kücklich, Julian Raul. 2009. "Virtual Worlds and Their Discontents: Precarious Sovereignty, Governmentality, and the Ideology of Play." *Games and Culture* 4 (4): 340–52.

Kuehn, Kathleen, and Thomas F. Corrigan. 2013. "Hope Labor: The Role of Employment Prospects in Online Social Production." *The Political Economy of Communication* 1 (1). http://polecom.org/index.php/polecom/article/view/9.

Land, Chris, and Scott Taylor. 2010. "Surf's Up: Work, Life, Balance and Brand in a New Age Capitalist Organization." *Sociology* 44 (3): 395–413.

Larson, Gregory S., and Amy R. Pearson. 2012. "Placing Identity: Place as a Discursive Resource for Occupational Identity Work among High-Tech Entrepreneurs." *Management Communication Quarterly* 26 (2): 241–66.

Lazzarato, Maurizio. 1996. "Immaterial Labor." In *Radical Thought in Italy*, edited by Paolo Virno and Michael Hardt, 133–51. Minneapolis: University of Minnesota Press.

———. 2009. "Neoliberalism in Action: Inequality, Insecurity and the Reconstitution of the Social." *Theory, Culture and Society* 26 (6): 109–33.

———. 2015. *Governing by Debt*. Cambridge, MA: Semiotext(e).

Lees, Matt. 2016. "What Gamergate Should Have Taught Us about the 'Alt-Right.'" *The Guardian*, December 1, 2016. https://www.theguardian.com/technology/2016/dec/01/gamergate-alt-right-hate-trump.

Lefebvre, Henri. 1991. *The Production of Space*. Oxford: Basil Blackwell.

Legault, Marie-Josee, and Johanna Weststar. 2013. "Are Game Developers Standing Up for Their Rights?" Gamasutra, January 9, 2013. http://www.gamasutra.com/view/feature/184504/are_game_developers_standing_up_.php.

Leonard, David. 2003. "'Live in Your World, Play in Ours': Race, Video Games, and Consuming the Other." *Studies in Media and Information Literacy Education* 3 (4): 1–9.

———. 2009. "Young, Black (& Brown) and Don't Give a Fuck." *Cultural Studies* ↔ *Critical Methodologies* 9 (2): 248–72.

Lewis, Suzan. 2003. "The Integration of Paid Work and the Rest of Life. Is Post-Industrial Work the New Leisure?" *Leisure Studies* 22 (4): 343–45.

Ligman, Kris. 2013. "More Layoffs Hit EA." Gamasutra, April 25, 2013.

Lordon, Frédéric. 2014. *Willing Slaves of Capital: Spinoza and Marx on Desire*. London: Verso.

Lorey, Isabell. 2014. *State of Insecurity: Government of the Precarious*. London: Verso.

Luckman, Susan. 2012. *Locating Cultural Work: The Politics and Poetics of Rural, Regional and Remote Creativity*. New York: Palgrave Macmillan.

MacDonald, Keza. 2018. "Rockstar Games Defends Itself over Working Conditions Claims." *The Guardian*, October 18, 2018, sec. Games. https://www.theguardian.com/games/2018/oct/18/rockstar-games-working-conditions-red-dead-redemption-2-rob-nelson.

Malaby, Thomas. 2009. *Making Virtual Worlds: Linden Lab and Second Life*. Ithaca, NY: Cornell University Press.

Marazzi, Christian. 2008. *Capital and Language: From the New Economy to the War Economy*. Los Angeles: Semiotext(e).

Martin, Randy, Michael Rafferty, and Dick Bryan. 2008. "Financialization, Risk and Labour." *Competition and Change* 12 (2): 120–32.

Massey, Doreen. 1994. *Space, Place and Gender*. Cambridge: Polity.

——. 2008. "A Global Sense of Place." In *The Cultural Geography Reader*, edited by Tim Oakes and Patricia Lynn Price, 257–64. London: Routledge.

Maxwell, Richard, and Toby Miller. 2012. *Greening the Media*. Oxford: Oxford University Press.

Mayer, Vicki. 2008. "Guys Gone Wild? Soft-Core Video Professionalism and New Realities in Television Production." *Cinema Journal* 47 (2): 97–116.

——. 2011. *Below the Line: Producers and Production Studies in the New Television Economy*. Durham, NC: Duke University Press.

Mbembe, Achille. 2003. "Necropolitics." *Public Culture* 15 (1): 11–40.

McCarthy, Cameron. 2011. "Reconstructing Race and Education in the Class Conquest of the City and the University in the Era of Neoliberalism." In *New Times: Making Sense of Critical/Cultural Theory in a Digital Age*, edited by Cameron McCarthy, Robert Mejia, and Heather Greenhalgh-Spencer, 86–107. New York: Peter Lang.

McGonigal, Jane. 2011. *Reality Is Broken: Why Games Make Us Better and How They Can Change the World*. New York: Penguin.

McGowan, Todd. 2003. *The End of Dissatisfaction? Jacques Lacan and the Emerging Society of Enjoyment*. New York: SUNY Press.

McGuigan, Jim. 2012. "The Coolness of Capitalism Today." In "Marx Is Back," edited by Christian Fuchs and Vincent Mosco, special issue, *TripleC: Communication, Capitalism and Critique* 10 (2): 425–38.

McKercher, Catherine, and Vincent Mosco, eds. 2007. *Knowledge Workers in the Information Society*. Lanham, MD: Lexington.

McRobbie, Angela. 2004. "'Everyone Is Creative': Artists as Pioneers of the New Economy?" In *Contemporary Culture and Everyday Life*, edited by Elizabeth Silva and Tony Bennett, 186–202. Durham, UK: Sociologypress.

——. 2016. *Be Creative: Making a Living in the New Culture Industries*. Cambridge: Polity.

Mejia, Robert. 2012. "Playing the Crisis: Video Games and the Mobilization of Anxiety and Desire." PhD diss., University of Illinois, Urbana-Champaign.

Melo, Marijel C. 2018. "The Shadow Rhetorics of Innovation: Maker Culture, Gender, and Technology." PhD diss., University of Arizona.

Miller, Patrick. 2012. "11th Annual Salary Survey." *Game Developer*, April 2012, 7–13.

——. 2013. "Industry in Flux: What We Learned from *Game Developer*'s 2012 Salary Survey." Gamasutra, April 4, 2013. http://gamasutra.com/view/news/189893/Industry_in_flux_What_we_learned_from_Game_Developers_2012_Salary_Survey.php.

Miller, Toby. 2006. "Gaming for Beginners." *Games and Culture* 1 (1): 5–12.

Mitchell, Liam. 2018. *Ludopolitics: Videogames Against Control*. Winchester: Zero Books.

Mosco, Vincent. 1999. "New York.Com: A Political Economy of the Informational City." *Journal of Media Economics* 12 (2): 103–16.

——. 2004. *The Digital Sublime: Myth, Power, and Cyberspace*. Massachusetts: MIT Press.

——. 2009. *The Political Economy of Communication*. 2nd ed. London: Sage.

Mukherjee, Souvik, and Emil Lundedal Hammar. 2018. "Introduction to the Special Issue on Postcolonial Perspectives in Game Studies." *Open Library of Humanities* 4 (2): 1–14. https://doi.org/10.16995/olh.309.

Murray, Soraya. 2018. *On Video Games: The Visual Politics of Race, Gender and Space*. London: IB Tauris.

Nakamura, Lisa. 1995. "Race in/for Cyberspace: Identity Tourism and Racial Passing on the Internet." *Works and Days* 13: 181–93.

——. 2008. *Digitizing Race: Visual Cultures of the Internet*. Minneapolis: University of Minnesota Press.

——. 2009. "Don't Hate the Player, Hate the Game: The Racialization of Labor in *World of Warcraft*." *Critical Studies in Media Communication* 26 (2): 128–44.

——. 2014. "Indigenous Circuits: Navajo Women and the Racialization of Early Electronic Manufacture." *American Quarterly* 66 (4): 919–41.

Nash, Jennifer C. 2011. "Practicing Love: Black Feminism, Love-Politics, and Post-Intersectionality." *Meridians* 11 (2): 1–24.

Neff, Gina. 2012. *Venture Labor: Work and the Burden of Risk in Innovative Industries.* Acting with Technology. Cambridge, MA: MIT Press.

Neff, Gina, Elizabeth Wissinger, and Sharon Zukin. 2005. "Entrepreneurial Labor among Cultural Producers: 'Cool' Jobs in 'Hot' Industries." *Social Semiotics* 15 (3): 307–34.

Negri, Antonio. 1989. *The Politics of Subversion: A Manifesto for the Twenty-First Century.* Cambridge: Polity.

Newbery, Masha-Jayne. 2013. "Gender and the Games Industry: The Experience of Female Game Workers." MA thesis, Simon Fraser University.

Ngai, Pun. 2005. *Made in China: Women Factory Workers in a Global Workplace.* Durham, NC: Duke University Press.

Ngai, Pun, and Jenny Chan. 2012. "Global Capital, the State, and Chinese Workers: The Foxconn Experience." *Modern China* 38 (4): 383–410.

Nichols, Randy. 2014. *The Video Game Business.* London: British Film Institute.

Nieborg, David B. 2011. "Triple-A: The Political Economy of the Blockbuster Video Game." PhD diss., University of Amsterdam.

——. 2014. "Prolonging the Magic: The Political Economy of the 7th Generation Console Game." *Eludamos: Journal for Computer Game Culture* 8 (1): 47–63.

Noble, Safiya. 2018. *Algorithms of Oppression: How Search Engines Reinforce Racism.* New York: NYU Press.

O'Connor, Alice. 2018. "Rockstar Employees Speak Out against Crunch Controversy." Rock Paper Shutgon, October 18, 2018. https://www.rockpapershotgun.com/2018/10/18/rockstar-employees-decry-crunch-controversy/?fbclid=IwAR0oYnQ2BIqn9QEDlCNRdM8iETp8R_U—G_r-lR%E2%80%A6.

O'Donnell, Casey. 2008. "The Work/Play of New Economy: Video Game Development in the United States and India." PhD diss., Rensselaer Polytechnic Institute.

——. 2014. *Developer's Dilemma: The Secret World of Videogame Creators.* Cambridge, MA: MIT Press.

O'Meara, Victoria, Chandell Gosse, Marie-Josée Legault, and Johanna Weststar. 2017. "The Blame Game." *First Person Scholar*, October 4, 2017. http://www.firstpersonscholar.com/the-blame-game/.

Oudenampsen, Martin. 2007. "Back to the Future of the Creative City: An Archaeological Approach to Amsterdam's Creative Redevelopment." In *My Creativity Reader*, edited by Geert Lovink and Ned Rossiter, 165–77. Amsterdam: Institute of Network Cultures.

Pasquale, Frank. 2015. *The Black Box Society: The Secret Algorithms That Control Money and Information.* Cambridge, MA: Harvard University Press.

Passavant, Paul A., and Jodi Dean. 2004. *Empire's New Clothes: Reading Hardt and Negri.* New York: Routledge.

Pateman, Carole. 1988. *The Sexual Contract.* Stanford, CA: Stanford University Press.

——. 2004. "Democratizing Citizenship: Some Advantages of a Basic Income." *Politics and Society* 32 (1): 89–105.

Patterson, Kerry. 2002. *Crucial Conversations: Tools for Talking When Stakes Are High.* New York: McGraw-Hill.

Paul, Christopher A. 2018. *The Toxic Meritocracy of Video Games: Why Gaming Culture Is the Worst.* Minneapolis: University of Minnesota Press.

Peck, Jamie. 2005. "Struggling with the Creative Class." *International Journal of Urban and Regional Research* 29 (4): 740–70.

Perez, Matt. 2019. "Activision Blizzard To Lay Off Nearly 800 People As Its 2019 Looks Bleak." *Forbes*, February 12, 2019. https://www.forbes.com/sites/mattperez/2019/02/12/activision-blizzard-to-layoff-nearly-800-employees/#1383866f76f5.

Peters, Nathan. 2013. "I Freelanced on *Halo 4*: It's Time for Gaming's Contractors to Strike." *Kotaku*, May 31, 2013. http://kotaku.com/i-freelanced-on-halo-4-its-time-for-gamings-contract-510353357.

Piketty, Thomas. 2013. *Capital in the Twenty-First Century*. Cambridge, MA: Harvard University Press.

Pink, Daniel H. 2009. *Drive: The Surprising Truth about What Motivates Us*. New York: Riverhead.

Plunkett, Luke. 2012. "Every Game Studio That's Closed Down since 2006." Kotaku Australia, January 16, 2012. https://kotaku.com/every-game-studio-thats-closed-down-since-2006-5876693.

Pollman, Elizabeth, and Jordan M. Barry. 2017. "Regulatory Entrepreneurship." *Southern California Law Review* 338 (392): 1–60.

Postigo, Hector. 2010. "Modding to the Big Leagues: Exploring the Space between Modders and the Game Industry." *First Monday* 15 (5). doi: https://doi.org/10.5210/fm.v15i5.2972.

Prassl, Jeremias. 2018. *Humans as a Service: The Promise and Perils of Work in the Gig Economy*. Oxford: Oxford University Press.

Pyrko, Igor, Viktor Dörfler, and Colin Eden. 2017. "Thinking Together: What Makes Communities of Practice Work?" *Human Relations* 70 (4): 389–409.

Qiu, Jack Linchuan. 2016. *Goodbye iSlave: A Manifesto for Digital Abolition*. Geopolitics of Information. Urbana: University of Illinois Press.

Raley, Rita. 2009. *Tactical Media*. Minneapolis: University of Minnesota Press.

Ramanan, Chella. 2017. "The Video Game Industry Has a Diversity Problem—but It Can Be Fixed." *The Guardian*, March 15, 2017. https://www.theguardian.com/technology/2017/mar/15/video-game-industry-diversity-problem-women-non-white-people.

Ramsay, Morgan. 2012. *Gamers at Work: Stories behind the Games People Play*. New York: Apress.

Read, J. 2003. *The Micro Politics of Capital: Marx and the Prehistory of the Present*. New York: SUNY Press.

Reay, Diane. 2004. "Gendering Bourdieu's Concepts of Capitals? Emotional Capital, Women, and Social Class." In *Feminism after Bourdieu*, edited by Lisa Adkins and Beverley Skeggs, 57–75. Oxford: Oxford University Press.

Roberts, Sarah T. 2019. *Behind the Screen: Content Moderation in the Shadows of Social Media*. New Haven, CT: Yale University Press.

Rodino-Colocino, Michelle. 2007. "High-Tech Workers of the World, Unionize! A Case Study of WashTech's New Model of Unionism." In *Knowledge Workers in the Information Society*, edited by Catherine McKercher and Vincent Mosco, 209–27. Lanham, MD: Lexington.

Rose, Mike. 2013. "Layoffs at Activision's High Moon Following *Deadpool* Completion." Gamasutra, April 3, 2013. http://www.gamasutra.com/view/news/189771/Layoffs_at_Activisions_High_Moon_following_Deadpool_completion.php.

Rosenblat, Alex, and Luke Stark. 2016. "Algorithmic Labor and Information Asymmetries: A Case Study of Uber's Drivers." *International Journal of Communication* 10:3758–84.

Rosler, Martha. 2010. "Culture Class: Art, Creativity, Urbanism." *E-Flux* 21 (12). https://www.e-flux.com/journal/21/67676/culture-class-art-creativity-urbanism-part-i/.

Ross, Andrew. 2003. *No-Collar: The Humane Workplace and Its Hidden Costs*. Philadelphia: Temple University Press.

——. 2007. "Nice Work if You Can Get It: The Mercurial Career of Creative Industries Policy." In *My Creativity Reader*, edited by Geert Lovink and Ned Rossiter, 17–41. Amsterdam: Institute of Network Cultures.

Ruberg, Bonnie, and Adrienne Shaw, eds. 2017. *Queer Game Studies*. Minneapolis: University of Minnesota Press.

Rushkoff, Douglas. 2016. *Throwing Rocks at the Google Bus*. New York: Penguin.

Ryan, Bill. 1992. *Making Capital from Culture: The Corporate Form of Capitalist Cultural Production*. Berlin: Walter de Gruyter.

Ryneal, Marcelina. 2016. "Turning Waste into Gold: Accumulation by Disposal and the Political Economy of e-Waste Urban Mining." PhD diss., Northern Arizona University.

Saha, Anamik. 2012. "'Beards, Scarves, Halal Meat, Terrorists, Forced Marriage': Television Industries and the Production of 'Race.'" *Media, Culture and Society* 34 (4): 424–38.

Sassen, Saskia. 2002. "Cities in a World Economy." In *Readings in Urban Theory*, edited by Susan Fainstein and Scott Campbell, 32–57. Oxford: Blackwell.

Scholz, Trebor. 2013. *Digital Labor: The Internet as Playground and Factory*. New York: Routledge.

Scholz, Trebor, and Nathan Schneider. 2016. *Ours to Hack and to Own: The Rise of Platform Cooperativism; a New Vision for the Future of Work and a Fairer Internet*. New York: OR.

Schor, Juliet B., and William Attwood-Charles. 2017. "The 'Sharing' Economy: Labor, Inequality, and Social Connection on For-Profit Platforms." *Sociology Compass* 11 (8): 1–16.

Schreier, Jason. 2017. *Blood, Sweat, and Pixels*. New York: Harper.

Schumacher, Leif. 2006. "Immaterial Fordism: The Paradox of Game Industry Labour." *Work Organisation, Labour and Globalization* 1 (1): 144–55.

Sennett, Richard. 2006. *The Culture of the New Capitalism*. New Haven, CT: Yale University Press.

——. 1999. *The Corrosion of Character: The Personal Consequences of Work in the New Capitalism*. New York: W. W. Norton.

Sharma, Sarah. 2011. "The Biopolitical Economy of Time." *Journal of Communication Inquiry* 35 (4): 439–44.

Sheikh, Rahil. 2017. "How Big Is Gaming's Racial Diversity Problem?" BBC.com, December 20, 2017. https://www.bbc.com/news/technology-42357678.

Shepherd, Tamara. 2013. "Young Canadians' Apprenticeship Labour in User-Generated Content." *Canadian Journal of Communication* 38 (1): 35–55.

Skeggs, Beverley. 1997. *Formations of Class and Gender: Becoming Respectable*. London: Sage.

——. 2004. *Class, Self, Culture*. London: Routledge.

Slack, Jennifer Daryl, and J. Macgregor Wise. 2015. *Culture and Technology: A Primer*. New York: Peter Lang.

Slee, Tom. 2015. *What's Yours Is Mine: Against the Sharing Economy*. New York: OR.

Solnit, Rebecca. 2001. *Hollow City: Gentrification and the Eviction of Urban Culture*. London: Verso.

Sperling, Gene. 2015. "How Airbnb Combats Middle Class Income Stagnation." https://www.stgeorgeutah.com/wp-content/uploads/2015/07/MiddleClassReport-MT-061915_r1.pdf.

Srauy, Sam. 2017. "Professional Norms and Race in the North American Video Game Industry." *Games and Culture*, May 15, 2017, 1–20.

Srnicek, Nick. 2016. *Platform Capitalism*. Cambridge: Polity.

Stahl, Matt. 2012. *Unfree Masters: Recording Artists and the Politics of Work*. Durham, NC: Duke University Press.

Stewart, Kathleen. 2012. "Precarity's Forms." *Cultural Anthropology* 27 (3): 518–25.

Stiegler, Bernard. 2016. *Automatic Society*. Cambridge: Polity.

Strangleman, Tim. 2004. "Ways of (Not) Seeing Work: The Visual as a Blind Spot in Work, Employment and Society?" *Work, Employment and Society* 18 (1): 179–92.

Streeck, Wolfgang. 2016. *How Will Capitalism End? Essays on a Failing System*. London: Verso.

Taffel, Sy. 2015. "Towards an Ethical Electronics? Ecologies of Congolese Conflict Minerals." *Westminster Papers in Communication and Culture* 10 (1): 18–33.

Tanner, Nicole. 2011. "Editorial: The Real Housewives of Game Development." IGN (blog), May 2, 2011. http://www.ign.com/articles/2011/05/02/editorial-the-real-housewives-of-game-development.

Taylor, Astra. 2014. *The People's Platform: Taking Back Power and Culture in the Digital Age*. New York: Metropolitan Books, Henry Holt and Company.

——. 2018. "The Automation Charade." *Logic Magazine*, 2018. https://logicmag.io/05-the-automation-charade/.

Taylor, Nicholas, and Gerald Voorhees, eds. 2018. *Masculinities in Play*. Cham, Switzerland: Palgrave Macmillan.

Thrift, Nigel. 2008. *Non-representational Theory: Space, Politics, Affect*. New York: Routledge.

Tokumitsu, Miya. 2015. *Do What You Love: And Other Lies about Success and Happiness*. New York: Regan Arts.

Trautman, Ted. 2014. "Excavating the Video-Game Industry's Past." *New Yorker*, April 29, 2014. https://www.newyorker.com/business/currency/excavating-the-video-game-industrys-past.

Turner, Fred. 2006. *From Counterculture to Cyberculture: Stewart Brand, the Whole Earth Network, and the Rise of Digital Utopianism*. Chicago: Chicago University Press.

Tyree-Hageman, Jennifer. 2013. "From Silicon Valley to Wall Street: Following the Rise of an Entrepreneurial Ethos." *Berkeley Journal of Sociology* 57:74–113.

Umney, Charles, and Genevieve Coderre-LaPalme. 2017. "Blocked and New Frontiers for Trade Unions: Contesting 'the Meaning of Work' in the Creative and Caring Sectors." *British Journal of Industrial Relations* 55 (4): 859–78.

Valentine, Rebekah. 2018. "Nintendo Barely Improves Conflict Minerals Sourcing over Two Years." GamesIndustry.biz, July 31, 2018. https://www.gamesindustry.biz/articles/2018-07-31-nintendo-barely-improves-conflict-minerals-certainty-over-two-years.

Van Parijs, Philippe. 1995. *Real Freedom for All: What (if Anything) Can Justify Capitalism?* Oxford: Clarendon.

van Doorn, Niels. 2017. "Platform Labor: On the Gendered and Racialized Exploitation of Low-Income Service Work in the 'On-Demand' Economy." *Information, Communication and Society* 20 (6): 898–914.

Vanderhoef, John, and Michael Curtin. 2016. "The Crunch Heard 'Round the World: The Global Era of Digital Game Labor." In *Production Studies, the Sequel! Cultural Studies of Global Media Industries*, edited by Miranda Banks, Bridget Conor, and Vicki Mayer, 196–211. New York: Routledge.

Vijayakumar, Gowri. 2013. "'I'll Be Like Water': Gender, Class, and Flexible Aspirations at the Edge of India's Knowledge Economy." *Gender and Society* 27 (6): 777–98.

Virno, Paolo. 1996. "The Ambivalence of Disenchantment." In *Radical Thought in Italy: A Potential Politics*, edited by Paolo Virno and Michael Hardt, 13–37. Minneapolis: University of Minnesota Press.

——. 2004. *A Grammar of the Multitude: For an Analysis of Contemporary Forms of Life.* Los Angeles: Semiotext(e).

Wainwright, Oliver. 2017. "'Everything Is Gentrification Now': But Richard Florida Isn't Sorry." *The Guardian*, October 26, 2017. https://www.theguardian.com/cities /2017/oct/26/gentrification-richard-florida-interview-creative-class-new-urban -crisis.

Waitt, Gordon. 2006. "Creative Small Cities: Cityscapes, Power and the Arts." In *Small Cities: Urban Experience beyond the Metropolis*, edited by David Bell and Mark Jayne, 169–85. New York: Routledge.

Wark, McKenzie. 2007. *Gamer Theory.* Cambridge, MA: Harvard University Press.

Warner, Kristen. 2015. *The Cultural Politics of Colorblind TV Casting.* New York: Routledge.

Warren, Samantha. 2002. "Show Me How It Feels to Work Here: Using Photography to Research Organizational Aesthetics." *Ephemera* 2 (3): 224–45.

Weeks, Kathi. 2011. *The Problem with Work: Feminism, Marxism, Antiwork Politics, and Postwork Imaginaries.* Durham, NC: Duke University Press.

——. 2017. "Down with Love: Feminist Critique and the New Ideologies of Work." *Women's Studies Quarterly* 45 (3): 37–58.

Wenger, Etienne. 1998. *Communities of Practice: Learning, Meaning, and Identity.* Learning in Doing. Cambridge: Cambridge University Press.

Weststar, Johanna. 2015. "Understanding Video Game Developers as an Occupational Community." *Information, Communication and Society* 18 (10): 1238–52.

Weststar, Johanna, and Marie-Josee Legault. 2014. "Developer Satisfaction Survey 2014: Employment Report." International Game Developers Association. https://c.ymcdn .com/sites/www.igda.org/resource/collection/9215B88F-2AA3-4471-B44D -B5D58FF25DC7/IGDA_DSS_2014-Employment_Report.pdf.

Weststar, Johanna, Victoria O'Meara, Chandell Gosse, and Marie-Josée Legault. 2017. *Diversity Among Videogame Developers, 2004–2015: Compared Results of IGDA International Surveys 2004, 2005, 2009, 2014 & 2015 and 2013–2014 Canadian Interviews.* Canada: SSHRC/IGDA. http://r-libre.teluq.ca/1275/1/DiversityReportSummary%20 _FINAL.pdf.

Whitson, Jennifer. 2013. "The 'Console Ship Is Sinking' and What This Means for Indies." *Loading . . .* 7 (11): 122–29.

——. 2018. "Voodoo Software and Boundary Objects in Game Development: How Developers Collaborate and Conflict with Game Engines and Art Tools." *New Media and Society* 20 (7): 2315–32.

Wilde, Thomas. 2018. "'It's Very David and Goliath': Inside the Growing Effort to Unionize Video Game Developers." GeekWire, May 9, 2018. https://www.geekwire.com /2018/david-goliath-inside-growing-effort-unionize-video-game-developers/.

Williams, Dmitri, Nicole Martins, Mia Consalvo, and James D. Ivory. 2009. "The Virtual Census: Representations of Gender, Race and Age in Video Games." *New Media and Society* 11 (5): 815–34.

Williams, Ian. 2018. "After Destroying Lives for Decades, Gaming Is Finally Talking Unionization." *Waypoint*, March 23, 2018. https://waypoint.vice.com/en_us/article/7xdv5e /after-destroying-lives-for-decades-gaming-is-finally-talking-unionization.

Williams, Raymond. 1977. "Culture Is Ordinary." In *Cultural Theory: An Anthology*, edited by Imre Szeman and Timothy Kaposy, 53–60. Chichester: Wiley-Blackwell.

Woodcock, Jamie. 2019. *Marx at the Arcade: Consoles, Controllers, and Class Struggle.* Haymarket Books: London.

Working Partnership USA. 2014. *Tech's Diversity Problem: More Than Meets the Eye.* San Jose, CA: Working Partnership USA. https://siliconvalleyrising.org/files/Techs DiversityProblem.pdf.

Wright, Steven T. 2018. "Despite Resistance, Crunch Continues to Define the Video Game Industry." *Variety,* October 19, 2018. https://variety.com/2018/gaming/features /video-game-union-crunch-industry-practice-1202985642/.

Yee, Nick. 2006. "The Labor of Fun: How Video Games Blur the Boundaries of Work and Play." *Games and Culture* 1 (1): 68–71.

Zamponi, Lorenzo. 2018. "Bargaining with the Algorithm." *Jacobin,* June 9, 2018. http:// jacobinmag.com/2018/06/deliveroo-riders-strike-italy-labor-organizing.

Zizek, Slavoj. 2011. "Liberalism as Politics for a Race of Devils." *ABC Religion and Ethics,* November 22, 2011. https://www.abc.net.au/religion/liberalism-as-politics-for-a -race-of-devils/10100998.

Index

accountant, Jill, technical artist (husband Dan)
  "cool factor," 109
  "fraternity house," 105, 116
  gender and love in creative industries, 118
Activision Blizzard, 144, 168–69
Adorno, Theodore, 130
affect, 33
  positive and negative, 38
alienation
  cultural work, 56
  fixation, 38
  good work, 38
  industrial work, 37
  logic of one-dimensional creativity, 38
  Marxist analysis and, 56
  materiality, 39
  pleasure at work and, 33
  transformation of life into work, 41, 160
  worker's self image, 35
anonymity, 175n1, 175n4, 179n4
Apple, 31, 44
art director, Theodor, 104
  background, 89
  emotions about work, 94–95
  studio stability, 141–42
artist, Ricardo
  admission of racial decisions, 51
  decision to leave, 152
  employment contracts, 39–40
  racially loaded colors, 47
  stock price worries, 149
artists, work of, 19
assistant producer, Vincent, 143
  bankruptcy auction anxiety, 154
  Digital Creatives recklessness, 144
  layoff and rehiring, 110, 146–47, 148
  unionization rejection, 155
assistant producer's girlfriend, Sabrina
  clear division with work complaint, 114–16
  "cool factor," 110
assistant producer's wife, Judith, 117, 121
  clear division with work complaint, 114
  like being a single mom, 112
associate producer, Margaret, 31, 146, 152, 155
Atari, 9, 14

autonomist Marxism, 11, 177n2
autonomy, 21, 27
  "not invented here" syndrome, 55–56

bankruptcy
  employees' lack of control, 39
  reaction to bankruptcy, 154
Banks, Mark, 56, 176n11
Barry, Jordan M., 9
Bell, Daniel, 56
Berardi, Bifo, 177n2
Berlant, Lauren, 124
Berlusconi, Silvio, 23
Bhattacharya, Tithi, 34
Black, Asian, and Minority Ethnic (BAME) in
    Games Network, 44
Bloch, Ernst, 173
Braverman, Harry, 28, 56, 67, 124, 130
Burawoy, Michael, 13
Bushnell, Nolan, 160
buyout
  antagonistic imperatives, 54
  cultural changes, 61
  financial security and autonomy, 68
  teamwork shift, 61
  trade-off, 71–72
  workforce expansion, 58

capitalism, artists relation to, 56
Certain Affinity, 122–23
China, working conditions, 41
city planner, Alan, 79
class, 51
  background and, 24
  definition of, 107–8
  gender, race and, 87, 175n6
  gendered relations of, 111
  politics of, 160–61, 166
  privileges of, 113
  See also creative class; game testing and
    testers
Cohen, Nicole, 11
college student questions
  portfolio, 30
  work ethic, 30

197

college students
    indifference to financial and social costs, 42
    work and toil, 32
color-blind ideology, 49–50, 51
    avatars design choice, 50
commodification, intensified, 71
communicative developers
    Crucial Conversations, 101–3
    in-house training, 99
    vital skill, 18, 100
conflict-free minerals, 42
core creatives
    expendability of, 123, 125
    first layoff of, 145
    immateriality of, 128
    internal financial information, 150–51
    layoffs of, 29, 141
    reaction to project management, 67
    skills of, 18, 28, 179n2
Corrosion of Character, The (Sennett), 155
creative autonomy, 6, 33–34, 38, 56, 71, 159
creative city, 7, 74, 82, 86–87
creative class, 35, 71, 76–77, 81–82, 84, 86,
    179n1
creative economy, 126, 129, 157
creative industry, 3, 138, 166
    unions of, 171
creative labor, 177n2
creative workers
    desires of, 38
    "labor of love," 37, 156–57
cruel optimism, 28, 124
crunch, 64, 96
    concern over, 96
    definition of, 176n10
    disadvantage of, 111–12, 131
    family time and, 157
    life during, 98, 106
    problem of, 170
    stress and anxiety, 167
    testers and, 130–33
    women's labor during, 107–8, 111, 113–14,
    119
culture, 14, 74
    "bro culture," 44
    design, 19, 156
    Desire's, 17, 55, 57–58, 130–31, 133
    game, 45, 171, 176n12
    Game City, 77, 80, 82–83, 85
    garage, 59–62, 65, 71
    industry, 5
    political, 23
    popular, 48

start-up, 56
studio, 94, 96, 166–67
techno-masculine work, 28, 105, 109
toxic, 64

Democratic Republic of Congo (DRC), 41
de Peuter, Greig, 21, 129
designer, Silvio
    job prospects, 6
    love of games, 90
designers, work of, 19
designer's girlfriend, Mona, 114
    insecurity of job, 117
    nerdy boyfriend, great parties, 110
Developer's Dilemma, The (O'Donnell), 10
Developers Satisfaction Survey 2014, 164
Dialectic of Sex, The (Firestone), 29
Digital Creatives
    acquisition of Desire, 54
    employment contracts, 34
    employment contracts and political bondage,
    149–50, 157
    expansion game or sequel, 149
    financial condition, 1–2
    flagship studio, Desire, 57
    internal financial information, 150
    precarity of work, 62, 70–72
    publicly traded company, 68–69, 150
    reckless growth and bad investments, 3,
    69–70, 148–49
    relocation of Desire, 27, 73, 75, 78, 88
    stock investment worries, 151
    stock price, 13, 70, 149
    sustainable urban development, 81
Digital Creatives, bankruptcy of, 3, 159
    auction for Desire, 137, 153–54
    disassociation with products, 177n3
Digital Creatives, buyout
    family insecurity, 116–17
    organizational and cultural tensions, 55,
    70–71
domestic space, 11, 25, 28, 111, 179n1,
    106–7
    See also home and family
"Don't Sign That Contract" (Peters), 122
Dream Reality, 44
Drive (Pink), 18
Drucker, Peter, 56
Dyer-Witheford, Nick, 21

EA Spouse case, 34–35, 79n1, 111, 119, 164,
    169, 179n1
    labor force examination, 106

Ebert, Roger, 89
Electronic Arts (EA), 14, 144
  downsizing of, 9–10
  EA Spouse and gender, 34–35
Electronic Software Association (ESA), 15
emotions at work, 93–96
  communication and, 102
employment contracts, 34
  whole worker, 39–40
Entertainment Media Council, 160
entrepreneurialism, 9, 57
  digital utopianism and, 178n7
  start-up experience, 60
Ernkvist, Mirko, 9
escapism, 27, 35, 37, 43, 46–48, 51–53, 173
exploitation, 11, 27, 33–35, 50
  domestic labor, 107, 118, 120–21
  Global South, 43
  unions and, 155
  worker's, 8, 137, 177n2, 178n1

fair labor practices, 157
family and home
  blurred line between work and home, 107
  classed subjectivities, 107
  role of, 106–7
  value of women to company, 111
Fautley, Tom, 167
Federici, Silvia, 26, 106–7
femininities, 106–8
financialization, 5, 68–69, 141, 157, 165
financial security
  cultural changes, 58
  trade-off, 56
Firestone, Shulamith, 29, 51
flexibility, workplace, 97, 99, 110, 114, 128,
  178n1
Florida, Richard, 7, 80–81, 84, 87
Fordism and post-Fordism, 18, 32, 137
  capital, 129
  domestic roles, 107
  joyful alienation, 37
  precarity and, 6
Foxconn, 37, 52
  love imposed from the top, 52
  working conditions, 41
fun
  definition of, 27
  degradation of, 28, 130–32, 138
  fuel for game industry, 11
  gender and racial inequalities and, 35
  global political economy of, 52
  instrumentalization of play, 131

measure of a good game, 43, 47
  white masculinity and, 37, 45–47
  work as, 26, 33–34, 47

Gamasutra, 120, 122, 143
Game City, 73
  attractions and challenges, 76–77, 179n2
  description of, 75
  downtown economy, 76
  Downtown Plan, 79, 82–83
  downtown revitalization, 78. *See also* tax
    increment finance (TIF) district
  downtown transformation, 74, 87
  public-private partnership, 79, 81–83
  Studio Desire low profile, 76
  video game production in, 76
  See also micro-urbanism
Game City Center Partnership, 84
  999 East, arts and culture district, 85
  Game City Excitement, 84–86
game content
  ambivalence toward, 45, 51
  inferential racism, 47
  militarist, sexist, and racist, 43
  political outcomes and, 48
  success measures, 43
game developer, Harold
  layoff worries, 145
  parent company worries, 2
  stock price worries, 149
  unionization rejection, 155
  usability testing, 31–32
game developer, Stuart
  decision to leave, 152
  demeaning all, 46–47, 49
  happily work, 99
  stock price worries, 149
Game Developer magazine, 163
game developers
  communicative capacities, 55
  creative autonomy, 54
  elitist practices, 65
  emotions and, 93–96
  exploitation of, 40, 118
  family and home, 108–11, 113–14, 119–21
  financial insecurity, 142, 144, 150
  financial security and autonomy, 57, 71, 173
  flexibility of, 96
  fun and, 47–48, 53
  gender, love and work, 14
  hip cultural workers, 61
  immaterial labor, 11, 33
  inequalities of, 4

game developers (*continued*)
  intellectual property and, 39
  interaction with, 12–14
  love and, 22, 34, 37, 52, 150, 157, 161
  ludic religiosity, 51
  management and, 20, 27, 91
  precaritization of, 6–7, 26, 117, 155–56, 172
  project managers and, 64, 67
  self image, 39
  unions and, 165–66, 169
  work-life balance, 163–64
  See also game developer, Harold; game
    developer, Stuart
Game Developers Conference (GDC), 90, 109,
  169–70
game development
  dynamics of, 90–91
  gendered metaphors for, 89–91
game play programmer, Jose, 147
Gamers at Work (Ramsay), 161
game testing and testers, 19–20, 28
  entry-level position, 122
  impact of low status, 128–30
  lack of skill, 134–35
  layoffs in, 133–34
  measurement of productivity, 127–28
  precarity of, 19, 28, 123–25, 129–30, 137–39
  repetitive tasks and precarity, 160
  second-class citizenship, 123, 135–37
  unionization of, 139
  work-leisure blur, 123–24, 130
  workplace hierarchy, 126–27
  See also playbor; tester pit
Game Workers Unite (GWU), 169–73
garage ethos
  cultural changes, 59–60
  gendered labor, 60, 63–65
  not-invented-in-the-studio syndrome, 65
  precarity of, 68
  start-up experience, 62
gender
  "bro culture," 44
  classed femininities, 106–8
  diversity problem, 43–45, 178n5
  exploitation of women, 107–8
  financial and social relationships, 37, 42
  garage ethos, 60
  gendered metaphors, 91
  language and, 63
  passionate work, 111–12, 119
  predominantly white-male labor force,
    34–35, 161
  See also EA Spouse case
Ghana, toxic and hazardous waste, 42

gig economy, 8–9
  unionization, 169
Gill, Rosalind, 124, 139
Global South
  exploitation in, 34, 36
  negative role, 42
  repetitious work and natural exploitation, 43
Grandma's Boy (film), 123
Grand Theft Auto, 30, 167
Gray, Kishona, 47
Gregg, Melissa, 158

Hall, Stuart, 35, 47
Hardt, Michael, 10, 177n2
Harrer, Sabine, 51
Harvey, David, 133
Hawkins, Trip, 17, 160–61
Heynen, Hilde, 64
Hirani, Kish, 44
Hochschild, Arlie, 107
home and family
  anger at being laid off, 119
  clear division with work complaint, 114–16
  crunch strategy, 113–14, 119
  disadvantages of video game employment,
    111
  insecurity of job, 116–18
  precarity of situation, 118
  presence bleed, 114
  unity of the family, 113
  See also EA Spouse case
hope, 23, 28, 33, 108, 120, 144, 173
  testers and, 124, 133, 135, 138, 160
  unionization and, 170
Horkheimer, Max, 130
Houser, Dan, 167
human resources, Stacey, 67–69
Huws, Ursula, 54

ideology, 48
  of creativity, 139
  crunch and, 113
  heterosexual family, 22
  individualism, 167
  post-racial, 49, 51
  of progress, 22
  technomasculinist, 63
immaterial labor, 177n2
  benefits of, 41–42
  definition of, 11, 33
  photographs and emotions, 92
  See also game testing and testers
Independent Workers Union of Great Britain
  (IWGB), 169

inequality
   flexible labor regime, 36
   inequality in video game production, 38
   in video game production, 33, 35
intellectual property
   employment contracts and, 34
   inequality and, 11
   lack of control, 39
   secrecy, 17, 24
   See also nondisclosure agreements (NDAs)
International Game Developers Association
   (IGDA), 24, 164
International Wages for Housework
   Campaign, 26
internships, 31–32, 79, 146

Jarett, Kylie, 33, 40, 118
Jobs, Steve, 23–24
Johnson, Robin, 178n4

Kinema, Emma, 170
Konami Europe, 44
Kotaku, 10, 122–23, 143
Kücklich, Julian, 17

Labor and Monopoly Capital (Braverman), 56
layoffs
   anger at Digital Creatives, 152
   core creatives reaction, 145–48
   exit interviews, 153
   job security, 13, 19, 38, 117, 137, 154, 163
   precarity of gaming industry, 153
   rehires of laid-off employees, 148
   See also game testing and testers
Lazzarato, Maurizio, 5, 25, 33
lead designer Robert, 96–97, 100, 102, 142, 154
   anger at Digital Creatives, 153
   bankruptcy auction anxiety, 154
   expansion game demand, 149
   flexible work environment policy, 96–97
   planning for layoff, 152
   reaction to bankruptcy, 154
   unionization rejection, 155
League of Legends, 44
Lefebvre, Henri, 74
libertarianism, 56–57, 120–21, 144, 155–57,
   167, 170–71
Lordon, Frédéric, 37–38
ludic contract, 10, 175n7
ludic religiosity, 27, 47–49, 51, 178n4
   cultural inequalities, 36–37
ludopolitics, 11, 27
   definition of, 36
   definition of fun, 43

global regime of, 35
inequality in video game production, 33,
   36, 38
inequality politicized, 40
"labor of love," 4, 33, 52, 91, 156–57, 159–62,
   176n1
powerful studio and precarious testers, 133
unequal regime and, 29, 38, 121, 133, 141,
   145, 159, 161, 172–73
See also social reproduction
Ludopolitics (Mitchell), 177n4
ludopolitics, global dimension, 41
   equipment manufacture, 41
   geographical triangle, 42–43
   inequality in video game production, 43
   material extraction and recycling, 41–42

MacDonald, Keza, 168
Machlup, Fritz, 56
MacLean, Jen, 169
Making Capital from Culture (Ryan), 56
management
   bureaucracy, 27, 55–56
   creativity and, 91
   flexible work environment, 92, 96–98, 103–4
   formatting, 55
   meeting overload, 96
   training sessions on communicative
      subjects, 92
Marxism, 11, 37, 56
masculinity. *See* technomasculinity; white
   masculinity
Massey, Doreen, 77
Mayer, Vicki, 176n11
Mbembe, Achille, 36
McGowan, Todd, 23
media and communication studies, 56,
   177n1
meritocracy, 2, 44
   collective action, 167
   love and, 24–25, 119, 178n6
   masculinity and, 63
   UBI and, 171
   work partners and, 36
micro-urban community, 16, 75, 77, 79, 82,
   84–87
micro-urbanism, 75, 77, 82–86, 179n1
   low-risk, low-cost, 86–87
Miller, Toby, 4
Mitchell, Liam, 177n4
Morgan Ramsay, 160
motivation, nonmonetary, 24
   love, 32–33, 176n1
mystique of ludic authorship, 64

"Necropolitics" (Mbembe), 36
Negri, Antonio, 10, 42, 177n2
neoliberalism, 31, 173
    context of, 6, 11
    creative city of, 74
    flexible regime, 171
    passionate work, 14
    public-private partnership, 27, 85
    rhetoric of, 107
    spacialization and, 159
    technologies of, 52
Nieborg, David B., 21
nondisclosure agreements (NDAs), 21,
    34, 39
nonwhite workers, 43–44

O'Donnell, Casey, 10, 111, 165

Papandreou, Georgios, 23
passionate work, 14, 62, 106, 109, 111–12, 116,
    119, 121
Pateman, Carole, 40, 175n7
Peck, Jamie, 87
permanent tester, Eric
    complexity of testing, 126
    outdoor work appreciated, 132
Peters, Nathan, 122
Pink, Daniel, 18
playbor, 16
    definition of, 10
    degradation of fun, 124, 133
    relocation space and, 159
play tests, 41, 130
political bondage, 149, 157
    stock options and, 5
political economy, 5, 11, 21–23, 38
political economy, global, 50, 52, 55, 168
Pollman, Elizabeth, 9
Pong, 38
postwork society, 11, 28, 172–73
Prassl, Jeremias, 9
Pratt, Andy, 139
precarity and precarization
    in capitalism, 137
    definition of, 5, 6
    low-wage jobs, 4
    precog persona, 129, 129133
    social contract and, 26
    subjectivity and, 6
    video game industry, 5–6, 26, 139, 159
    See also game testing and testers
producer, David, 100
    attraction to Game City, 76–77
    degradation of fun, 132

escapism, 46
    impressing management visitors, 100
    tester disenchantment, 136
    tester lack of skill, 134
producer, Margaret
    internship, 31
    layoff worries, 146
producer's wife, Emma
    class privileges, 113
    insecurity of job, 117
    midwest lifestyle helps crunch, 112–13
production of space, 74, 86
programmer, Chris, 90–91
    attraction to Game City, 76–77
    competitive tone at job interview, 166
    stereotypes of culture, 45
programmer, James, 97
    call for fair labor practices, 157
    flexible work environment and, 97
    layoff and industry dynamics, 147–48
programmer, Karl, 65
    background, 55
    buyout tensions, 54–55
    frustration with Digital Creatives, 70
    to new start-up, 70–71
    new start-up culture, 60
    skepticism for nontechnical workers, 68
    start-up communication, 63
    start-up experience, 57
programmer, Matthew, 18–19, 25, 90–91,
    97–98, 100, 154, 163
    anxiety, 39
    bankruptcy auction anxiety, 154
    financing relief, 58
    flexible work environment, 97
    friction with developers, 65–66
    loss of control, 69–70
    stereotypes of culture, 45–47
    teamwork shift to a job, 61–62
    unionization rejection, 155
programmer, Edward
    project manager friction, 66–67
    teamwork of start-up, 61–62
programmer Pipa, 96, 101, 111, 117
programmer's wife, Karen
    husbands work too much, 111
    insecurity of job, 117–18
programming, work of, 18–19
programming partner, Patricia
    spatial flexibility, 114–15
    work from home, 114–15
project design director, Siva, 89–90
project manager, Renata, 142
    diversity problem, 44

project managers
    friction with developers, 65–67
    role of, 20, 58
project manager's wife, Mary
    insecurity of job, 117
    nephew's love her husband's work, 110
proof of concept (POC) meetings, 99–102
publicly traded companies
    advantages of, 68
    friction in, 57, 69
    internal financial information, 70, 150
    shareholders and stock market pressures, 71

quality assurance (QA). *See* game testing and
    testers

race
    diversity problem, 44–45
    financial and social relationships, 37, 42
    postracialism, 49
    predominantly white-male labor force, 34–35
    See also nonwhite workers
racism, 7, 10, 47, 50
Ramanan, Chella, 44
Ramsay, Morgan, 160
rationalization upon acquisition
    cultural shift on acquisition, 4–5, 71
    definition of, 4
real estate CEO, Bill, 80, 85–86
    benefits to city of Desire, 81–82
"Real Housewives of Game Development, The"
    (Tanner), 119
recruitment, 20, 80
    after layoffs, 152–53
    college student questions, 30–31
    cost of living, 76, 84
    environment artists, 152
    location and, 76
    project managers, 58
research and interview process, 12–14, 16
    media ethnography, 25
Riot Games, 44–45
Rockstar
    Grand Theft Auto (GTA), 15, 167
    oppressive work practices, 167–68
    Rockstar Spouse, 119, 169, 179n1
    social media ban, 167
Ross, Andrew, 157
Rubin, Jason, 161
Ryan, Bill, 4, 55–56
Ryerson, Liz, 170

Second Life, 10
Sennett, Richard, 16, 155

Shefta, Sitara, 44
Sheikh, Rahil, 44
Silicon Prairie ecology, 75
Silicon Valley, 44, 75–77, 162
skills, 179n2
    core creative team or testing, 134
social factory, 11, 34, 74
social reproduction, 25, 27–28, 74, 111, 176n1,
    179n1
    domestic space and, 25, 28
    labor to life shift, 27
    materialist investigation of love and labor,
        34–36
    partners' work, 36
    spouse or partner's role, 34–35, 106
society of enjoyment, 23–24
spatialization, 4
    relocation after acquisition, 159
"spectacle of the Other," 35, 37
Square Enix, 9
Srauy, Sam, 47
start-up experience
    cultural changes, 58
    culture of, 56–57, 60
    Desire, 36
    financial relief, 58
    nostalgia for, 64, 178n3
    pride, ego, and technomasculinity, 60–61
    small group communication, 63
    successes and failures, 177n2
stay-at-home wife, Isabel
    gender and love in creative industries, 118
    insecurity of job, 117
    pride in husband's work, 109
    tolerance and resentment, 112
Streeck, Wolfgang, 8
studio design director, Michael
    emotions about work, blank wall, 93–94
    reaction to bankruptcy, 153
studio design manager, Otis
    benefit from Crucial Conversations, 103
    frustration with Digital Creatives, 70
    new game problem, 67
    teamwork of start-up, 61–62

Take-Two, 9
Tanner, Nicole, 119–21
Tanvir, Asim, 44
tax increment finance (TIF) district, 78, 179n3
    plaza construction and impact, 78–81
Taylor, Astra, 34
Taylorism, 56, 68
teamwork, 30, 61, 103, 156
    flexible work environment and, 97

tech artist, Ronaldo
 background, 58–59
 cultural changes, 59–60
 libertarianism rather than union, 155–56
 parent company anxieties, 151
 parent company problems, 148–49
 project management friction, 67
 start-up experience, 58–62
 stock price worries, 69–70
 transition to corporate, 66
 update his CV, 152
technical artist, Dan, 105–6
technical artist's wife, Gina
 "boy's club," 116
 clear division with work complaint, 115–16
 gendered analysis of the industry, 111–12
 glamour of IT sector, 24
 "youth is king," 120–21
technomasculinity, 63–65, 105, 116, 118,
  178n4
temporary tester, Andy, 129, 154, 156
 bankruptcy auction questions, 154
 necessary evil crunch, 132
 tester disenchantment, 136, 137
 unionization rejection, 156
temporary tester, Cirose, 130
 comparison to other jobs, 134
 diminished passion for games, 131
 hope, 138
 mind numbing crunch, 132
 precarity of, 140
 report on co-workers, 127
 tester disenchantment, 135–37, 139
 tester pit as second home, 125
temporary tester, George, 156
 advice to others, 138
 hope of reemployment and moving up, 135
 irregular work history, 130
 lack of skill, 134
 mind numbing crunch, 131–32
 studio's position of testing, 139
 unionization rejection, 156
temporary tester, Melissa
 massive layoff and, 129
 peer pressure, 127
temporary tester, Steven, 134
tester, Ricky
 diminished passion for games, 131
 job for game lovers, 139
 lack of skill, 134
 mind numbing crunch, 132
 tester disenchantment, 135
tester pit, 125

testers. *See* game testing and testers
38 Studios case, 120, 169
Titanic, 1–3, 145, 163
Tokumitsu, Miya, 138
toxic and hazardous waste, 42

Ubisoft, 87
Ulm, Chris, 161
unionization
 core creatives and, 7, 151–52, 157, 166–67
 developers and, 151–52, 154–56
 gaming testers and, 139, 142
 Unions Now? Pros, Cons, and Consequences,
  169
 See also Game Workers Unite (GWU)
universal basic income (UBI), 171–72
unpaid labor
 spouses or partners, 60, 106, 113, 118
 unionization and, 160
urban space, 74
usability testers, 31–32
usability tests, 31–32
USGamer, 169

video game industry
 business and labor in, 15–17
 crises in, 9–10
 cultural infrastructure, 23
 economics of, 21–22
 entrepreneurialism, 57
 finance capitalism and, 3–4
 history of, 14–15, 57
 labor practices, 22
 privileged precarity, 6–7
 studies of, 10–11
video games, 7
 criticism of, 43
 culture of, 23
 design of, 21–22
 developers' passion for, 114, 117, 130
 fun and, 48
 history of, 14, 126
 library use of, 17
 love of, 25, 89–90
 societal view of, 25
 software production, 50
 study of, 10
 testers' passion for, 124–25, 160

Warner Communications, 9
Weeks, Kathi, 32, 51, 172–73, 177n1
white masculinity, 23, 27, 35, 42, 48, 50
 diversity problem, 24–25, 178n5

emotional toxicity, 178n6
financial and social relationships, 37
games that reflect themselves, 44, 48
geek culture, 178n7
ludopolitics and, 52
racialized and gendering, 43–45
technomasculinity, 63–65, 105
unoffendable, 49
"work for free" recommendation, 42
work valued, 50
Williams, Raymond, 57, 60
work, future of, 7–9, 23, 26, 175n6

work environment, rebellious playground, 98–99
work ethic, 165–66, 170
college student questions, 30
See also Fordism and post-Fordism
workforce expansion
buyout, 58
cultural shift, 65–66
work-life balance, 162–65
quality of life issues, 164
writer, Tim, 135

Xbox Live, 47

Lightning Source UK Ltd.
Milton Keynes UK
UKHW041110060320
359559UK00025B/550